The Destiny
of Mankind

In the shrunken world of this scientific age serious philosophers are concerned with the brotherhood of man; Christianity comes under their fire as a religion which promulgates an "entirely individualistic point of view," negating the ideal of a common humanity.

Father de Lubac answers these accusers with a deeply searching and lucid investigation of Catholic doctrine, tradition, and revelation. He shows that Catholicism is social in the deepest sense of the word, not only in its attitude toward natural institutions, but in the heart of its dogma, in the Mystical Body of Christ.

With illustrations drawn from both history and doctrine, Father de Lubac maintains that the Church teaches that all men are one in the community of their divine origin and destiny. This vitally important work shows that the brotherhood of man is not merely a philosophical concept made imperative by today's politics and science, but that it is the ancient and continuing goal of the eternal Church.

"It might well be said that no one who has received his formation in the lay apostolate in this country since 1950 has failed to undergo the heady influence of this book."

—*Ave Maria*

Other MENTOR-OMEGA Books

ELEMENTS OF CHRISTIAN PHILOSOPHY *by Etienne Gilson*
The noted French philosopher illuminates the key
ideas of the theology of St. Thomas Aquinas.
(#MT489—75¢)

THE CHRIST OF FAITH *by Karl Adam*
A scholarly discussion of the doctrine of the Catholic
Church as revealed in the life, works, personality, and
message of Jesus Christ. By an eminent German
theologian and priest. (#MQ430—95¢)

AMERICAN CATHOLIC DILEMMA *by Thomas F. O'Dea*
A well-known sociologist discusses the contributions of
his fellow Catholics to American intellectual life.
(#MP404—60¢)

TWO CENTURIES OF ECUMENISM: The Search for Unity
by George H. Tavard
A study of successive efforts at Christian reunion from
the Oxford Movement of the last century to the most
recent Council of the Church called by the late Pope
John XXIII. (#MT465—75¢)

CATHOLICISM

A Study of Dogma
in Relation to the
Corporate Destiny
of Mankind

by Henri de Lubac, S. J.

A MENTOR-OMEGA BOOK
Published by The New American Library

*Published as a MENTOR-OMEGA BOOK
by arrangement with Sheed & Ward, Inc.,
who have authorized this softcover edition.
A hardcover edition is available from Sheed & Ward, Inc.*

FIRST PRINTING, JUNE, 1964

TRANSLATOR'S NOTE

The English translation has been made from the fourth French edition —Paris, 1947—which contains certain small additions in the text and in the footnotes. Account has of course been taken of these additions, but the number of footnotes has been very considerably reduced in order to put the book into a convenient format and encourage its use by the general reader. I am grateful to Dom Illtyd Trethowan for much advice and help in the preparation of this translation.

LANCELOT C. SHEPPARD

First published in the U.S.A. by Sheed & Ward, Inc., New York, 1950

NIHIL OBSTAT: PATRICIVS J. MORRIS, S.T.D., L.S.S.

261.5   CENSOR DEPVTATVS

IMPRIMATVR: E. MORROGH BERNARD

VICARIVS GENERALIS

WESTMONASTERII, DIE XXVI SEPTEMBRIS, MCMXLIX

*MENTOR-OMEGA BOOKS are published by
The New American Library of World Literature, Inc.
501 Madison Avenue, New York, New York 10022*

PRINTED IN THE UNITED STATES OF AMERICA

CONTENTS

Extracts

INTRODUCTION

> Have I found joy? . . . No, but I have found *my* joy and that is something wildly different. . . .
>
> The joy of Jesus can be personal. It can belong to a single man and he is saved. He is at peace, he is joyful now and for always, but he is alone. The isolation of this joy does not trouble him; on the contrary: he is the chosen one. In his blessedness he passes through the battlefields with a rose in his hand. . . .
>
> When I am beset by affliction, I cannot find peace in the blandishments of genius. My joy will not be lasting unless it is the joy of all. I will not pass through the battlefields with a rose in my hand.[1]

What Christian has not encountered such an accusation? How many souls have not encountered upon their course this stone of stumbling? In the recent past "difficulties of belief" arose, it seems, in many cases from agnostic philosophy and doubts about the Bible and Christian origins. Exegesis and history have not ceased to be a source of difficulties, but the problems that beset us to-day are rather of the social and spiritual order, and it is possible that they are even more fundamental. The philosophical problem itself no longer appears as a matter of pure science. Thus, in general, there is less inquiry about the historical or rational developments by which Christianity has come down to us than about the nature of Christianity itself, and many who would not have dreamt of disputing its historical claims or criticizing its metaphysical foundations are beginning to be doubtful of its permanent value. "How," they ask in particular, "can a religion which apparently is uninterested in our terrestrial future and in human fellowship offer an ideal which can still attract the men of to-day?"

A few quotations will be sufficient to show how widespread is such an idea among our contemporaries. It is to be found developed at length in a work by Gabriel Séailles which was very popular forty years ago, and is still read. After stating what he called, with some emphasis, the affirmations of the modern conscience, he went on to sketch two contrasting portraits of the Christian and the modern man: the

Christian "who withdraws from the converse of men, exclusively preoccupied with his own salvation, which is a matter between God and himself" and "the modern man who, accepting the world and its laws, resolves to extract from them all the good that they contain." Unlike the former, the latter "cannot detach himself from other men: fully conscious of the solidarity which unites him with his fellows, which makes him in a sense dependent on them, he knows that he cannot work out his salvation by himself." [2] So another thinker, who is fond of mordant phrases, referred to the Pope as "only a technician of individual salvation." And in an article attacking Christian tradition, an educationist said the same thing, though in rather a different manner: "The point in question is whether education should prepare the individual to ignore everything that exists in this world. If so, it will result in the development of an egoism gone mad. Man will have only one concern left to him, his individual salvation; so much the worse if others suffer and if untold misfortunes surround us. And if everybody adopted this point of view the world and mankind would have no further reason for existence, 'it would only remain for us to go back to the deserts, to shut ourselves up in the cloister, to scourge ourselves day and night' in order to avoid hell and gain heaven. But all that is the very denial of humanity and of life in society." [3]

Séailles, Alain, Marcel Giron are all, each in his way, aggressive free-thinkers. But such a calm philosopher as Hamelin is in agreement with them on this point. In the course of a study on Renouvier's analytical philosophy of history [4] Hamelin asserts that, Christ having promised salvation not to communities but to individuals and "all that is social in the efforts of humanity" being, according to Christian belief, "condemned to perish," "the entirely individualist point of view" which the Christian therefore adopts involves "a contempt for justice." For, he explained, "it is impossible to be just without admitting an interest in the social life of the group to which one belongs and in its future. Justice rejects, then, a strict individualism, and is thus opposed to the doctrine of the struggle for existence and that of Christian detachment."

In answer to all this we may quote this simple assertion of a believer and a theologian: "Fundamentally the Gospel is obsessed with the idea of the unity of human society." [5]

This shows the full extent of the misunderstanding. We are accused of being individualists even in spite of ourselves, by the logic of our faith, whereas in reality Catholicism is essentially social. It is social in the deepest sense of the word: not merely in its applications in the field of natural institutions but first and foremost in itself, in the heart of its mystery, in the essence of its dogma. It is social in a sense which should have made the expression "social Catholicism" pleonastic.

Nevertheless, if such a misunderstanding has arisen and entrenched itself, if such an accusation is current, is it not our own fault? We can leave on one side what is only too obviously groundless in certain objections, those which are bound up with a purely extrinsic and secular conception of Catholicism or of salvation or based on a complete misunderstanding of Christian detachment. Nor need we insist on the failings, serious though they often are, which may have given rise to these misunderstandings: the selfish piety, the narrow religious outlook, the neglect of ordinary duties in the multiplication of "devotions," the swamping of the spiritual life by the detestable "I," the failure to realize that prayer is essentially the prayer of all for all. These are all deviations to which all believers, being human, are exposed, and which it is easy to criticize. But are they in fact sufficiently recognized as such? Does not neglect of dogma increase the extent of moral failure? And if so many observers, who are not all lacking in acumen or in religious spirit, are so grievously mistaken about the essence of Catholicism, is it not an indication that Catholics should make an effort to understand it better themselves?

It is an effort of this kind that the following pages would assist in their small measure. Since they are addressed to believers who are concerned to have a better understanding of the faith by which they live, their aim is only indirectly apologetic. I have not undertaken to show once again the part that must be claimed for Christianity in the work of social progress, nor to provide another of the many commentaries on that saying of Montesquieu's about the earthly happiness secured by a religion which is wholly concerned with the life after death. I have no intention of drawing up for this century a plan of social reform inspired by Christianity. Confining myself to the implications of dogma I shall be concerned first and foremost with the society of believers—that on earth and that of the world to come, that which is visible and especially that which is invisible. For it is in this, it is in the intimate understanding of this mysterious *Catholica*, that is to be found, it seems to me, the fundamental explanation of the "social" repercussions of Christianity in the temporal order, as well as a preventive against a "social temptation" which could cause corruption in faith itself if it were to yield to it.

The subject thus more accurately defined is still too wide for me to have any desire to exhaust it. I have deliberately restricted the scope of my work, leaving regretfully on one side the rich resources of scripture and the great doctors on the subject of man's solidarity with the universe, or on our relations with the world of pure Spirits. Even the word "Catholicism" will not be explained, at any rate explicitly, in all its meanings. I have chosen it as the title of this book to show the spirit in which I have tried to write it rather than as an indication of what it contains. This is not a work on the *Catholica*. Consequently here will be found no treatise on the Church or on the Mystical Body—although these pages refer continually to both, and particularly to the question of their identity. Many excellent works, like Karl Adam's *The Spirit of Catholicism* or Fr Mersch's great historical inquiry,[6] excuse our dwelling on these matters. There is nothing in this book about the disunion of Christians or the "principles of a Catholic Œcumenicism"; after Fr Congar's work there was no need to return to the subject.[7] Nor have I mentioned the Catholic principle of Tradition, the "constitutive thinking" of Christianity, whose social nature is just as clear as that of its "constituted thinking," that is, of dogma: it would have raised a whole new series of problems which would have been beyond me. And lastly I have not dealt with Catholic Action: this subject could only be tackled by a theologian with a wide and enlightened experience of this Action. Without any attempt at systematic doctrinal treatment and without introducing questions that would require a strictly philosophical investigation, my purpose has been simply to bring out clearly certain ideas that are inherent in our faith: ideas so simple that they do not always attract attention, but at the same time so fundamental that there is some risk of our not finding time to ponder them.[8]

The first part shows in a general conspectus how our whole religion, in the principal articles of its *Credo* (Chapter I), in its living constitution (Chapter II), in its sacramental system (Chapter III), in the end that it offers to our hope (Chapter IV), exhibits an eminently social character, which it would be impossible without distortion of our religion to disregard. From this character the second part draws certain conclusions which concern the part assigned by Christianity to history. After seeing that in this respect Christianity provides the inquirer with a unique phenomenon (Chapter V), I consider from this point of view the question of scripture and its spiritual interpretation—a question that not only concerns the history of exegesis and of Christian thought for many centuries, but still remains at bottom a subject of capital importance whose essential connexion with orthodoxy was noticed by both Newman and Moehler (Chapter VI). I go on to show that the question of the salvation of unbelievers is somewhat clarified by the principles thus indicated (Chapter VII). Next an examination of the Fathers' answer to the pagan objection about the late coming of the Incarnation helps to show the extent and the unity of the divine plan for our humanity as they saw it (Chapter VIII). Lastly there is found in the great achievement of the missions a clue to a better understanding of the spirit of Catholicism (Chapter IX). In the third and shortest part, after noticing some characteristics of the present theological position (Chapter X), I try to dissipate certain misunderstandings by an examination of how Catholicism ennobles personal values (Chapter XI) and how its twofold historical and social character is not to be understood in a purely temporal and earthly sense (Chapter XII). The problem of the Person and the problem of Transcendence are both eternal problems, but both are lamentably real in our own day; without being able to go deeply into them, I felt that they could not be entirely passed by.

This is not intended as a technical work. If the quotations are numerous—even at the risk of tiring the reader—it is because I wanted to present the subject as impersonally as possible, drawing especially on the treasures, so little utilized, in the patristic writings. This is not to overlook in a frenzy of archaism the precisions and developments in theology which have been made since their time, nor do I take over in their entirety all the ideas they offer us: I seek only to understand them, and listen to what they have to tell us, since they are our Fathers in the Faith and since they received from the Church of their time the means to nourish the Church of our times as well. Still less do I claim to write history: I merely endeavour to bring to light certain permanent features —with all the dangers of inexactitude which that implies— among the very diverse and sometimes contrary trends of Tradition. For the unity of this Tradition in all that affects the essentials of Catholicism does not seem to me an empty term, an abstract theological thesis which a careful examination of the facts would invalidate. On the contrary, the greater becomes one's familiarity with this immense army of witnesses, the closer one's association with this one or that, the keener is the realization of how deep is the unity in which all those meet together who, faithful to the one Church, live by the same faith in the same Holy Spirit.

Finally (I readily confess it, for I have been constantly aware of it in writing the book) the point of view adopted leads inevitably to an incomplete treatment. Dogma is considered only in certain of its aspects. That was a necessity imposed upon me by my method. It is enough, I think, if these aspects are not presented in an exaggerated form, and I hope that no reader will be deceived into thinking that I undervalue what I have had to pass over in silence. To sum up, then, this book contains no more than certain materials gathered together in no very strict order and followed by certain reflexions on them. I place them now in the hands of those who will be able, better than I, to make use of them and complete them.

LYONS, July 31, 1937

Feast of St Ignatius Loyola

¹ Jean Giono, *Les vraies richesses*, 1936, pp. v and viii.

² *Les affirmations de la conscience moderne*, 3rd edn., 1906, pp. 108–9; and p. 56: "Our morality is less and less Christian just because it is more and more social." P. 108: "the Christian, like the Stoic, is sufficient unto himself."

³ Marcel Giron, *Le sentiment religieux et l'école libératrice*, in *L'École libératrice*, Feb. 2, 1935.

⁴ It appeared in the *Année philosophique* of 1898; reprinted in O. Hamelin, *Le Système de Renouvier*, 1927, pp. 444–5.

⁵ E. Masure, conference in *Semaine sociale de Nice*, 1934, p. 229.

⁶ E. Mersch, S. J., *Le Corps mystique du Christ, études de théologie historique* (*Museum Lessianum*, theological section), 2 vols., 2nd edn., 1936. By the same author: *Morale et Corps mystique* (*ibid*), 1937; *Le Corps mystique du Christ, centre de la théologie comme science* (*Nouvelle Revue théologique*, 1934); *L'Objet de la théologie et le Christus totus* in *Recherches de Science religieuse*, 1936. The informed reader will notice that we owe much to Fr Mersch. His posthumous work, *La Théologie du Corps mystique*, appeared in 1944, 2 vols. There must now be noticed, too, the teaching of the encyclical *Mystici Corporis*.

⁷ M.-J. Congar, O.P., *Chrétiens désunis, Principes d'un œcuménisme catholique* (*Unam Sanctam* series, 1; English translation: *Divided Christendom: A Catholic Study of the problem of reunion*, London, 1939).

⁸ The first draft of this work appeared in *Chronique sociale de la France*, April and May 1936, and these articles were published afterwards by the *Chronique* as a pamphlet. Chapter VII is a partial reproduction of a report read to the Congress of the Missionary Union of the Clergy at Strasbourg in 1933, and Chapter IX is a development of a study published in 1932 by the *Revue de l'Aucam*.

At the end of this book the reader will find a series of extracts illustrating facets of the teaching which is here set out. They are nearly all patristic texts. In view of the extreme dearth of editions and translations of the Fathers this small selection seemed likely to be of some use.

I

DOGMA

The supernatural dignity of one who has been baptized rests, we know, on the natural dignity of man, though it surpasses it in an infinite manner: *agnosce, christiane, dignitatem tuam—Deus qui humanae substantiae dignitatem mirabiliter condidisti.* Thus the unity of the Mystical Body of Christ, a supernatural unity, supposes a previous natural unity, the unity of the human race. So the Fathers of the Church, in their treatment of grace and salvation, kept constantly before them this Body of Christ, and in dealing with the creation were not content only to mention the formation of individuals, the first man and the first woman, but delighted to contemplate God creating humanity as a whole. "God," says St Irenaeus, for example, "in the beginning of time plants the vine of the human race; he loved this human race and purposed to pour out his Spirit upon it and to give it the adoption of sons." [1] For Irenaeus again, as indeed for Origen,[2] Gregory Nazianzen, Gregory of Nyssa, for Cyril of Alexandria, Maximus, Hilary and others, the lost sheep of the Gospel that the Good Shepherd brings back to the fold is no other than the whole of human nature; its sorry state so moves the Word of God that he leaves the great flock of the angels, as it were to their own devices, in order to go to its help. The Fathers designated this nature by a series of equivalent expressions, all of a concrete nature, thus demonstrating that it was in their view a genuine reality.

They seemed to witness its birth, to see it live, grow, develop, as a single being. With the first sin it was this being,

17

whole and entire, which fell away, which was driven out of
Paradise and sentenced to a bitter exile until the time of its
redemption. And when Christ at last appeared, coming as the
"one bridegroom," his bride, once again, was the "whole
human race."

Our early Fathers' habitual manner of thought must be
borne in mind if we would understand certain strange ways of
speaking—whatever their precise origin—that are met with in
such writers as Methodius of Olympus, who appears to make
of Christ a new appearance of Adam himself brought back
to life by the Word.[3] If several of them held so strongly,
as we know, that Adam was saved, one of the reasons for
it was undoubtedly that they saw the salvation of its head
as the necessary condition of the salvation of the human
race. "This Adam, within us all," says one of the homilies of
Pseudo-Epiphanius.[4] And another homily, of Pseudo-Chrysostom: "By the sacrifice of Christ the first man was saved,
that man who is in us all."[5] Is not this also the inner
meaning of the legend according to which Adam, who had
been buried on Calvary, was baptized by the water which
flowed from the side of Jesus? Surely, too, the many liturgical
texts about the descent of Christ into "hell," where the first
man is alone mentioned, are, like the works of art which
correspond with them, indications that that same way of
thought continued until much later.

Before embarking on the study of this human nature, from
its beginning until the end of the world, the Fathers made a
fundamental examination of it in order to perceive the principle of its unity. Now this principle appeared no different
to them from that on which rests the natural dignity of man.
Was it not shown to them in Genesis, where it was taught
that God made man in his own image? For the divine image
does not differ from one individual to another: in all it is
the same image. The same mysterious participation in God
which causes the soul to exist effects at one and the same
time the unity of spirits among themselves. Whence comes
the notion, so beloved of Augustinianism, of one spiritual
family intended to form the one city of God.

To confine ourselves to man, the doctrine of Gregory of
Nyssa, we know, makes a distinction between the first individuals of our kind, coming forth "as by degrees" from
their causes, in their time, "by a natural and necessary
genesis" in the fashion of all other living creatures, and Man

made according to the Image, the object of a direct creation out of time, who is in each one of us and who makes us so entirely one that we ought not to speak of man in the plural any more than we speak of three Gods.[6] For "the whole of human nature from the first man to the last is but one image of him who is."[7] That is a doctrine which, in broad outline, was not to remain only Gregory's but to be the inspiration of a whole tradition and which is still reproduced in the fourteenth century by Ruysbroeck, for example, who writes in his wonderful *Mirror of Eternal Salvation:*

> The heavenly Father created all men in his own image. His image is his Son, his eternal Wisdom . . . who was before all creation. It is in reference to this eternal image that we have all been created. It is to be found essentially and personally in all men; each one possesses it whole and entire and undivided, and all together have no more than one. In this way we are all one, intimately united in our eternal image, which is the image of God and in all of us the source of our life and of our creation.[8]

So when pagan philosophers jeered at what they considered the extravagant claim put forward by the Christians, those latest of the barbarians, of uniting all men in the same faith, it was easy for the Fathers to answer them that this claim was not, after all, so extravagant, since all men were made in the one image of the one God. It was a sort of divine monogenism, forging the link between the doctrine of divine unity and that of human unity, the foundation in practice of monotheism and its full significance.[9] In the language of the first centuries Adam was not generally called the "father of the human race"; he was only the "first made," "the first begotten by God," as is recalled by the final sentences, so solemn in their simplicity, of the genealogy of Jesus according to Luke: "who was of Henos, who was of Seth, who was of Adam, who was of God."[10] To believe in this one God was, therefore, to believe at the same time in a common Father of all: *unus Deus et Pater omnium.*[11] The prayer taught us by Christ makes clear in its very first phrase that monotheism postulates the brotherhood of all men. It implied that he assumed the original unity of all men and that he was effectively to re-unite them all in one same worship: *adunari ad unius Dei cultum.*[12] "Since he who dwells in us is one only, everywhere he joins and binds together those who are in the bond of unity." [13]

Again and again Irenaeus dwells on this dual correspondence:

> there is but one God the Father, and one Logos the Son, and one Spirit, and one salvation only for all who believe in him. . . . There is but one salvation as there is but one God. . . . There is one only Son who fulfils the will of the Father, and one only human race in which the mysteries of God are fulfilled.[14]

Clement of Alexandria, in pages brimming over with poetry, after exposing the baseness of the pagan mystery cults, extols the mysteries of the Logos and displays the "divine Choregus" calling all men to him:

> Be instructed in these mysteries and you shall dance with the choir of angels before the uncreated God, whilst the Logos will sing the sacred hymns with us. This eternal Jesus, the one high priest, intercedes for men and calls on them: "Hearken," he cries, "all you peoples, or rather all you who are endowed with reason, barbarians or Greeks! I summon the whole human race, I who am its author by the will of the Father! Come unto me and gather together as one well-ordered unity under the one God, and under the one Logos of God." [15]

In these conditions, all infidelity to the divine image that man bears in him, every breach with God, is at the same time a disruption of human unity. It cannot eliminate the natural unity of the human race—the image of God, tarnished though it may be, is indestructible—but it ruins that spiritual unity which, according to the Creator's plan, should be so much the closer in proportion as the supernatural union of man with God is the more completely effected. *Ubi peccata, ibi multitudo*.[16] True to Origen's criterion, Maximus the Confessor, for example, considers original sin as a separation, a breaking up, an individualization it might be called, in the depreciatory sense of the word. Whereas God is working continually in the world to the effect that all should come together into unity,[17] by this sin which is the work of man, "the one nature was shattered into a thousand pieces" and humanity which ought to constitute a harmonious whole, in

which "mine" and "thine" would be no contradiction, is turned
into a multitude of individuals, as numerous as the sands of
the seashore, all of whom show violently discordant in-
clinations. "And now," concludes Maximus, "we rend each
other like the wild beasts." [18] "Satan has broken us up,"
said St Cyril of Alexandria for his part, in order to explain
the first fall and the need of a redeemer.[19] And in a curious
passage, in which the recurrence of an ancient myth may
be discerned, Augustine explains the matter similarly in a
symbolical manner. After establishing a connexion between
the four letters of Adam's name and the Greek names for
the four points of the compass, he adds: "Adam himself is
therefore now spread out over the whole face of the earth.
Originally one, he has fallen, and, breaking up as it were,
he has filled the whole earth with the pieces." [20]

That was one way of considering evil in its inmost essence,
and it is a pity perhaps that the theology of a later period
has not turned it to greater account. Instead of trying, as we
do almost entirely nowadays, to find within each individual
nature what is the hidden blemish and, so to speak, of looking for the mechanical source of the trouble which is the
cause of the faulty running of the engine—some exaggerat-
ing the trouble, others inclined to minimize it—these Fathers
preferred to envisage the very constitution of the individuals
considered as so many cores of natural opposition. This was
not taken as the first or only cause of sin, of course, but at
least as a secondary result, "equal to the first," and the inner
disruption went hand in hand with the social disruption. To
be sure, these two explanations are by no means contradictory,
and may often in fact be found together. In this connexion
we tend to associate St Augustine chiefly with the wonderful
psychological analyses of the *Confessions,* but it is well to
bear in mind that he has not neglected the other point of
view, as we have just seen. St Maximus, indeed, given the
opportunity, could combine the two ways of considering the
question: "the devil," he writes, for instance, "man's tempter
from the beginning, had separated him in his will from God,
had separated men from each other." [21] Several of the
Fathers show us the state of sin as the disintegration of the
limb cut off from the body. Between the Fathers and us, then,
doctrinal unity is preserved. But it cannot be denied that our
approach is different.

Let us abide by the outlook of the Fathers: the redemption being a work of restoration will appear to us by that very fact as the recovery of lost unity—the recovery of supernatural unity of man with God, but equally of the unity of men among themselves. "Divine Mercy gathered up the fragments from every side, forged them in the fire of love, and welded into one what had been broken. . . . He who re-made was himself the Maker, and he who re-fashioned was himself the Fashioner." [22] Thus does he raise up again man who was lost by gathering together once more his scattered members, so restoring his own image. Like the queen bee, Christ comes to muster humanity around him. It is in this that the great miracle of Calvary consists:

> There were at that time all kinds of miracles: God on the Cross, the sun darkened . . . the veil of the temple rent . . . water and blood flowing from his side, the earth quaking, stones breaking, the dead rising. . . . Who can worthily extol such wonders? But none is to be compared with the miracle of my salvation: minute drops of blood making the whole world new, working the salvation of all men, as the drops of fig-juice one by one curdle the milk, re-uniting mankind, knitting them together as one.[23]

For a change of metaphor there is that in which Christ is likened to a needle the eye in which, pierced most painfully at his passion, now draws all after him, so repairing the tunic rent by Adam, stitching together the two peoples of Jew and Gentile, making them one for always.

Divisa uniuntur, discordantia pacantur: [24] such from the very beginning is the effect of the Incarnation. Christ from the very first moment of his existence virtually bears all men within himself—*erat in Christo Jesu omnis homo.* For the Word did not merely take a human body; his Incarnation was not a simple *corporatio,* but, as St Hilary says, a *concorporatio.*[25] He incorporated himself in our humanity, and incorporated it in himself. *Universitatis nostrae caro est factus.*[26] In making a human nature, it is *human nature* that he united to himself, that he enclosed in himself,[27] and it is the latter, whole and entire, that in some sort he uses as a body. *Naturam in se universae carnis adsumpsite.* Whole and entire he will bear it then to Calvary, whole and entire he will raise it from the dead, whole and entire he will save it. Christ the Redeemer does not offer salvation merely to each one; he effects it, he is himself the salvation of the whole, and for each one salvation consists in a personal ratification of his original "belonging" to Christ, so that he be not cast out, cut off from this Whole.[28]

Not in vain does John assert that the Word came and dwelt among us, for in this way he teaches us the great mystery that we are all in Christ and that the common personality of man is brought back to life by his assuming of it. The new Adam is so called because he acquires for the common nature all that pertains to happiness and glory, just as the old Adam acquired what pertains to its corruption and shame. Through the medium of one the Word came to dwell in all, so that the only Son of God being established in power, his dignity should be shed upon the whole human race by the holiness of the Spirit: and thus should be verified in each one of us that saying of Scripture: "I said ye are Gods and sons of the most High." . . . The Word dwells in us, in that one temple he took through us and of us, so that we should possess all things in him and he should bring us all back to the Father in one Body.[29]

It is a commonplace to allude to the Platonism of the Fathers in connexion with these doctrines. But instead of invoking the Platonic doctrine of essential being, we should do better to account for them—to the extent that they are dependent at all on a philosophic basis—by looking rather to the Stoic conception of universal being. There are many expressions in Marcus Aurelius, for example, regarding the integration of the individual in the concrete totality of the cosmos, and still more concerning the reciprocal immanence of those who are participators in the *Nous*. But all this is of secondary importance, and we should beware of adopting the practice known in accountancy as double-entry, as so many Protestant historians do in dealing with the Fathers and the Bible. For in the Fathers they will see nothing but Hellenistic borrowings and influence, whereas in St Paul and St John they will find nothing but "pure revelation" or at least "pure religion." So severely critical an attitude on the one hand, such naïve simplicity on the other, are in fact equally the causes of their blindness.

For in whatever degree a philosophical basis was necessary to the Fathers, were it Platonist or Stoic, their speculation was conditioned less by considerations of philosophy than by a keen realization of the needs of Christianity. How else indeed could they make the most of the metaphor of the body and its members in the great Pauline epistles if they were to leave Stoicism out of account? Or how could they interpret with accuracy the epistle to the Hebrews if first they must eliminate all trace of Platonism? In fact, they never scrupled to borrow, and that to a large extent, from the great pagan philosophers whom they held in esteem. But, wiser than Solomon, they were not led into idolatry by their philosophy, and as a modern historian, Christopher Dawson,[30] has remarked, we must go back to St John and St Paul if we would understand patristic thought.

For we can learn from the Fathers another view of the work of redemption, the horizontal view—if we may put it thus—which is explicit in revelation no less than the first, the vertical or Godward view. In fact this horizontal view is to be found there equally as the condition and the result of the vertical view. From the beloved Apostle, who was privileged to be closer to Jesus than the others, we take this reflexion concerning Caiaphas: "Being the high priest of that year, he prophesied that Jesus should die for the nation. And not only for the nation, but to gather together in one the children of God that were dispersed." [31] This interpretation of the sacrifice of our redemption was based on those very words of Christ that the evangelist had set down in the preceding chapter of his book: the Good Shepherd must gather all his sheep, all the peoples of the earth, that is to say, into one flock.[32] Such an interpretation echoes that great prophecy of Isaias: "I will bring forth thy seed from the east and gather thee from the west: I will say to the north: Give up; and to the south: Keep not back; bring my sons from afar, and my daughters from the ends of the earth." [33]

St Paul in a memorable passage describes the warfare in every man of the flesh against the spirit: but there is another conflict that figures as prominently in his thought, that which splits the work of God into two opposing or alien groups. Such in the cosmic order (at least according to a possible and common interpretation) is the dissension between the heavenly powers and human beings.[34] Such, in any case, in the earthly order, is that tragic enmity, symbolic of so many others, between Jew and Gentile. Christ came to bring them

to unity and peace. He is himself this peace in person:
Pax nostra. Raised up on the cross, his arms stretched out,
he is to gather together the disunited portions of creation,
"breaking down the middle wall of partition" between them.[35]
It is by his blood that "those who some time were afar off
are made nigh"; it is his blood that will join together the
two parts of the building. Through his one sacrifice he will
make but one kingdom out of all nations.[36] While his grace
restores unity in each one of us, at the same time it reunites us all together, so that

> we who were sundered and at enmity by reason of our
> sensuality and the diverse desires and uncleanness of our
> sins, being cleansed by the Mediator should set out to-
> gether towards that same blessedness, and being forged to-
> gether into one mind by the fire of love, are united, not
> in our common nature alone but by the bond of a common
> love.[37]

This pristine unity, broken as soon as established, is re-
constituted by dint of many an ordeal, but is fuller at the
last and on a grander scale: *felix culpa—mirabilius re-
formasti.*

Such, in the thought of St Paul faithfully expounded in
the Fathers, is the mystery in which is summed up the whole
object of revelation, "that he might make known to us the
mystery of his will, according to his good pleasure, which
he hath purposed in him, in the dispensation of the fullness
of times, to re-establish (*reunite*) all things in Christ. . . ."[38]
This mystery is nothing else than the Mystical Body of Christ
—to use the term consecrated by long tradition which faithfully mirrors the teaching of the two Apostles. St Paul spoke
simply of the Body of Christ. Presiding over the churches,
he emphasized both the social function and the differing responsibilities of each of the members of this body in the
unity of the same Spirit. St John, on the other hand, writing in a more contemplative strain, stressed rather the unity
of life in the different branches of the mystical Vine. Yet in
reality St Paul's teaching is no less forceful than St John's,
for just as with the latter the personal link of the disciple
with Jesus—*in me manet et ego in eo*—is no impairing of
the unity of the whole body—*ut unum sint*[39]—so in St
Paul insistence on an objective view diminishes not at all
his teaching on mystical union. The Pauline metaphor of the

body was not at all original; it gains its whole strength because St Paul does not say simply "the body of Christians," just as he might have said "the body of the Greeks" or "the body of the Jews," [40] but "the body of Christ," to which he frequently adds that favourite gloss of his, "in Christ Jesus."

If for St John the bond uniting the faithful to each other and to their Saviour seems to emerge as the expression of an exceedingly close and mutual relationship, for St Paul, on the other hand, it is Christ who appears rather as a centre, an atmosphere, a whole world even, in which man and God, man and man, are in communion and achieve union. For it is "he who fills all in all." [41]

These different expressions are matched and defined in St Paul's vocabulary by another, which this time is not entirely metaphorical. It concerns the "new man" that every Christian must "put on" as he puts on Christ.[42] Sufficient attention has not been paid to the fact that mention of this "new man" who is ever "renewed" is, in the Epistle to the Colossians, coupled with a reference to the unique Image, "the image of him that created him," and to "Christ . . . all, and in all." The Epistle to the Ephesians, in accordance with its general tenor, increases the emphasis on this social aspect; for the "new man" is there identified with that one Body in which the two hostile peoples, reconciled and united, should "have access . . . to the Father": εἰς ἕνα καινὸν ἄνθρωπον, ἐν ἑνὶ σώματι.

Thus St Hippolytus was very close to the Apostle's thought when he wrote: "Anxious that all should be saved, the Son of God calls on every one of us to make up, in holiness, one single perfect man." [43] Likewise Clement of Alexandria: "The whole Christ, if we may be allowed the phrase, the total Christ, is not divided: for he is neither barbarian, nor Jew, nor Greek, nor man, nor woman, but the new Man, wholly transformed by the Spirit." [44] St Augustine, in his turn, faithfully following St Paul, speaks of "this new Man spread about over the whole world" [45] and made up of the body of the Christian faithful. So, too, St Maximus, or the unknown author hidden under his name, literally sums up the whole doctrine by telescoping into one short phrase the principal heads under which, one by one, St Paul had enunciated his teaching: "Putting on that new Man, whole and entire, who was created by the Spirit in the image of God." [46]

But it is in St Cyril of Alexandria beyond all others that this thought appears almost as an obsession. Time and again the very language of the epistle to the Ephesians figures in his works, and throughout his commentaries on the prophets he is conscious of the foreshadowing of the doctrine. Christ, he remarks, not only threw down the old dividing wall, but has made of himself the corner-stone of the building;[47] indeed, through his agency not a single but a threefold wall of division was thrown down, and a threefold reunion has thus been effected. For man was reconciled to man, to the angels and to God. God cannot be worshipped save in one edifice, and his straying children can only find the way to the Father if they are gathered together in one Body, the new Man whose head is our Redeemer. This mystery of the new Man is in the highest sense of the word the mystery of Christ.

Εἰς ἕνα καινὸν ἄνθρωπον: behold then this new creature of whom St Paul had spoken to the Corinthians and Galatians [48] without at that time manifesting its full significance. Behold him, this "perfect man," who, in the epistle to the Ephesians, is shown to us finally as the one pattern to the making of which the united endeavours of all should strive, for the perfection of each individual must be measured at its maturity against the fullness of the Whole.[49] Behold him, "this new being in the world," the masterpiece of the Spirit of God. Henceforward one living being grows under the action of a single life-force, and vivified by the one Spirit attains to the stature of perfection. Its scope remains God's secret.

NOTES TO CHAPTER I

[1] *Adversus Haereses*, passim.

[2] *In Genesim*, hom. 2, 5; 9, 3; 13, 2 (Baehrens, pp. 34, 92, 114).

[3] Methodius of Olympus, *Symposium*, 3, c. 4–8 (French trans. by Farges, pp. 42–52).

[4] Homily 2 (P.G. xliii, 460–1).

[5] *In Pascha*, sermo 2; cf. sermo 1 (P.G. lix, 725 and 723).

[6] *De hominis opificio*, passim, especially c. 8 (P.G. xliv); *Quod non sint tres dii*; *Tractatus adversus graecos ex communibus notionibus* (xlv); *Contra Eunomium*, lib. 3 (xlv, 592). Doubtless the Bishop of Nyssa no more speaks of numerical unity in regard to man than in regard to God. But it is not that he

only allows, on a final analysis, a "specific" unity; it is because number is for him a sign of quantity which derives from matter. This theory is outlined in *Contra Eunomium*, lib. 1 (xlv, 312) and *Quod non sint tres dii* (xlv, 131). See Extract 1, p. 208.

⁷ *De hominis opificio*, c. 16 (P.G. xliv, 188). See Extract 2, p. 211.

⁸ Chap. 8. And Julian of Norwich, *Revelations of Divine Love*, Chap. 58. See Extract 3, p. 212.

⁹ Gregory of Nyssa, *In Psalm.*, lib. 2, c. 15 (P.G. xliv, 593).

¹⁰ *Luke* iii. 38.

¹¹ *Ephes.* iv. 6; *Rom.* iii. 30; *Acts* xvii. 26–8.

¹² Isidore of Seville, *De fide cath. c. Judaeos*, lib. 2, c. 1 (P.L. lxxxiii, 409).

¹³ Cyprian, *De Cath. Eccl. Unitate*, c. 23 (Hartel, pp. 284–5).

¹⁴ *Adv. Haereses*, 4, 6, 7 (P.G. vii, 990); 4, 9, 3 (998); 5 in fine (1224).

¹⁵ *Protreptic*, c. 12.

¹⁶ Origen, *In Ezech.*, hom. 9, n. 1 (Baehrens, p. 405).

¹⁷ *Quaestiones ad Thalassium*, q. 2 (P.G. xc, 272).

¹⁸ *Ibid.*, covering letter (P.G. xc, 256) and q. 64 (724–5).

¹⁹ Ἐσκόρπισεν: *In Joan.*, lib. 7 (P.G. lxxiv, 69).

²⁰ *In Psalm.* 95, n. 15 (P.L. xxxvii, 1236).

²¹ *Epist.* 2 (P.G. xci, 396–7). Cf. *Ambiguorum liber* (xci, 1156), etc. and Anastasius Sinaita, q. 57: "Each one is sundered from himself and others" (lxxxix, 621). On the other hand, a modern liturgical text, the collect for the feast of Christ the King, reads: "Cunctae familiae gentium, peccati vulnere disgregatae." Cf. also the Buchman group's definition of sin: "What separates us from God and from each other" (quoted by M.-J. Congar, *Chrétiens désunis*, English trans., *Divided Christendom*, London, 1939); and Karl Barth on the threefold opposition caused by sin: "opposition to God, to oneself and to one's neighbour" (*L'Église et les Églises*, French trans. by Moobs, in Œcumenica, 1936, p. 139). Gabriel Marcel has noted with emphasis: "the state of division and as it were spiritual dislocation that is today the lot of humanity . . ., an evil for which all humanity is responsible . . . an evil with deep roots, and untold consequences" (*Les Groupes d'Oxford*, in the *Bulletin de l'Union pour la Vérité*, 1936, p. 366). See also Newman, *Parochial and Plain Sermons*, vol. 9.

²² Augustine, *In Psalm.* 58, n. 10 (P.L. xxxvi, 698). See Extract 4, p. 213.

²³ Gregory Nazianzen, *Orat.* 45, c. 29 (P.G. xxxvi, 662–4). Cf. *Ephes.* ii. 13.

²⁴ Fulgentius, *Ad Monimum*, lib. 2, c. 10 (P.L. lxv, 188).

²⁵ Hilary, *In Matthaeum*, lib. 6, c. 1: "concorporationem Verbi Dei" (P.L. ix, 951).

²⁶ Hilary, *In Psalmum* 54, n. 9 (Zingerle, p. 153).

²⁷ Origen, *In Joannem*, vol. x, c. 41 (Preuschen, p. 218). In spite of what some historians like Harnack have said, this doctrine is in no way derogatory to the dogma of the hypostatic

union of one sole nature with the Godhead, any more than the
unity of the Father and the Holy Spirit with the Son requires
their Incarnation. The Fathers perceived the difficulty: thus Maximus, "Debate with Pyrrhus" and letter 13 (P.G. xci, 305 and 528–9)
and John Damascene, *De fide orthodoxa*, lib. 3, c. 6. (xciv, 1008).
In the sixth century, Joannes Philoponus will admit only one specific nature, entirely abstract (ἡ κοινὴ φύσις ὁ κοινὸς τῆς φύσεως λόγος),
and individual concrete natures: in this way he imagined he
could get over a problem that was embarrassing him (P.G.
xciv, 748–9), but only succeeded in laying himself open to a
charge of Tritheism and a tendency to Monophysism. In spite
of the difficulty that he pointed out in the contrary doctrine
it remained traditional none the less, and was the inspiration
of chapter iv of the second council of Quierzy in 853:
"Christus Jesus Dominus noster, sicut nullus homo est,
fuit vel erit, cujus natura in illo assumpta non fuerit." Cf.
also the interesting attempts at Thomistic interpretation by L.
Malevez in *L'Église dans le Christ* in *Recherches de Science religieuse*, 1935, and by M.-J. Congar in *Revue des Sciences philosophiques et théologiques*, 1936. With a proper concern for the
avoidance of confusion Fr Malevez, following the terminology of
Gregory of Nyssa (but see P.G. xlv, 700), refuses to use the
term "assume"—ἀναλαμβάνειν—in connexion with the universal
nature. He speaks in this case of union or inclusion. Such distinctions are not to be found in Hilary, Athanasius, or Gregory
Nazianzen. But it must be noted, lastly, that in spite of a frequent intermixture of the two points of view these texts concerning the bond contracted by Christ with all men by the very
fact of the Incarnation alone must not be applied as they stand
to the doctrine of the Mystical Body.

[28] *Romans* xi. 22.

[29] Cyril of Alexandria, *In Joannem*, lib. 1 (P.G. lxxiii, 161–
4).

[30] *Progress and Religion, an historical Enquiry* (London,
1931).

[31] *John* xi. 52; cf. xvii. 2 (notice the neuter singular, ζῶντες.).

[32] *John* x. 15–6; *Ezechiel* xxxiv.

[33] *Isaias* xliii. 5–6; xlix. 12.

[34] *Coloss.* i. 20; *Ephes.* i. 10. See F. Prat, *La théologie de saint
Paul*, vol. i, 7th edn., p. 352, and vol. ii, 6th edn., pp. 107–8;
J. Huby, *Les Épîtres de la captivité*, p. 47.

[35] *Ephesians* ii. 14.

[36] *Apoc.* i. 6.

[37] Augustine, *De Trinitate*, lib. 4, c. 9 (P.L. xlii, 896: summarized trans. of this in text).

[38] *Ephesians* i. 9. Of the four possible meanings of the word
ἀνακεφαλαιώσασθαι, restore, resume, crown, reunite, the last appears
to be the one that should be used, at least for the primary
meaning (so d'Alès, Robinson, Huby, Benoit).

[39] J. Bonsirven, *Individualisme chrétien chez saint Jean*, in

Nouv. Rev. théol., 1935, pp. 449–76. L. Bouyer, *Le Mystère pascal*, pp. 179–84.

[40] An edict of Augustus (7–6 B.C.) speaks of "the body of Greeks," as later on the edict of Milan spoke of the "body of Christians" and the Theodosian code of the "body of Jews." E. W. Mamson, *Journal of Theol. Studies*, 1936, p. 385.

[41] There can be no question here of discussing the Pauline doctrine of the Body of Christ. Further details may be found in Mersch, 2nd edn., Appendix I: *La Doctrine du corps mystique dans les différentes épîtres de saint Paul* (vol. ii, pp. 379–91), and P. Benoit, *loc. cit., Revue biblique*, 1937 (September and October), and the review of A. Wikenhauser's *Die Kirche als der mystiche Leib Christi nach dem Apostel Paulus* in the *Revue biblique*, 1938, pp. 115–9. L. Cerfaux, *La théologie de l'Église suivant saint Paul* (1942), is a welcome reaction against certain interpretations of the Pauline epistles which attribute to St Paul the idea of a sort of impersonal Christ, different from the Jesus of the Gospels. Cf. *L'Église dans saint Paul* in *La Vie spirituelle*, May 1943.

[42] *Ephesians* ii. 15 and iv. 24; *Coloss.* iii. 10–11. Cf. *Coloss.* i. 20.

[43] *On Christ and anti-Christ*, c. 3 and 4 (Achelis, pp. 6–7).

[44] *Protreptic*, c. 11 (Stählin, vol. i, p. 79; Mondésert, p. 173).

[45] *In Psalm.* 85 and 122 (P.L. xxxvii, 1085 and 1630).

[46] *Capitula theologica et oeconomica*, cent. 2, c. 27 (P.G. xc, 1137).

[47] *In Isaiam* (P.G. lxx, 1009–12).

[48] *Gal.* vi. 15; *II Cor.* v. 17.

[49] *Ephesians* iv. 13. Modern translators do not always bring out the full meaning of the Pauline idea of the "perfect man." But it emerges in Fr Huby's *Les Épîtres da la captivité*, p. 205. The general context of the Epistle and the whole balance of the sentence seem to require this interpretation, and several of the Fathers pointed it out. See Extract 26, p. 242.

II

THE CHURCH

We are now in a better position to understand what the Church is. For all dogmas are bound up together. The Church which is "Jesus Christ spread abroad and communicated" [1] completes—so far as it can be completed here below—the work of spiritual reunion which was made necessary by sin; that work that was begun at the Incarnation and was carried on up to Calvary. In one sense the Church is herself this reunion, for that is what is meant by the name of Catholic by which we find her called from the second century onwards, and which in Latin as well as in Greek was for long bestowed upon her as a proper noun. Καθολικός, in classical Greek, was used by philosophers to indicate a universal proposition. Now a universal is a singular and is not to be confused with an aggregate. The Church is not Catholic because she is spread abroad over the whole of the earth and can reckon on a large number of members. She was already Catholic on the morning of Pentecost, when all her members could be contained in a small room, as she was when the Arian waves seemed on the point of swamping her; she would still be Catholic if to-morrow apostasy on a vast scale deprived her of almost all the faithful. For fundamentally Catholicity has nothing to do with geography or statistics. If it is true that it should be displayed over all the earth and be manifest to all, yet its nature is not material but spiritual. Like sanctity, Catholicity is primarily an intrinsic feature of the Church.

The Church in each individual calls on the whole man, embracing him as he is in his whole nature. "People think that you can play on a man as you play on an organ. An organ he is in truth, but a strange and fitful one. He who

31

can play only on an ordinary organ will produce no chords from this one."[2] But the Church can play on this organ because, like Christ, she "knows what is in man," because there is an intimate relationship between the dogma to which she adheres in all its mystery and human nature, infinitely mysterious in its turn. Now by the very fact that she goes to the very foundation of man the Church attains to all men and can "play her chords" upon them. Because she is eager to draw them all together she is fitted to do so.

Catholicity was understood in this sense by the great apologists of the first centuries, even though afterwards when the treatise on the marks of the Church came to be written too much importance was attached to geographical considerations. St Ambrose contemplating the Church saw her embracing both earth and sky with Christ set above for sun. He sees her including the whole *orbis terrarum* because he is aware that all, whatever their origin, race or condition, are called on to become one in Christ, and that thenceforward the Church is fundamentally that unity. From another point of view the same may be said of Origen, Tertullian and St Augustine. In such expressions as *per orbem terrae ecclesiae latitudo diffusa*[3] Origen states what is a requirement arising from his idea of the Church rather than actual statement of fact. Tertullian, mistaken in this like so many others, celebrated the actual extensive universality of the Church in phrases that were far too oratorical; but over and beyond this he describes that universality "in depth" which he explained by showing its relation with the human soul, everywhere the same and everywhere "naturally Christian."[4] In the same way there is not a little of the same illusion in St Augustine's *Chorus Christi jam totus mundus est.*[5] And yet, though it is not so accurate an estimate of the reality, it was a sound view of the nature of the Church that made the holy doctor add *Chorus Christi ab oriente ad occidentem consonat.* Whatever the number of members—that *Catholicae multitudo* so dear to St Augustine—and however great or small the part of the earth on which she was to be found, the Church still sings the canticle that is never old, the canticle of universal charity: *Pax vinculum sanctae societatis, compago spiritualis, aedificium de lapidibus vivis.* Without restriction of space she extends from "sea to sea," spreading out her song *per universum orbem terrarum.* It is not, then, the small extent of their territory that is the burden of St

Augustine's censure of the Donatists but their claim to self-sufficiency, to restrict the Church to their own bounds, *quasi perditis caeteris gentibus,*[6] and of solving all difficulties *inter Afros.*[7] It is their sectarian spirit and parochialism: *et nescio quis ponit in Africa fines caritatis.*[8] On the other hand, what he loves and admires in the *Catholica,* the *Unica Catholica,* is not just her mere universality, open to all men and excluding none—*ad ultimas gentes crescendo porrigitur* —but the bond of peace, that cohesion that is created wherever her sway extends.[9] In the fullest meaning of the word she brings beings into existence and gathers them together into one Whole. Humanity is one, organically one by its divine structure; it is the Church's mission to reveal to men that pristine unity that they have lost, to restore and complete it.[10]

The Church is a mother, but quite unlike other mothers she draws to her those who are to be her children and keeps them united together in her womb. Her sons, says St Maximus, come to her from all sides:

> Men, women, children, profoundly divided in national-ity, race, language, walk of life, work, knowledge, rank or means . . . all these she recreates in the Spirit. On all in the same measure she imprints a divine character. All receive of her a single nature which cannot be divided and by reason of which their many and deep differences can no longer be held in account. By it all are brought up and united in a truly Catholic manner. For (in the Church) no one is in the slightest degree separated from the community, all are fused together, so to speak, one in another, by the mere and undivided strength of faith. . . . Christ is also all in all, for he encloses all in himself by his sole power, infinite and all-wise in its goodness, like the centre to which all lines converge, so that all the creatures of the one God should not be strangers or enemies to each other without common ground whereon to show their friendship and the peace between them.[11]

That was the mystic reality, with its visible result of fra-ternal charity, a radiant novelty in the midst of a world grown old in its divisions, that aroused the enthusiastic ad-miration of such as St John Chrysostom or St Augustine. Chrysostom exclaims in his commentary on St John, when he reaches those words "to gather together those who are high

and those who are far off": "What does that mean? It means
that of one and all Christ makes a single body. Thus he who
lives in Rome may look on the Indians as his own members.
Is there any union that may be likened to this? Christ is
the head of all." [12] And St Augustine, again extolling the
Church in his well-known hymn in the *De moribus ecclesiae*:
"You unite together the inhabitants of the cities, the different peoples, nay the whole human race, by belief in our
common origin, so that men are not satisfied in being joined
together, but become in some sort brothers." [13]

Through a symbolism the origins of which seem to go
back to the first Christian generations, this Catholicism found
expression in the miracle of Pentecost. For in very early
times the scene that occurred then must have been compared
with the account in Genesis of the scattering of the peoples
and also with that in Exodus of the giving of the Law on
Sinai. The tongues of fire proclaim the gifts of tongues that
are to come; we have here indeed a parable in action which
signifies and ordains the world-wide preaching to the gentiles.
For these gifts were in fact scattered on the Apostles [14]
simply that they might carry out a mission of unity: the Holy
Spirit, manifested through them, is about to re-establish mutual comprehension among men, since each individual will
understand in his own language the one truth which is to
reunite him to his fellows:

> "Let us go down," said the Holy Spirit to the other
> persons of the Blessed Trinity, "and there confound their
> tongue, that they may not understand one another's speech
> . . . and therefore the name thereof was called Babel,
> because there the language of the whole earth was con-
> founded" (*Gen.* xi. 7, 9). And behold, once again at Pente-
> cost the Holy Spirit comes down from heaven. He does
> not merely come down, he falls down, *cecidit*. He rushes
> down like a thunderbolt; he restores these "parted tongues"
> (*dispertitae linguae*) to the Church that they may be the
> fire of a single furnace.[15]

There are twelve Apostles in the same way that there are
twelve tribes of Israel, and the number twelve signifies the
universality of the world, for the twelve are to go everywhere, teaching all nations and bringing them back to unity.

Each of them speaks all languages; one man, alone, speaks all languages because the Church is one, and she must one day praise God in all the tongues of the earth. "And even now all these tongues belong to each one of us, since we are all members of that one body that speaks in them." [16] So the miracle of Pentecost heralded, in symbolic abridgement, the fulfilment of the promise made of old to Abraham, and the infant Church herself, on the day of her birth, proffered a living likeness of her nature and her end.

For just as after the flood the wicked pride of men built a high tower against the Lord, and the human race then deserved to be divided by means of a diversity of languages so that each people speaking its own tongue was no longer understood of the others; so the humble piety of the faithful has made these divers tongues combine in the unity of the Church, so that what discord had broken up charity should reunite, and the scattered members of humanity, as members of one only body, should be bound up together in Christ, the only head, and forged together in the fire of love to make the unity of this holy body.[17]

This unity is so close that the Church is constantly personified. She is the betrothed, the bride that Christ has chosen, for the love of whom he gave himself up, whom he has made clean by baptism.[18] She is the "chosen people," the "son of God," etc.[19] She appears to Hermas in the guise of an aged woman "created before all things." [20] And here we are not dealing with mere metaphor. The emphasis that is laid in this way on the universal destiny of the community is a genuine legacy from the Old Testament, a doctrinal legacy and not merely a literary one. It is said in St Matthew that the Kingdom "shall be given to a people bringing forth the fruits thereof," not $\xi\theta\nu\epsilon\sigma\iota$, "to the Gentiles," but $\xi\theta\nu\epsilon\iota$, "to a new people" of God.[21] St Paul especially, unrivalled opponent as he was of Judaism, pours Christian teaching, so to speak, into the moulds that this very Judaism had providentially made for it. The novelty of Christianity consists in its being a transfiguration rather than a fresh creation. To St Paul the Church is the People of the New Covenant. Israel according to the Spirit takes the place of Israel according to the flesh: but it is not a collection of many individuals, it is still a nation albeit recruited now from the ends of the earth; "the tribe of Christians," says

Eusebius, for instance, "the race of those who honour God."[22] The Old Covenant is entirely oriented towards the preparation of the New—and it is in this that it achieves again its full meaning at the very moment when, as such, it ceases to be. The promise was made to Abraham and his seed. The biblical text, remarks the Apostle in a piece of subtle exegesis, does not speak of seed in the plural, as if there were several heirs of Abraham; it is put in the singular. This one seed is Christ.[23] Where Christ is, and there alone, can be found the true Israel, and it is only through incorporation in Christ that participation in the blessings of Abraham may be obtained. "The real spiritual people of Israel is to be found in us":[24] that will be the Christians' calm assertion. "We are the true people of the Circumcision, the chosen people, the nation of kings and priests." Gentile converts can say quite naturally, speaking of those we still call nowadays the patriarchs and the princes of Jewish history, "our fathers, our forebears."[25] In the prayer of the liturgy we still beseech the Lord that the peoples of the world may become the children of Abraham and may be led *in Israeliticam dignitatem.*[26]

Thus, just as the Jews put all their trust for so long not in an individual reward beyond the grave but in their common destiny as a race and in the glory of their earthly Jerusalem, so for the Christian all his hopes must be bent on the coming of the Kingdom and the glory of the one Jerusalem; and as Jahwe bestowed adoption on no individual as such, but only in so far as he bestowed universal adoption on the people of the Jews, so the Christian obtains adoption only in proportion as he is a member of that social structure brought to life by the Spirit of Christ.[27]

Seen like this, Jewish nationalism, which taken by itself would stand for so narrow and incomplete a doctrine, finds its full meaning in an anticipatory symbolism. It was not merely of service, as is generally admitted, for the upholding of the chosen people, a necessary condition for the maintenance of their religion. The national character of the kingdom of God, in apparent contradiction with its world-wide character, was an antidote to all attempts at interpretation in an individualist sense. Made spiritual and world-wide, as the prophets had indeed foretold,[28] Judaism passed on to Christianity its concept of salvation as essentially social. If, having regard to the greater number of the faithful, the

Church derives more particularly from the Gentiles—*Ecclesia ex gentibus*—the idea of the Church, none the less, comes from the Jews.

No doubt if they had taken greater care many historians of primitive Christianity would not have connected its universalism with that of contemporary pagan mystery cults. For this one word "universalism" denotes two realities which, in spite of certain common attributes that there is no question of denying, profoundly differ: on the one hand it denotes a vague cosmopolitanism, on the other hand Catholicism. From the very beginning the Church by her visible, intimate structure, as by the very concept which she had of herself, was apart, right outside the limits of Hellenistic religion. Combining at the same time a certain looseness of organization with the maximum of centralization, she appears to the observer as a type of society like no other.

For the redeeming Act and the foundation of this religious society have an extremely close connexion. These two works of Christ are in truth but one. All that we have said so far applies equally to the visible Church and to the invisible body of Christ, and any attempt at separation will in this case run counter to the facts of history. No more to St Paul than to the other witnesses to the early faith is the Church a sort of "æon," a transcendent hypostasis which really existed before the work of Christ in the world. But neither is she a mere federation of local assemblies. Still less is she the simple gathering together of those who as individuals have accepted the Gospel and henceforward have shared their religious life, whether in accordance with a plan of their own or as the occasion demanded, or even by following the instructions of the Master. Neither is she an external organism brought into being or adopted after the event by the community of believers. It is impossible to maintain either of these two extreme theses, as it is impossible to keep them entirely separate. Yet that is the vain endeavour of most Protestant theology.[29] Paradoxically enough, on the other hand, it is precisely Protestant studies, completing and sometimes correcting Catholic work in the field of history or philology, that strengthen the traditional view on this important point. It emerges particularly that the primitive idea of the Church is in direct continuity with the Hebrew concept of "Qahal," a word translated in the Septuagint by ἐκκλησία. "Qahal" does not mean a restricted group or a purely empirical gathering, but the whole people of God, a concrete reality which, however small it may seem outwardly, is yet always far greater than it appears.

The Greek word accepted from the Septuagint was suitable, too, because it emphasized another essential aspect of the Church. The man who hears the "glad tidings" and gives himself to Christ answers a call. Now by reason of the connexion between the words (it does not appear in English) "to be called" is to be called to belong to the Church. The Ἐκκλησία that neither Paul nor any other of the first disciples ever imagined as an entirely invisible reality, but which they always understood as a mystery surpassing its outward manifestations, this Ἐκκλησία is in logical sequence to the κλητοί: she convenes them and gathers them together for the Kingdom.[30] She is a *convocatio* before being a *congregatio*. Isidore of Seville, for example, faithfully interpreted primitive Christian thought when he risked the following definition, so often to be quoted in the course of the following centuries: *Ecclesia vocatur proprie, propter quod omnes ad se vocet, et in unum congreget.*[31]

She summons all men so that as their mother she may bring them forth to divine life and eternal light. Now this part of a mother is indeed allotted to the visible Church. This "Jerusalem from on high, our mother," who makes of us free men, is not envisaged by Paul as being merely in some far off heavenly future; he sees it rather on the earth, in every city that has received the Gospel, already beginning its work of liberation; she it is who speaks by the mouth of the Apostles and of the heads of churches. And when the Christians of Lyons write concerning their brethren who at first gave way but had afterwards offered themselves for martyrdom, they say: "It was a great joy for our virgin mother when she received back alive those whom she had cast out from her womb as dead."[32] Irenaeus too speaks of the living faith on which the Church alone feeds her children.[33] And Origen tells his hearers, "May you, as a new Isaac, be the joy of your mother the Church. But I fear she must yet give birth in pain and sorrow."[34] When Cyprian lays down the principle that will be echoed through the Christian centuries, "He cannot have God for Father who has not the Church for Mother";[35] when Basil upbraids Julian the Apostate, "You have turned against God and you have insulted the Church, the mother, the nurse of all"; [36] when Augustine, Optatus, Fulgentius and Caesarius extol the *Catholica mater*,[37] their filial fondness and their unswerving fidelity go out to that society whose witnesses they are in the face of paganism, whose defenders they are against schism.

It was the unanimous language of tradition which came spontaneously to Paul Claudel when he wrote in praise of his refound faith, "Blessed be that mother at whose feet I have learnt all." A Protestant, Karl Barth, more than anyone else on his guard against the attraction of Catholicism, recognized this in his own fashion when he wrote, "If we seek to solve the question of the unity of the Church by appealing to an invisible church, we speculate as Platonists instead of listening to Christ." [38]

Of course—and this remark has often been made before—just as Christianity is not the Church, so the Church, in so far as it is visible, is not the Kingdom, nor yet the Mystical Body, though the holiness of this Body shines through its visible manifestation. Do not the two terms "visible" and "mystical" bring out this distinction? Yet confusion may creep in here from the fact that in theological literature the same word "Church" is used with varying meanings.[39] For was not Christianity itself in its double aspect and double power—spiritual and temporal—for long just called "the Church"? Another source of confusion is that the Mystical Body is sometimes considered as it appears in its transitory, imperfect state and sometimes in its complete, spiritual, definitive state. So it happens that conclusions are drawn which seem at first sight contradictory. For a distinction must be made not indeed between two realities with no intrinsic connexion between them, but as it were between a series of parallel conclusions none of which exactly corresponds to its opposite number. Firstly, for example, the Church is, in an objective sense, *congregatio generis humani*, the assembly which results from the reuniting of all peoples: *Ecclesia ex circumcisione, ecclesia ex gentibus;* yet in the second place it is she on the contrary who summons them, and she it is *ex qua credunt homines*. She is baptized and also she baptizes.[40] The one metaphor of the Bride conjures up two contrary visions, both founded on scripture and both frequently portrayed: the wretched being on whom the Word took pity and whom he came to save from prostitution at his Incarnation; [41] on the other hand, the new Jerusalem, the bride of the Lamb "coming out of heaven from God": [42] the daughter of strangers or the daughter of the king. On the one hand we see an assembly of sinners, a mixed herd, wheat gathered with the straw, a field with tares growing in it: *Corpus Christi mixtum*, the ark which shelters clean and unclean animals; on the other we have an unspotted virgin, mother of saints, born on Calvary from the pierced side of Jesus, or else the very Assembly she has made holy: *Ecclesia in sanctis, virgo mater.* In the first case a group with fixed laws and well-defined frontiers; a peculiar "sect," if we may be allowed the expression, in the midst of other sects, a proper subject for sociological investigation. In the other we perceive a vast spiritual organization, unseen even by those who are its members, which is known only to God. From yet another point of view, she is either an historic institution or else she is the very city of God. In the first case, as a society founded by Christ for the salvation of men, she labours to bring them to it; she is then a means, and we can say with Pius XI: "men were not made for the Church, but the Church was made for men: *propter nos homines et propter nostram salutem.*" [43] A necessary means, a divine means, but provisional as means always are. Whereas in the second case, since the Bride is henceforward but one with the Bridegroom, she is that mysterious structure which will become fully a reality only at the end of time: no longer is she a means to unite humanity in God, but she is herself the end, that is to say, that union in its consummation. *Christus propter ecclesiam venit.* Thus Clement of Alexandria writes: "In the same way that the will of God is an act and it is called the world, so his intention is the salvation of men, and it is called the Church." [45] That too is the idea expressed by the second vision of the Shepherd in which Hermas unites, that he may apply them to the Church, what the book of Proverbs sings about Wisdom and what Paul proclaimed about Christ, together with what Judaism taught about Israel itself or the Law. He beholds an aged woman whom at first he does not identify.

"Who is this aged woman, think you, from whom you received the little book?"

"The Sibyl," I replied.

"You are wrong," said the Shepherd, "for it is not she."

"Who is it then?"

"The Church."

"Why is she aged?" I then asked.

"Because," he answered, "she was created first, before all else; that is why she is aged. It was for her that the world was made." [46]

So we must be careful not to confuse these aspects, which are so very different despite their correlation. The danger of such confusion is by no means an imaginary one, and its consequences may be serious, as the history of Donatism or Jansenism demonstrates. But provided the requisite distinctions are made, and not forgotten when they are needed, it is no less important to construct a synthesis. The Church on earth is not merely the vestibule of the Church in heaven. She is not unlike the Tabernacle of the desert compared with Solomon's Temple, for she stands to our heavenly home in a relation of mystical analogy in which we should perceive the reflexion of a profound identity. It is indeed the same city which is built on earth and yet has its foundations in heaven; and St Augustine, who has taught us most of the foregoing distinctions, could exclaim with justice: "the Church of to-day is the kingdom of Christ and the kingdom of heaven." The Church, without being exactly co-extensive with the Mystical Body, is not adequately distinct from it. For this reason it is natural that between her and it—as within the Mystical Body itself between the head and the members —there should arise a kind of exchange of idioms: *Corpus Christi quod est ecclesia.* "I am Jesus whom thou persecutest." "He who beholds the Church," says Gregory of Nyssa, "really beholds Christ." And just as the term "supernatural" is applied equally to the means that shape man on his course towards his end and to that end itself, so the Church is properly called Catholic, and it is right to see in it in truth the Body of Christ, both in its actual and visible reality and in its invisible and final achievement. For between the means and the end there is not merely an extrinsic relationship. *Gratia inchoatio gloriae.* Since we are dealing with two states of the same body, we might use a closer comparison; we might say that just as our poor fleshly body is the same one that, in a spiritual state, will have its lot in glory—*corpus humilitatis nostrae configuratum corpori claritatis Christi*—so the Church which lives and painfully progresses in our poor world is the very same that will see God face to face. In the likeness of Christ who is her founder and her head, she is at the same time both the way and the goal; at the same time visible and invisible; in time and in eternity; she is at once the bride and the widow, the sinner and the saint.

In the interests of refuting such chaotic concepts as those which see a divine Church only in a "Church of the saints," an entirely invisible society which is nothing but a pure abstraction, we must not fall into the contrary error. The Church "in so far as visible" is also an abstraction, and our faith should never make separate what God from the beginning has joined together: *sacramentum magnum in Christo et in ecclesia.* Nor do we claim to prove this union by an explanation of it, for the mystery of the Church is deeper still, if that were possible, than the mystery of Christ, just as that mystery was more difficult to believe than the mystery of God, a scandal not only to the Jews and Gentiles, but also for too many Christians. *Avocamentum mentis, non firmamentum.* For no one can believe in the Church, except in the Holy Spirit. That, at any rate, is not "to deify her visibility," as we are sometimes reproached with doing. We do not confuse the "institution of the Papacy and the kingdom of God." We do not "attribute to the Church what belongs to God alone." We do not adore her. We do not believe in the Church in the same sense in which we believe in God, for the Church herself believes in God, and she is the "Church of God." All the more then do we reject Monophysism in ecclesiology just as we do in Christology, but none the less strongly do we believe that dissociation of the divine and the human is in either case fatal. If necessary, the experience of Protestantism should serve us as sufficient warning. Having stripped it of all its mystical attributes, it acknowledged in the visible Church a mere secular institution; as a matter of course it abandoned it to the patronage of the state and sought a refuge for the spiritual life in an invisible Church, its concept of which had evaporated into an abstract ideal.

But the Church, the only real Church, the Church which is the Body of Christ, is not merely that strongly hierarchical and disciplined society whose divine origin has to be maintained, whose organization has to be upheld against all denial and revolt. That is an incomplete notion and but a partial cure for the separatist, individualist tendency of the notion to which it is opposed; a partial cure because it works only from without by way of authority, instead of effective union. If Christ is the sacrament of God, the Church is for us the sacrament of Christ; she represents him, in the full and ancient meaning of the term, she really makes him present. She not only carries on his work, but she is his very continuation, in a sense far more real than that in which it can be said that any human institution is its founder's continuation. The highly developed exterior organization that wins our admiration is but an expression, in accordance with the needs of this present life, of the interior unity of a living entity, so that the Catholic is not only subject to a power but is a member of a body as well, and his legal dependence on this power is to the end that he may have part in the life of that body. His submission in consequence is not an abdication, his orthodoxy is not mere conformity, but fidelity. It is his duty not merely to obey her orders or show deference to her counsels, but to share in a life, to enjoy a spiritual union. *Turpis est omnis pars universo suo non congruens.*

This makes it possible to understand why schism has always inspired the true believer with horror, and why from earliest times it has been anathematized as vigorously as heresy. For destruction of unity is a corruption of truth, and the poison of dissension is as baneful as that of false doctrine. Nor is it only a pastor, the responsible head of a church, like Cyprian of Carthage, who thinks in these terms. Clement of Alexandria is not a whit less vehement against those who, faithless to the unity of the Church, attack, so to say, the very unity of God. We may recall Origen's emphatic commendation of that *consonantiae disciplina* without which no offering can be acceptable to the Lord—without which, indeed, a proper idea of God is wanting. For they who do not give him glory do not know him, and this glory can be given to him only in the Church—*Ipsi gloria in ecclesia!* And did not the Lord appear to Moses in a burning bush to teach us that as a general rule he does not reveal himself elsewhere save in the Church, that is to say, in the midst of that Assembly where burns the fire of the Holy Spirit?

It follows that the schismatic or the provoker of dissension outrages what is dearest to Christ, for he commits a crime against that "spiritual body" for which Christ sacrificed his carnal body. It is a violation of that vital charity which is the guardian of unity. Conversely he who does not keep charity cannot speak in the name of unity. Woe to the *perditor caritatis!* For if the charity that depreciates unity is never authentic, there is only a seeming unity where charity does not reign—*Caritas unitas est ecclesiae. Sive caritatem, sive unitatem nomines, idem est, quia unitas est caritas, et caritas unitas.*[47] Injury done to the one or to the other—and one is never injured without injury to the other as well—is to rend the Church, the seamless robe that Christ willed to put on that he might dwell among us. It is a rending, so far as it is in man's power, of the very body of Christ—*Corpus Christi ecclesia est, quae vinculo stringitur caritatis.* It is an onslaught on the very society of the human race. In truth it is self-destruction, in that the schismatic cuts himself off from the tree of life: "If a member is separated from the Whole he ceases to live."

On the contrary, in the man in whom the grace of Christ triumphs over sin it will be seen that the most spiritual inwardness is coincident with the fullness of the Catholic spirit, a spirit, that is to say, of the broadest universality coupled with the strictest unity. No one has a better title to the fine name of "churchman" than this truly spiritual man, and no one is more removed than he from whatever smacks of sectarianism. For the fact that he "has received the Spirit of God and that the Spirit of God dwells in him" may be recognized precisely in this: "the love of peace and unity, the love of the Church scattered far and wide over the face of the earth." This love makes him clear-sighted, for gradually he regains the eyes which man possessed in his state of innocence wherewith in the mirror of his soul he could contemplate the glory of the Lord. Once more he becomes aware of the truth of his being, and the divine Image that has been restored in him disperses the illusions created by sin. For him, then, begins once more the restoration of that pristine harmony of human nature, together with those new splendours which are the work of sacrifice and charity. It is a foreshadowing, dim but certain, of a new paradise. In the midst of a world impervious to the light and generally hostile, he has already recovered his lost unity—*per communionem quidem gratiae incipit reparari communio naturae.*[48] He knows that in Christ the faithful are truly present to each other, and that for those who live by his love the good of each is the good of all: "If you love unity, whatever in it is another's is at the same time yours."[49]

A medieval author, taking his cue from Claudianus Mamertus, expressed this view of the faith very well when he wrote as follows as a Christian addressing his brother in Christ:

> When you are at prayer you are in my presence, and I am in yours. Do not be surprised because I say *presence*; for if you love me, and it is because I am the image of God that you love me, I am as much in your presence as you are in your own. All that you are substantially, that am I. Indeed, every rational being is the image of God. So be who seeks in himself the image of God seeks there his neighbour as well as himself; and he who finds it in himself in seeking it there, knows it as it is in every man. . . . If then you see yourself, you see me, for I am not different from you; and if you love the image of God, you love me as the image of God; and I, in my turn, loving God, love you. So seeking the same thing, tending towards the same thing, we are ever in one another's presence, in God, in whom we love each other.[50]

What that monk wrote to another monk, every Christian should be able to say to his fellow Christian. He should try to make it understood by all men.

NOTES TO CHAPTER II

[1] Bossuet, *Allocution aux nouvelles catholiques* (Œuvres oratoires, Lebarcq, t. 6, p. 508).

[2] Pascal, Br. 3.

[3] *In Genesim*, hom. 2, n. 5 (Baehrens, p. 35).

[4] *Adv. Judaeos*, c. 7, and *De Testimonio*, c. 6 (Reiff., p. 142).

[5] *In Psalm.* 149, n. 7 (P.L. xxxvii, 1953).

[6] See *Sermon* 128, n. 1 and 10 (P.L. xxxviii, 768) and *Sermon* 12 *Denis*, c. 3 (P.L. xlvi, 853) for the argument against the Donatists who found in the Canticle of Canticles a prophecy of an African Church. In order to square their assertions with the many texts of scripture quoted against them the Donatists claimed that the Church had already penetrated everywhere, but that thenceforward it was confined to Africa—an idea analogous to that of certain apologists who speak of a transient or precarious Catholicism. Augustine, *De agone christiano*, n. 31 (P.L. xl, 307); *Contra epist. Parmeniani*, lib. 2, n. 38 (P.L. xliii, 79); *Contra litteras Petiliani*, lib. 2, c. 39, n. 94 (P.L. xliii, 294).

⁷ *Collatio cum Donatistis,* 3a dies, c. 3 (P.L. xliii, 624).

⁸ *In 1 Joan.,* tract 10 (P.L. xxxv, 2060).

⁹ *Epist.* 140, n. 43 (P.L. xxxiii, 556).

¹⁰ It seems a little inaccurate, therefore, to assert, as a recent author has done, that the "development of the idea of a qualitative Catholicism" in opposition to the idea of a "spatial numerical Catholicism" has found favour in recent years on account of a certain neglect of the patristic sources of doctrine (G. Thils, *Les Notes de l'Église dans l'apologétique catholique depuis la Réforme,* p. 252).

¹¹ *Mystagogia,* c. 1 (P.G. xci, 665–8), slightly abridged translation.

¹² Hom. 65, n. 1 (P.G. lix, 361–2).

¹³ Lib. 1, c. 30, n. 63 (P.L. xxxii, 1336).

¹⁴ In *Acts* ii. 3 "the choice of the term διαμεριζόμεναι cannot be without significance. It is the word which, in the Song of Moses, is used for the scattering of the nations, *Deut.* xxxii. 8" (Cerfaux).

¹⁵ Paul Claudel, *Introduction au livre de Ruth,* p. 93.

¹⁶ Augustine, *Sermons* 266–9 (P.L. xxxviii, 1225–37).

¹⁷ Pseudo-Fulgentius, s. 51 (P.L. lxv, 918). See Extracts 7 and 8, pp. 216, 217.

¹⁸ *Ephesians* v. 25–32.

¹⁹ Irenaeus, *Adv. Haereses,* 4, 33, 14 (P.G. vii, 1082).

²⁰ Vision 2, c. 4, n. 1 (Lelong, p. 23).

²¹ *Matthew* xxi. 43. And compare also *Deut.* vii. 6; xiv. 2; and *I Peter* ii. 9.

²² *Historia Eccles.,* passim.

²³ *Galatians* iii. 16; *Genesis* xv. 18.

²⁴ Justin, *Dialogue with Trypho,* c. 11, n. 5 (Archambault, p. 54).

²⁵ So Eusebius, *Praep. evang.,* lib. 1, c. 5 (P.G. xxi, 44–8).

²⁶ Cf. Collect on Holy Saturday (after fourth prophecy).

²⁷ *Romans* ix. 5; *Galatians* iii. 25 and 29; *Ephesians* ii. 12.

²⁸ See particularly *Isaias* xix. 23–5, and *Jeremias* xxxiii. 38–42.

²⁹ As, for example, Theodore of Beza, *Traité de l'autorité du Magistrat en la punition des hérétiques*: The Church "is our Christian republic, and consists of several companies of citizens assembled together. The Church is the reunion of Christian cities." "The Church," said Edmond Schérer, "is an abstraction by which the churches are considered as one whole," *Esquisse d'une théorie de l'Église chrétienne,* p. 4. Still more recently Emil Brunner, after saying, "The Church is not only the totality of individuals who have been separately selected in the world and designated as heirs presumptive of the heavenly kingdom," and again "The Church is the mother of all believers, she exists before every believer," adds a little further on: "The community must of necessity create an organism for itself, an 'exterior' organ by which it manifests its life," *Le Renouveau de l'Église* (1935), pp. 12, 14, and 23.

³⁰ L. Cerfaux, *op. cit.,* pp. 188–91. "These three terms, convocation, Church, Kingdom, are mutually dependent, and one

defines the other; each of the three is necessary to the whole conception, and taken together they evoke one of the predominating trends of primitive Christian thought. . . ." See also *Théologie de l'Église suivant saint Paul,* pp. 143 and 149–50. (But we have been unable to utilize this important work.) Cf. *I Thess.* ii. 12.

[31] *De ecclesiasticis officiis,* lib. 1, c. 1 (P.L. lxxxiii, 739–40).

[32] In Eusebius, *H.E.,* lib. 5, c. 1, n. 45 (Grapin, vol. 1, p. 35).

[33] *Adv. Haereses,* 3, praef., and 3, 24, 1 (P.G. vii, 843 and 966).

[34] *In Gen.,* hom. 10, n. 1 (Baehrens, p. 93).

[35] *De catholicae Ecclesiae unitate,* c. 6.

[36] *Epist.* 41, n. 1 (P.G. xxxii, 345).

[37] Optatus, *De schismate donatistarum,* lib. 1, c 11, and lib. 7, c. 5.

[38] *L'Église et les églises,* trans. Moobs, Œcumenica, t. 3, p. 141.

[39] It will be noticed that St Augustine, for example, makes a clear distinction between the Church, which is the Body of Christ and the City of God, and the visible Church as she is contained within certain limits of space and time. *In Psalm.* 90, sermo 2, n. 1 (P.L. xxxvii, 1159).

[40] See below, Chapter III.

[41] Ambrose, *In Lucam,* lib. 1, n. 17 (P.L. xv, 1540). See below, Chapter VII.

[42] *Apocal.* xxi. 9; Cf. iii. 12; *Galat.* iv. 26.

[43] Allocution to the Lenten preachers of Rome, Feb. 28, 1927.

[44] Scotus Erigena, *In Joannem* (P.L. cxxii, 326).

[45] *Paedagog.,* lib. 1, c. 6.

[46] Vision 2, c. 4, n. 1.

[47] Hugh of St. Victor, *De Sacramentis,* lib. 2, p. 13, c. 11 (P.L. clxxvi, 544).

[48] Baldwin of Canterbury, *Tractatus de vita coenobitica* (P.L. cciv, 562). See Extracts 11 and 12, pp. 219, 221.

[49] Augustine, *In Joan.,* tr. 32, n. 8 (P.L. xxxv, 1646).

[50] *Meditationes piissimae de cognitione humanae conditionis,* c. 15, n. 14 (P.L. clxxxiv, 495). See Extract 13, p. 223.

III

THE SACRAMENTS

Since the sacraments are the means of salvation they should be understood as instruments of unity. As they make real, renew or strengthen man's union with Christ, by that very fact they make real, renew or strengthen his union with the Christian community. And this second aspect of the sacraments, the social aspect, is so intimately bound up with the first that it can often be said, indeed in certain cases it must be said, that it is through his union with the community that the Christian is united to Christ.

That is the constant teaching of the Church, though it must be confessed that in practice it is too little known. Just as redemption and revelation, even though they reach every individual soul, are none the less fundamentally not individual but social, so grace which is produced and maintained by the sacraments does not set up a purely individual relationship between the soul and God or Christ; rather does each individual receive such grace in proportion as he is joined, socially, to that one body whence flows this saving life-stream. Thus it has been said that the causality of the sacraments is to be found not so much "in a paradoxical efficacy, in the supernatural order, of a rite or perceptible action, as in the existence of a society, which under the appearances of a human institution hides a divine reality." [1] All the sacraments are essentially sacraments of the Church; in her alone do they produce their full effect, for in her alone, "the society of the Spirit," is there, normally speaking, participation in the gift of the Spirit.

The first effect of baptism, for example, is none other than this incorporation in the visible Church. To be baptized is to enter the Church. And this is essentially a social event, even in the primary, extrinsic meaning of the word. But its consequences are not solely juridical; they are also spiritual, mystical, because the Church is not a purely human society: whence comes the "character" conferred by baptism, and, when the other requisite conditions are present, the sacramental grace of regeneration. So it is that by being received into a religious society one who has been baptized is incorporated in the Mystical Body: such is the twofold indivisible meaning of traditional expressions like *Ecclesiae Dei sociari, Ecclesiae incorporari, in corpus Ecclesiae transire*, and it is by this incorporation that each one receives the adoption of sons and is given life by the Holy Spirit. The first act is a social one.

Nor is the final consequence any less social in nature, though its meaning is in this case an entirely inward one. For if the sacraments derive their efficacy from the Church, it is still in view of the Church that this efficacy is bestowed upon them. The water and blood which flowed from the side of Jesus on the Cross, the water of baptism, the blood of the Eucharist, first fruits of the mystical union between Christ and his Church, are, at the same time, the streams at which that Church is nourished. As the water flows over our foreheads it does not merely effect a series of incorporations, but there takes place at the same time a "concorporation" of the whole Church in one mysterious unity. Baptismal regeneration, on a final analysis, is not confined in effect to one soul alone. "For in one Spirit," says the Apostle, "we were all baptized into one body." That is what St Irenaeus was at pains to make clear about both baptism and confirmation, working out a symbolism that has become less familiar to us nowadays, though it was for long a commonplace in sermons.

The Holy Spirit came down on the Apostles that all nations might enter on the Life. And so they are gathered together to sing a hymn to God in all tongues. In this way the Holy Spirit brought the scattered peoples back to unity, and offered to the Father the first fruits of all nations. Indeed, just as without water no dough, not a single loaf, can be made of dry flour, so we who are many cannot become one in Christ without that water that comes from heaven. That is why our bodies receive by baptism that unity which leads to life incorruptible, and our souls receive the same unity through the Holy Spirit.[2]

Primitive inscriptions in Rome also furnish a commentary on this:

> Unto heaven is born a people of divine strain, begotten by the Holy Spirit who makes the waters fruitful.
> Amidst the waves Mother Church brings forth her unspotted offspring conceived by virtue of the Holy Spirit.
> Among those reborn is no difference: they are one through one immersion, one Spirit and one faith.
> And you who were begotten in these waters, come then to unity as you are called by the Holy Spirit that he may bestow his gifts upon you.[3]

The language used by Ivo of Chartres is more significant still, forging as it does another link in the long chain of tradition. In dealing with the sacrifice of the new law in which the Church offers herself at the same time as she offers Christ, he portrays her made ready by previous rites to carry out this high office: *per aquam baptismatis adjuncta, chrismatis oleo peruncta, sancti Spiritus igne solidata, per humilitatis Spiritum hostia placens effecta*, so that through each one of us this one Church ever appears as the chief object as well as the chief minister of all the sacraments. *Sacramenta faciunt ecclesiam.*

The efficacy of penance is explained like that of baptism, for the relationship is quite as clear, in the case of the former, between sacramental forgiveness and the social reintegration of the sinner. The double functions of this sacrament as a disciplinary institution and as a means of inner purification are not merely associated in fact; they are united, if one may so put it, by the nature of things. The Church's primitive discipline portrayed this relationship in a more striking manner. The whole apparatus of public penance and pardon made it clear that the reconciliation of the sinner is in the first place a reconciliation with the Church, this latter constituting an efficacious sign of reconciliation with God. At the end of his *Quis dives salvetur* Clement of Alexandria relates the touching (perhaps legendary) story of the pagan who was converted by St John and afterwards fell away. By his patience, tears and prayers the Apostle managed to convert him again, that is to say, he "restored him to the Church." In St Cyprian's view, for instance, the priest's intervention has for its immediate effect this "return" of the sinner, this return of one who has been "cut off" (excommunicated) to the assembly of the faithful; the cleansing of the soul is a natural consequence of this reimmersion in the stream of grace, and it should be defined as a return to the "communion" of saints. It is precisely because there can be no return to the grace of God without a return to the communion of the Church that the intervention of a minister of that Church is normally required. "Only the whole Christ," said Isaac de Stella in the twelfth century, "the head upon his Body, Christ with the Church, can remit sins."

The sacrament in the highest sense of the word— *sacramentum sacramentorum, quasi consummatio spiritualis vitae et omnium sacramentorum finis*—the sacrament "which contains the whole mystery of our salvation," the Eucharist, is also especially the sacrament of unity: *sacramentum unitatis ecclesiasticae.*

Doubtless no Catholic, however ill-instructed in his religion, is ignorant of this. But is this capital truth understood in all its implications? When a thought is given to it, don't we often tell ourselves that this is only a secondary and additional consideration without which the doctrine of the Eucharist would still be complete? That at least is what the abundant literature on the subject would lead one to believe. In 1912 Dom J. Simon was able to write:

> Contemporary authors do not seem to have attached great importance to this unitive force of the Eucharist. If *l'Année Liturgique* and a few rare works on mysticism had not been at pains to revive it, it would have been in our days a forgotten doctrine.[4]

Since then, in spite of many efforts, the situation seems much the same as far as the generality of Christians is concerned. Yet St Paul said: "For we being many are one bread, one body, all that partake of one bread;" and St. Ignatius of Antioch: "There is but one chalice that you may be united in the blood of Christ." The Council of Trent teaches:

It was the will of Christ to make of this sacrament the symbol of that Body of which he is himself the Head, to which he would bind us as his members by the close bonds of faith, hope and charity, so that all should be but one reality, with never a division.

It calls on "all those who bear the name of Christian" to come together "in this sign of unity, this bond of charity, this symbol of harmony." In his Apostolic Constitution of 1902 on the Eucharist Leo XIII defined it again as the *radix atque principium catholicae unitatis.*

Such teaching was not only general with the Fathers of the Church, it was in the very forefront of their thought. The choice among so many equally clear and beautiful texts is an embarrassing one. It must be enough to quote a few among many of them.

This, for example, is what St Cyprian says:

How strong is Christian unanimity . . . , the sacrifice of the Lord itself proclaims it. For when the Lord calls his body the bread which is made up of many grains joined together, he means by that the union of all Christian people, which he contained within himself. And when he calls his blood the wine which is made into one drink of many grapes, he again means that the flock which we form is made up of individuals who have regained their unity." [5]

And St John Chrysostom says:

Let us learn the wonders of this sacrament, the purpose of its institution, the effects that it produces. We become one body, says the Scripture, members of his flesh, bones of his bones. That is what the food that he gives us effects: he joins himself to us that we may become one whole, like a body joined to its head. [6]

The mysticism of St Cyril of Alexandria is especially insistent:

To merge us in unity with God and among ourselves, although we have each a distinct personality, the only Son devised a wonderful means: through one only body, his own, he sanctifies his faithful in mystic communion, making them one body with him and among themselves.

Within Christ no division can arise. All united to the single Christ through his own body, all receiving him, the one and indivisible, into our own bodies, we are the members of this one body and he is thus, for us, the bond of unity.

We are all of us, by nature, separately confined in our own individualities, but in another way, all of us are united together. Divided as it were into distinct personalities by which one is Peter or John or Thomas or Matthew, we are, so to say, moulded into one sole body in Christ, feeding on one flesh alone. One Spirit singles us out for unity, and as Christ is one and indivisible we are all no more but one in him. So did he say to his heavenly Father, "That they may be one, as we are one." [7]

And here is St Augustine speaking to the newly baptized in that direct style of the best of his homilies, in which poetry breaks through the homely dialogue:

"The Body of Christ," you are told, and you answer "Amen." Be members then of the Body of Christ that your Amen may be true. Why is this mystery accomplished with bread? We shall say nothing of our own about it, rather let us hear the Apostle, who speaking of this sacrament says: "We being many are one body, one bread." Understand and rejoice. Unity, devotion, charity! One bread: and what is this one bread? One body made up of many. Consider that the bread is not made of one grain alone, but of many. During the time of exorcism, you were, so to say, in the mill. At baptism you were wetted with water. Then the Holy Spirit came into you like the fire which bakes the dough. Be then what you see and receive what you are.

Now for the Chalice, my brethren, remember how wine is made. Many grapes hang on the bunch, but the liquid which runs out of them mingles together in unity. So has the Lord willed that we should belong to him and he has consecrated on his altar the mystery of our peace and our unity. [8]

Lastly, St John Damascene, in whom the whole Greek tradition may be heard:

If the sacrament is a union with Christ and at the

same time a union of all, one with another, it must give
us real unity with those who receive it as we do.[9]

In the train of the Fathers, who themselves merely commented on the scriptural and liturgical texts, the whole Latin
Middle Ages were nourished on this teaching. Theologians,
preachers, exegetes, liturgists, controversialists and poets reveal it one after another. To all it appears so fundamental
that their discussions take it for granted. If it is not a
speciality of learned speculation, no more is it the special
preserve of any one school. The followers of Paschasius
Radbertus, Rhabanus Maurus, or Ratramnus, as well as those
of Florus or Amalarius, those who hold the theory of
"Ambrosian metabolism," "Augustinian dynamism" or just
Roman realism; whatever the exact relationship that they
work out between "the body born of a virgin" and the
Eucharistic body; whether in their assertion of the sacramental presence they place the emphasis on the *mysterium*
or the *veritas*; all are agreed in this: the result of the
sacrament is unity. *In (hoc) sacramento fideles communicantes pactum societatis et pacis ineunt.* Thus is it worthy of
the name of communion which is given to it. And that is why,
even though the bread and wine are validly consecrated
by schismatics, it can be said that there is a true Eucharist
only where there is unity—*non conficitur ibi Christus, ubi
non conficitur universus.* Like scripture the Eucharist has a
spiritual meaning; that is what is meant by the fraction, that
action through which the disciples of Emmaus knew Christ,
an action that unlocks the mystery for us that we may discover there signified the Body of Christ which is the Church.
The symbolism of the elements gives rise to all sorts of
developments, but there is no purpose in detailing them
here. We merely quote, as typically representative of an
explanation which goes back even in its details to the
patristic age, the *de Sacramentis* of Master Simon (middle
twelfth century), lately edited by Fr Weisweiler:

Why is Christ received under the form of bread and
wine? It may be said that in the sacrament of the altar
there are two things: the true body of Christ and what it
signifies, namely, his mystical body which is the Church.
Now as one loaf is made of many grains which are first
wetted, then milled and baked to become bread, so the

mystical body of Christ, that is to say the Church, formed
by the gathering together of a multitude of persons, like
to many grains, is wetted in the water of baptism. It is
then crushed between the two millstones of the Old and
New Testament or of hope and fear . . . , and in the last
place it is baked in the fire of passion and sorrow that it
may be made worthy to be the body of Christ. In truth
the blessed martyr Ignatius wished to be united with this
body in fullest reality when he said: "I am the wheat of
Christ; let me be crushed by the teeth of the beast to
become the bread of Christ." Likewise wine is the product of many grapes; when they have been trodden and
pressed in the wine press the must is left as worthless
and the wine is stored; Holy Church, too, suffers by being
beset in the world as in a wine press . . . where, as the
wine is separated from the must, the wicked are cast
away and the righteous put to the test. Rightly, then,
such elements designate Christ's body, that is, the
Church.[10]

This same teaching emerges, clearly and continually, from
a wealth of detail: the outward signs of the mystery, the
bread and wine, proclaim *quod fideles in hoc sacramento in
unam dilectionem convenire debent*. In this connexion will
be noted the important part played by suffering. It is the very
crucible wherein unity is forged. That man who will not
remain isolated must pass through it. For is not the
Eucharist the memorial of the Passion? It was quite natural
that the ears of wheat from which the bread of the offertory
is made should be compared with that other ear of which
our Saviour said that if it fell to earth and died it would
increase a hundredfold. And does not the wonderful fruitfulness of that Divine Grain that lay for three days in the
earth, lie in a multiplication which is for ever returning to
unity?

> Ex uno multis affluit copia granis,
> De quibus efficitur nunc unus in aethere panis:
> Nam quoties, Christo crescente, fide generamur,
> Ex uno grano quasi plurima grana creamur,
> Cujus dum sapimus carnes, et sanguinis haustum,
> Unus fit panis, vinumque fit hoc holocaustum. . . .[11]

From the eleventh century onwards these doctrines were

systematized in a theory which is structurally Augustinian. At that time a distinction began to be made between three elements as it were in the sacrament, three stages of depth, all three of them essential to its integrity: the *sacramentum tantum*, that is to say the outward sign; the *sacramentum et res*, what is contained under the sign, the sign in its turn of a deeper reality; and the *res tantum*, the definitive fruit of the sacrament. The first of these three elements was constituted, together with the sacrificial rite, by the species of bread and wine: *forma panis et vini*; the second by the body of Christ itself: *veritas carnis et sanguinis*; and the third by the unity of the Church: *virtus unitatis et caritatis*. And just as the body of Christ was signified more exactly by the bread and his blood by the wine, so the Church, which is also the Body of Christ, seemed signified by the consecrated bread, whilst the wine changed into the blood of Christ was naturally the symbol of love which is like the blood wherein is the life of this great Body. Such is the doctrine which, outlined by Fulbert of Chartres and Guitmond of Aversa, and developed at the beginning of the twelfth century by Alger of Liège, is to be found in its precise and final shape in most of the *Libri Sententiarum*. From that time onwards it ranks as a classical doctrine. It may be found in Otto of Lucca and Peter Lombard as in Hugh of St Victor or in Baldwin of Canterbury, in Abelard's disciples as in the *Sententiae Florianenses* or the *Sententiae Parisienses*. The great Scholastics took it up; St Thomas Aquinas drew on it more than once. At the beginning of the thirteenth century Innocent III, after setting it out at length in his great work on the mystery of the altar, crystallized it in a letter the very terms of which we have just been using. Durandus of Mende reproduces it in his well-known *Rationale*; in it he copies Innocent's phrases word by word. In the following centuries the same doctrine is still current, and the Council of Trent reproduces it in all its essentials.

O signum unitatis! O vinculum caritatis! Gradually the doctrine was forgotten; this cannot be accounted for simply by the fact that the framework of sacramental theory had been modified, for the doctrine was independent of this framework and to some extent was responsible for it. Nor, save in a secondary sense, can insistence on the reality of the Eucharistic presence be made the chief culprit for this loss; Berengarius's principal opponents were extremely careful to guard against such insistence being interpreted in any way as a repudiation of other aspects of the mystery. All the same a change was gradually wrought in men's habits of mind. Their whole picture of the world was changed. Just as they would no longer see the spiritual reflected in the sensible or the universal and particular as reciprocally symbolical, so the idea of the relationship between the physical body of Christ and his Mystical Body came to be forgotten. It was like the slow atrophy of an unused sense. Faith, though remaining orthodox, was straitened, because it was no longer nourished by "intelligence." There are doubtless not a few in our day inclined to think that there is but a vague extrinsic analogy between these two meanings of the "body." That was certainly not the opinion of our forebears, whether, in the first of the two uses of the term, they were concerned with the fleshly body of Christ as it was during his earthly life and on Calvary, or whether they envisaged this body in its risen, its "spiritual," state. When, with St Augustine, they heard Christ say to them: "I am your food, but instead of my being changed into you, it is you who shall be transformed into me," they unhesitatingly understood that by their reception of the Eucharist they would be incorporated the more in the Church. They could see a profound identity between the mysteries of the "real presence" and of the "mystical body." And this identity was taken for granted in all their—frequently lively—discussions on the question of the *corpus triforme* or the *triplex modus corporis Christi*. It is here that may be found the explanation of the fact that, in the works of some of them, the first of these two mysteries, the real presence, stands out less boldly, and also the reason for the changes in their terminology whereby the two attributes *mysticum* and *verum* come to be transposed without any essential change in doctrine.

"Jesus Christ bears us in himself; we are, if I may dare to say so, more truly his body than his own body." That is an astounding sentence of Bossuet's, though he is careful to qualify it with "whoever has the spirit of charity and Christian unity will understand what I mean." And he goes on: "What he does in his divine body is a true pattern of what should be accomplished in us." [12] Bossuet owes this fundamental principle, together with his daring manner of speech, to his constant study of the Fathers. "Everything in Christ," St Augustine tells us, for example, "his life, his death and his resurrection, his actions, his body even, are symbolic of Christian life, the 'sacrament' of that spiritual man who is also one and universal." Before him Origen had brought out with greater precision the relation of symbolic efficacy between the individual body of Christ, σῶμα τυπικὸν, and his "real" Body which is the Church, ἐκκλησία σῶμα. He came to the conclusion that the final result, the "truth" of sacramental communion, was union with the Church within whose heart the Word resounds, for she is indeed the real presence of the Logos. During the Middle Ages the essentials of his thought are to be found on all sides. So William of St Thierry, though like many others he distinguishes, but with additional slight differences of his own, a threefold body of Christ, goes on at once to say that in truth this body is one though there are three ways in which it may be considered by faith and adhered to by piety; so that from that body which was hung on the tree to the Church herself "there is unceasing continuity."

We have just come to the fringe of a problem, or rather a whole series of problems, which cannot be examined more deeply within the scope of this book. It must suffice that they have thus been brought to the notice of theologians. Yet in whatever light we look on the efforts at system-making shown by the history of theology, the basic idea that these efforts sought to emphasize cannot be considered a more or less wild speculation or merely a matter of opinion in no wise affecting the faith. For the teaching of the Doctors on the sacrament of the altar is inculcated very forcibly by the Church in her liturgy, and the very Act of the Eucharistic sacrifice itself, by its rites as well as by its formulæ, corroborates this teaching with the whole weight of its sovereign authority.

"The Christian sacrifice is one throughout the world; for the Christian by whom it is offered is one, and there is one God to whom it is offered, one faith by which it is offered and one alone who is offered." [13] It is the "sacrifice of the Church," "of the whole Church," of pastor and people, of the present, of the absent. And its purpose again is unity, for it is for the Church once more that it is offered, for

a greater, more united Church: *pro totius mundi salute.*
"Inexpressible mystery of divine grace that effects salvation,"
says a preface in the Ambrosian liturgy. "The offerings of
the many become by the infusion of the Holy Spirit the one
Body of Christ, and that is why we who receive the Communion of this holy bread and chalice are knit into one sole
body." [14]

The ceremonies of the Pontifical Mass at Rome were from
this point of view particularly striking:

> It was a matter of importance in the Roman Church
> that the ritual of the communion should contain a clear
> and striking expression of ecclesiastical unity. Hence the
> custom of the *fermentum,* that is of sending consecrated
> bread from the bishop's Mass to the priests whose duty
> it was to celebrate in the *Tituli*; hence also the sig-
> nificance of the rite of the *Sancta,* that is of putting into
> the chalice at the *Pax Domini* a fragment consecrated at
> the preceding Mass and brought forth at the beginning of
> the present one. Thus, in all the churches of Rome, and
> at every assembly there for liturgical worship past or
> present, there was always the same Sacrifice, the same
> Eucharist, the same Communion. Thus, in order to
> show clearly that the bread broken and distributed away
> from the altar was the same as that which had been
> consecrated on the altar, a fragment of it was allowed
> to remain on the holy table.[15]

For a like symbolical reason, before taking communion to
the people the archdeacon poured into the large chalice re-
served for this use a few drops of the consecrated wine
which the Pontiff had left in his chalice for the purpose. At
least that is the meaning which Mgr Duchesne attaches to
this rite, which dates back to about the eighth century,
though, as M. Andrieu is inclined to think, it is possible
that originally it was done for reasons of convenience.[16]

If these ceremonies of antiquity no longer portray for
us in our daily Mass the unity of the Church in space and
time, of pastor and people, itself a symbol of that mystic
unity of which the sacrifice of the altar is the bond that is
ever renewed, there is none the less no lack of prayers in
the liturgy to remind us of the supreme effect of the
Eucharist. Take that post-communion of the Friday after
Ash Wednesday:

Spiritum nobis, Domine, tuae caritatis infunde, ut quos uno pane caelesti satiasti, tua facias pietate concordes.

Or the secret of the Mass of the Blessed Sacrament itself:

Ecclesiae tuae, quaesumus, Domine, unitatis et pacis propitius dona concede, quae sub oblatis muneribus mystice designantur.

From end to end of the Canon the same thought is uppermost, from the *Communicantes* down to the *Pater* and the *Pax*, at which, in the words of Florus of Lyons, *dat sibi mutuo omnis Ecclesia osculum pacis*. If the liturgists of olden days seem to display what to us nowadays is a disconcerting subtlety, it must yet be acknowledged that even when they made use of the strangest and most arbitrarily allegorical explanations they could still take their inspiration, as did their brethren the exegetes, from the analogy of faith. Thus Amalarius, followed immediately by Rhabanus Maurus, explaining the signs of the Cross made by the priest over the chalice with the consecrated host, tells us that the four sides of the chalice are one by one touched by the host to show that the body of Christ reunites the whole human race, gathered together from the four points of the compass into one same body, and so effects the peace of the Catholic Church. Many other examples could be found of such a simple variation on that same fundamental and essential theme. And does not the celebrant twice during the Holy Sacrifice make supplication for the unity of the Church: *coadunare digneris?*

These prayers of our Roman liturgy, with their counterparts in the other Latin rites, repeat what was said in those of the ancient liturgies. Our evidence for the official prayer of the first centuries is only too scanty, but a particularly valuable fragment has recently been discovered. It is a homily of Theodore of Mopsuestia which is almost contemporary with the well-known Catecheses of St Cyril of Jerusalem. It describes the rite of the Mass in detail; in it we find that the priest, at the culminating point of the sacred action, prays earnestly for union and concord among all those who take part in the mystery of unity. Another Eastern rite, the liturgy of St Basil, at the same solemn moment says the same thing in almost identical terms: "May all of us who partake of this one bread and chalice be united to one another in the communion of the same Holy Spirit." That same desire is echoed in the epiclesis of an ancient Armenian liturgy:

> We beseech thee, O Lord, send thy Holy Spirit upon us and upon these present gifts so that, by sanctifying this bread and this chalice . . . he may make all of us who partake of this one bread and one chalice indissolubly one.[17]

Or again in the so-called liturgy of St Eustace, in the prayer immediately before the kiss of peace:

> O God of mercy and forbearance, we cry to thee in unison: grant us that we may bestow peace upon each other in the holy kiss . . . make of us one holy people, save us by uniting us with one another, that we may sing thy praises.[18]

In the West the anaphora of the "Apostolic Constitutions" takes us right back to the beginning of the third century. It is possible that it portrays the use of the Church of Rome towards the end of the second century. There is the same petition as in the Eastern liturgies:

> Send down thy Spirit, O Lord, on the sacrifice of this community. Gather it together, unite it, and grant to all the saints who rejoice in it that they may be filled with the Holy Spirit.

This too was the theme of the oldest Eucharistic form (apart from the references in the New Testament) that has come down to us; it is to be read in Chapters nine and ten of the *Didache*. But is this wonderful prayer, which approximates very closely to the Jewish forms of blessing at meals, really a Eucharistic prayer? There has been a good deal of discussion on the point. In any case it is the basis of so many other prayers which are certainly Eucharistic; and it is to be found, almost word for word, in the anaphora contained in the Euchologion of Serapion of Tmuis, an Egyptian bishop of the fourth century who was a friend of St Athanasius. For this reason alone it merits quotation here:

> Just as this bread was spread about over the mountains,

and being gathered together became one, so may thy Church be gathered together from the ends of the world into thy kingdom. . . . Remember thy Church, O Lord, and gather it, made holy, from the four winds into thy Kingdom.

That is the desire with which the Spirit of Christ fills the hearts of those he has gathered together. And the same thing happens when it is no longer the Church offering Christ, but Christ offering his Church, when, that is, the sacrifice of the Head follows that of the members. For Christ offers his Church, as of old Jephte offered his only daughter, whenever one of his members bears witness to him. And this is as true of the "official" martyr as it is of one whose torturers believe themselves to be the authorized defenders of God and his Christ—such cases have come to light in the lives of the saints. There can be few more moving phrases than the declaration, so full of gravity in its utter simplicity, made by a martyr of Saragossa as he gave himself up to the executioner: *In mente me habere necesse est Ecclesiam catholican ab oriente usque in occidentem diffusam.*[19]

That is the sacrifice for which the sacrifice of the altar is a preparation. True Eucharistic piety, therefore, is no devout individualism. It is "unmindful of nothing that concerns the good of the Church."[20] With one sweeping, all-embracing gesture, in one fervent intention it gathers together the whole world. It recalls the commentary that, according to St John, Jesus himself gave when he instituted the sacrament of his love: the allegory of the vine, the "new commandment," the prayer for unity and the approach of the "supreme token of love." It is on these things that true Eucharistic piety bases thoughts and resolutions; it cannot conceive of the action of the breaking of bread without fraternal communion: *in communicatione fractionis panis.* In addition it will be noticed that in the ancient liturgies, and still nowadays in the East, the prayers for union form the culminating point of the Epiclesis. Now the Epiclesis, like the whole of the sacrifice, but as a rule more explicitly, is under the sign of the Holy Spirit. This Holy Spirit, by whom Christ's carnal body was prepared, intervenes too in the confection of the Eucharist for the making of his Mystical Body. He who fell upon the sacrifice of Elias as a devouring fire burns up the dross in humankind, the obstacle to the unifying power of the sacrament. And as the Spirit of Christ once came down upon the Apostles not to unite them together in a closed group but to light within them the fire of universal charity, so does he still whenever Christ delivers himself up once more "that the scattered children of God may be gathered together." Our churches are the "upper room" where not only is the Last Supper renewed but Pentecost also.

NOTES TO CHAPTER III

[1] Scheeben, *Das Mysterium des Christentums*.

[2] *Adv. Haereses*, 3, 17, 2 (P.G. vii. 930).

[3] Sixtus III's inscription on the baptistery of the Lateran, and inscription of the Consignatorium (Vatican?).

[4] *L'Eucharistie sacrement d'unité* in the *Revue thomiste*, vol. 20, pp. 583–4.

[5] *Epist.* 69, c. 5, n. 2.

[6] Hom. 46 *In Joannem* (P.G. lix, 260). Hom. 24 *In I Cor.* (P.G. lxi, 200).

[7] *In Joannem*, 11, 11 (P.G. lxxiv, 560). *Dialogue on the Trinity* (P.G. lxxv, 695).

[8] *Sermons* 272 and 234 (P.L. xxxviii, 1247 and 1116).

[9] *De fide orthodoxa*, lib. 4, c. 13 (P.G. xciv, 1154).

[10] The Latin text is in H. Weisweiler, *Maître Simon et son groupe*, pp. 27–8. See extract 14, p. 224.

[11] *De sancta Eucharistia*, poem 18 (ascribed to Hildebertus of Tours, P.L. clxxi, 1208).

[12] *Sermon sur la nécessité des souffrances*, for Palm Sunday.

[13] Peter the Venerable, *Tract. contra Petrobrusianos* (P.L. clxxxix, 796).

[14] Sunday before Septuagesima. Dom Guéranger, *The Liturgical Year, The Time after Pentecost*, vol. i.

[15] Duchesne, *Christian Worship: its origin and evolution*, translated by M. L. McClure (London, 1903), p. 185.

[16] M. Andrieu, *Immixtio et Consecratio, in Revue des sciences religieuses*, 1922, p. 436.

[17] Quoted in *Oriens christianus*, Neue serie, vol. 3, 1913, p. 23.

[18] P.G. xviii, 697 and 698.

[19] *Acta SS. Fructuosi, Augurii et Eulogii* (Ruinart, *Acta martyrum*, edn. of 1859, p. 266).

[20] S. Thomas, 3a, q. 83, a. 4, ad 3.

IV

ETERNAL LIFE

The Christian, helped by the sacraments that the Church dispenses to make of him a freer, more vital member of that great body, and by the grace that he continually receives through and for this community, sets out on his journey towards his last end. So does not a certain amount of individualism come back here into its own? How can we go on talking of the social character of a doctrine which teaches the survival of the individual soul, its immediate reward, and, once the necessary purification has been undergone, its attaining the vision of the Divine Essence?

Nevertheless we are compelled to do so, now more than ever, as may appear already from what we have seen in the preceding chapter. Everything here below, including the Church itself, is for the elect, but the elect are not isolated beings, much less so indeed than Christians on earth. "Glory" is the blossoming of "grace," and the beatific vision marks the completion of the mystery of unity to which creation was the prelude. "We are all one in Christ Jesus. And if faith, by which we journey along the way of this life, accomplishes this great wonder, how much more perfectly will the beatific vision bring this unity to fulfilment when we shall see face to face?" [1]

Christian tradition has always looked on heaven under the analogy of a city. *Coelestis urbs Jerusalem* . . . "City of Unity" wherein all reign with the great King: *usque ad regnum tecum perpetuum sanctae civitatis tuae.* [2] City of God, city of the elect: *ex sanctorum civium congregatione construitur,* says St Gregory the Great.[3] There the saints dwell in fellowship and rejoice in common—*socialiter gaudentes;* their joy is derived from their community. Hence that definition given by a medieval author: *felicissima societas supernorum civium communiter viventium*; [4] or that other, like to it, *coelestis beatorum mutua caritativa societas*. St Augustine said: *Tota redempta civitas, hoc est congruentia societasque sanctorum*.[5]

It is a city compact like a single house; a close-knit society, gathered like one family under a single roof—*redempta familia Christi Domini*—but at the same time extended to the uttermost, for it holds within its walls "the whole spiritual creature": *ex angelis et hominibus, Ecclesiae unum corpus*.[6] It is then in its perfection the *Catholica societas*. Now just as the Church militant was not made up of the mere aggregation of those who to begin with had given themselves to Christ, so this triumphant *Catholica* is not the mere addition, the sum total of the elect. She is a real unity, a transpersonal unity, for she it is, in truth, who sees God, as it was she who in her previous dispersal and destitution was sought after by our Saviour. It was she afterwards, under the action of the Holy Spirit, who was gradually built up in tribulations, who during her earthly pilgrimage lived by faith and prayed to God without ceasing. From henceforth her brightness is no longer, like that of the moon, intermittent and reflected; it is the very splendour of Christ, the true sun, in whom shines all Divinity. What words can help us even to glimpse it? "This holy city, our mother, abode of light, wisdom created before any creature, temple of the divinity, house of God, possessing in the heavens its eternal character, spiritual essence which ever contemplates the face of the Lord. . . ." [7] She it is on whom the light shines and it is in her that we shall be illuminated. The analogy of an earthly city is too weak to express this. Among those who are received within this heavenly city there is a more intimate relationship than subsists among the members of a human society, for among them there is not only outward harmony, but true unity.

Far from remaining separate all will become a single entity, since they are united to that Good which is one alone; so that, bound together by the bond of peace, in the words of the Apostle, in the unity of the Spirit, all will be one Body and one Spirit, by reason of the hope in which they were called. And it is in the bond of this unity that glory consists.[8]

A common glory, one sole glory shining on all the elect. We must not ask, whatever we do, whether there is a "physical" or "merely moral" union. The analogies that these opposed conceptions evoke lead inevitably to so many confused ideas; and in the domain that now concerns us such a distinction is entirely out of place. We might well speak, with Hilary or Fulgentius, of a "natural unity of all," like the unity of God himself: *mysterium verae ac naturalis unitatis,*[9] so as to emphasize the depths of being in which the bonds of charity are joined, though indeed it ought to be called a spiritual unity: *in unum spiritum igne caritatis conflati.* St Augustine again tells us this: *ubi individua caritas, ibi perfecta unitas.* This is true unanimity, the very consummation of unity, both the image and the result of the unity of the Divine Persons among themselves. Not just a spiritual community, but a community of the Holy Spirit: *per unitatem naturae, peramorem Spiritus.* The Christian mysticism of unity is trinitarian. The likeness, which in every created soul must be the completion of the divine Image, is not that of a Spinozist God; it is that of a God of Love, of the God whose being is Love. That is the teaching set forth by Origen, comparing what St Paul says to the Romans about the charity diffused in our hearts by the Holy Spirit and the text of the second epistle of Peter on our participation in the divine nature.

> Paul calls the Holy Spirit the Spirit of Love; it is said of God himself that he is Love, and the Son is called the Son of Love. Now, . . . if this is so we should be certain that both the Son and the Holy Spirit come from that one foundation of Godhead which is the Fatherhood of God, and that of his abundance bounteous love is infused into the very heart of the saints so as to make them partakers of the divine nature, as St Peter the Apostle taught. And this is so, so that by this gift of the Holy Spirit there may be fulfilled the words of our Lord, "That they all may be one, as thou, Father, in me, and I in thee." That is to say: Let them be made partakers of the divine nature in the abundance of love diffused by the Holy Spirit.[10]

"That they all may be one as we are one." This last desire of Christ's was taken seriously by Christian tradition. Long before it could account for its conclusions on the matter it had formed a clear notion of the idea of perfect unity—

unitas plena atque perfecta—a unity that was without externality yet also without confusion, that was not a mere collection of individuals, yet did not absorb the individual. Tertullian, in a whole series of somewhat clumsy expressions which are in labour with the idea but fail to bring it forth, seems to envisage a trinitarian conception of the Church. *De unitate Patris et Filii et Spiritus Sancti plebs adunata,* says St Cyprian in his commentary on the Lord's Prayer. Origen, Eusebius, Gregory of Nyssa, Augustine and others work out the same idea,[11] and Fulgentius of Ruspe puts it in a particularly happy phrase: *Sancta naturalis unitas et aequalitas et caritas Trinitatis, quae unus solus et verus est Deus, unanimitate sanctificat quos adoptat.*

"Let us hasten, therefore," concludes Clement of Alexandria, "to gather ourselves together unto salvation, in the new birth, in the one charity, on the pattern of that perfect unity that is in the one nature of God." [12] Let us hasten to enter into that heritage that suffers no division. Let us hasten to that blessed peace (pax) which by its very name is a symbol of unity, for it is the proper name of Christ in whom all are brought together, and by its three letters signifies the Trinity. All our efforts converge together. That holiness through which each one of us seeks to become a temple of God is identical, as St Augustine following St Paul insists, with that by which we all become one Temple. By the action of the Spirit of Christ, *unus in uno sumus,* and the end at which we aim is summed up wonderfully in these words: *erit unus Christus, amans seipsum.*[13]

The early Christians had a very lively sense of this single fellowship of all individuals, and of the different ages in their course towards the one same salvation. If St Paul was so filled with joy at the approaching dissolution of his fleshly body that would soon allow him to be united to Christ, it was because this personal feeling of his sprang from a faith that had made it possible by throwing open far wider prospects.

St Paul could see the course of human history as it progressed towards its end: the liberation of all creation, the consummation of all things in the unity of the Body of Christ now fully perfected. The hope he implanted in the hearts of those he won for Christ was, it can be said with certainty, a cosmic one. It was therefore, if we limit our

consideration to the human race, the hope of a social salvation. It was the hope of the salvation of the community, and
the condition of the salvation of the individual. The natural
persuasion that this collective, final salvation was imminent,
the belief that this present world was soon to end, made
easier no doubt such an inclusion of personal hope within
the wider, common expectation. Nevertheless, when all illusion on this matter had passed away, the primitive faith about
it still remained, even when the Church had endured, had
struggled and suffered for centuries, when she had taken root
in the institutions of this world, and could look back on
many generations of departed members.

This is the explanation, it seems, of a long-enduring and
at first sight disquieting hesitation in Christian thought. In
the fourteenth century Benedict XII was obliged to censure
the thesis that the souls of the righteous had to wait until
the general resurrection to enjoy the beatific vision. Now,
this was not the opinion of merely a certain number of
theologians. Benedict's immediate predecessor in the chair of
Peter, John XXII, had preached it with enthusiasm in a series
of sermons to the people of Avignon in 1331 and 1332, and
maintained it again at the end of his long life, more particularly at the consistory of January 3, 1334. It is a fact
that such an opinion, thenceforward debated with some heat,
had on its side a respectable army of supporters, among
them the most famous names of tradition, Latin as well as
Greek. The elect to be, those whose time of trial had come
to an end, were often pictured as "held in a kind of sweet
sleep" or quiet joy, waiting at "the gate of heaven" in an
atrium, in a "place of repose," in the paradise made for
Adam,[14] in the bosom of Abraham, in a secret dwelling, or,
again, "beneath the altar" spoken of in the Apocalypse: these
were all figurative expressions by which were portrayed, with
different shades of meaning, the period of waiting that, as
was believed, had to be undergone by every righteous soul
until the end of time.

Some historians of dogma have attempted to evade this
evidence, or at least to lessen its significance. Others have
sought the reasons which could have led to an error so grave
as eventually to deserve condemnation. They have drawn attention to three principal causes. The Gospel seems to make
reward as well as punishment depend, as to time, on a general
judgement that will only take place at the end of the world.

Man, no longer complete without his body, seems unable to enjoy entire blessedness as long as this body has not risen; this was a weighty consideration at a time when for various reasons the two ideas of resurrection and immortality were far more intimately connected than they are nowadays. We must take into account also the views of the Millenarists and their effect in later years. But beyond these reasons, real as they are, though perhaps a little too obvious, not to say superficial, another may be discerned. It goes deeper, is more operative, though it is not always distinctly expressed. This reason is nothing else than the undying belief in the essentially social nature of salvation.

If it was possible to believe—mistakenly—that the soul could not arrive at the beatific vision before the end of the world, was it not, in part at least, because it was held, and rightly, that the salvation of the individual could only be obtained within the salvation of the community? In these ages men's outlook was primarily a social one, and was related only secondarily to the individual. They loved to think of the Church entering heaven after she had won her victory. As long as she was the Church militant, so it was more or less vaguely supposed, none of her members could enjoy the fullness of triumph. It was, then, a mistaken transposition into the order of time of a genuine causal dependence.

Several writers, not realizing sufficiently that there was no comparison between the circumstances of the two cases, applied to the elect of the New Testament arguments that it was customary to employ with regard to the saints of the Old. Of course, they did not deny the life of grace to these latter as some theologians did later. In accordance with the belief held by the Church from the very beginning, St Augustine time and again makes a distinction between man *in vetere testamento* and man *de vetere testamento;* and he compares the righteous born before Christ to Jacob's hand issuing from his mother's womb before his head; in this he was followed by St Gregory the Great, who refused to reject *extra mysterium* those who were born *ante tempus.* This teaching was everywhere repeated, but it was no hindrance to the idea that the righteous of the Old Law, though capable of salvation by reason of their faith and hope, had not received the indispensable *regenerationis sacramentum;* their position was approximately that of a blameless catechumen who nevertheless cannot yet be received into full communion. It is true, of course, that in two passages which take over a distinction of Tertullian's St Augustine quite explicitly rejected any confusion between Abraham's bosom, a place of repose and happiness, and the lower world, a place of sadness and suffering. But led away by St Gregory and St Isidore, the Middle Ages deviated from this insecurely held opinion of the great doctor. It was therefore generally admitted that since, like all men, the saints of the Old Testament, and even Abraham himself, could be saved only by the sacrifice of Christ, they must wait in the lower world for his coming on the evening of his Passion, to be at last delivered: *quod longo tempore exspectaverunt patres murmurantes infra claustra inferni.*[15] Some even wondered whether, since the Elect were saved only through the Church of Christ, they would not have to wait until the second coming of Christ, as the Epistle to the Hebrews seemed to suggest quite clearly, for the salvation of that Church, so as to enter into possession of their blessedness. Labourers, whether of the first or the eleventh hour, must they not, all alike, await the end of the day to receive their wage and to enter at last into the mansion prepared for them? As long as Redemption continues, as long as the Body is not fully grown, how shall one member of it realize his full stature?

That is the thought voiced by Origen in the noble homily on Leviticus wherein he teaches that Christ himself could not enjoy perfect blessedness as long as even one of his members was ensnared by evil or was in a state of suffering. Our Saviour will enter on his definitive glory only on the day, heralded by Paul, when he delivers up his Kingdom into the hands of his Father in an act of total submission; and this act cannot take place as long as all the elect are not all gathered together in Christ and the whole world brought by him to the summit of its perfection. And so he awaits the conversion of us all that we may drink with him the wine of gladness in his Kingdom. With him until that last day—*ultima dies dilati judicii*—all the righteous are waiting:

Abraham is still there, and Isaac and Jacob, and all the prophets expect us that with us they may enter on perfect beatitude. For it is one single body that awaits its redemption. . . . The eye may be healthy and see without blemish, yet if the other parts of the body are missing,

how can it rejoice? Or what perfection will there be if
the body has neither hands nor feet, or wants for other
limbs? For, if the glory of the eye puts it in a higher
category, it is chiefly because it is the guide of the body
and because it receives the services of the other members.[16]

Ever since St Bernard's attacks on it and Sixtus of Siena's
defence of it, the orthodoxy of this passage has been much
debated. It is not easy to see how Origen, with his idea of the
glorious Christ "made divine" in his very body, could still
allot to him a portion of suffering. It seems more probable,
then, that throughout this homily we have to do with Christ
contemplated not as he is in himself alone, but as mystically
united to man. If there is cause for misunderstanding, it is in
respect of the intimate union of Christ with his Church; for
Origen compares this with the union of soul and body, and
is thus led to assign to the former what is true only of the
latter. Such at any rate is the thought of Athanasius and
Ambrose; they are both of the same opinion as their famous
predecessor, though their exposition of it lacks his shrewd-
ness and breadth. Before the second "fullness of time," according to Ambrose, the souls of the righteous will not enter
on their glory. They mount the steps which bring them
nearer to it, but they will only enjoy it finally, they will
only see God, in company with the whole gathering of the
righteous. And that is why our soul's gaze must be fixed on
the end of time. The same idea, in scarcely different form, is
frequently to be found later on. Paschasius Radbertus in
the ninth century, without formulating a clear-cut thesis on
the subject but treating it in much the same terms, links together the completion of the Church during the six ages of
the world, the resurrection at the end of time and the final
enjoyment of eternal life. In the twelfth century the author
of the *Speculum de mysteriis Ecclesiae*, seeking some symbolism for the hour of Compline with which the day's Office
ends, sees in it, since it comes after Vespers, which represents the seventh day, that is, the repose of the soul before
the resurrection and the judgement, the eighth day, the day
of eternity which is characterized by two correlative facts:
the *numerus completus sanctorum* and the *consummatum
gaudium*. Such also was St Bernard's thought in that teaching
of his that so influenced John XXII. Bernard's fervent piety,

not without its traces of individualism,[17] displays in this connexion (in common with all of his century) a keen awareness of Christian solidarity. In one of his sermons for All
Saints' Day he pictures the elect on the threshold of heaven,
ready to enter the house of God but unable to do so until
the number of those who are to be saved is made up. *Jam
multi ex nobis in atriis stant, exspectantes donec impleatur
numerus fratrum; in illam beatissimam domum non sine nobis
intrabunt, id est non sancti sine plebe.*[18]

Yet is not all this but an echo of St. Augustine? It is
notoriously difficult to reconcile all the many passages in
which he speaks of the time and the circumstances of the
beatific vision, for in many passages—or in those at least in
which he seems to postpone the vision until the end of the
world—he implies the explanation that has just been given.
It is first and foremost the great hope of all Christians that
is here expressed, as (for example) in that sermon in which
Augustine, after arousing in his hearers a desire for the
vision of God, goes on to say, commenting on the Apostle's
words about the partial nature of our present knowledge:

> When in the end there will be but one people, then will
> come about that of which we sing: "I shall be satisfied by
> the manifestation of thy glory." For then will be fulfilled
> the promise that has been made to us: to see face to face.
> For we see now through a glass darkly, and in part; but
> when both peoples purified at last, and raised up, crowned
> and glorified for eternity, shall see God face to face, then
> there will be no more but the one and only Israel . . .
> which will in truth be seen of God." [19]

When the necessary adjustments have been made it should
surely be possible to preserve the underlying value of this
doctrine. Its wanderings in the dreamland of speculation can
be left to the past, but if behind the deviations its fundamental inspiration was sound it should not be impossible to
find in it teaching that is applicable to our own day. Should
we not pay more attention, for example, to that *consortium*
which is a real part of beatitude, as so many expressions in
our Roman liturgy continually insist? [20] St Thomas Aquinas
faithfully translates these expressions into his theological
language in his teaching on the last end: "the end of a reasonable creature," he explains, "is to attain to beatitude, and
that can only consist in the kingdom of God, which in its

turn is nothing else than the well-ordered society of those who enjoy the vision of God." [21] Then, too, it should be possible to give more emphasis to the Thomist teaching about the resurrection of the body. On the one hand, according to St Thomas, the soul is not perfect without the body, so that the resurrection is not just a superfluous extra.[22] On the other, if this resurrection can only take place at the end of time it is because the penalty which is the result of original sin, extending as it does to the whole of that nature in which all men are one, cannot be finally lifted from one without being lifted also from the others. Thus the saints in heaven must await together both the salvation of those still on earth and their own resurrection. These views link up with those of St Bernard, who, as we have seen, connects together two conditions of perfect happiness: the resurrection of the body and the completion of the number of the elect. Surely, in point of fact, the separated soul is so in a twofold sense. It is separated from its body and so it is also cut off, in some sort, from the natural medium through which it communicates with its fellows. And is it not true to say, too, that according to traditional teaching the Eucharist by incorporating us in Christ, that is to say, by uniting us to him, and in him to all our brethren, makes us ready for the resurrection to a glorious immortality? [23]

By the same token can we not preserve something at least of the imposing explanation that Origen gives of Ezechiel's vision? As at Jahwe's command, when he breathed upon them, the bones strewn about on the plain came together and were covered with flesh, and life entered into them, and the House of Israel, "an exceeding great army," was thus re-made, so will it be at the last day when death shall be overcome. "When shall come the resurrection of the real, whole body of Christ, then the members of Christ will be knitted together, joint to joint, each one in his place, and the multitude of members will form at last, completely and in full reality, one single Body." [24] For the divine inbreathing which is the very source of resurrection and of life has ever appeared as the source of unity, so much so, in fact, that the resurrection of the dead can be described by the word already used for the formation of the Church—*congregatio*.

Finally, if it is obviously wrong to speak of a real deprivation, a doubt, an anxiety in the glorified Christ, would it not be possible, on the other hand, to consider that as long as the work given him to do by the Father is not complete there is room in heaven for a certain hope on Christ's part? As he still suffers in his earthly members, so, according to this view, Christ hopes in himself and in his heavenly members: and taken together this suffering and this hope complete the redemption. That, at least, is the opinion upheld in the seventeenth century by a Spanish theologian, Muniessa. With some modifications and following the path already indicated by St Thomas Aquinas, Fr Pierre Charles has lately revived the essentials of this thesis and drawn certain conclusions from it. He explains in terms that correct and at the same time recall those used by Origen:

> Christ, the Word incarnate, was not our Redeemer by a sort of accident; it was his sole office, it governed everything else. Can it be allowed that the Redeemer's hope is fully satisfied, independently of the outcome of his work? Has the hope of the Shepherd nothing to do with the fate of his flock? Is it enough for him to have kept clear of the wolf's jaws that he may peacefully contemplate his sheep from afar, watching over them merely with pity as if they were not his very own? As long as God's work is not complete, as long as there are petitions of the *Pater* still unfulfilled, can it be admitted that hope has no place in heaven, that its object is wanting? The happiness of the individual is no substitute for that of the community. The same steadfast longing, the same desire, the same rhythm of life run through both the Church militant and the Church triumphant until that day when Christ shall be complete, that is, until he shall come again in glory.[25]

As Fr Charles has pointed out, it matters little really that "hope" hardly seems the right term if we follow to the letter the most current but not necessarily best-founded definitions. It is not surprising that our language should fail in some point in dealing with these subjects. But the idea more or less successfully conveyed by this term is, on the contrary, of the highest importance. The work of God, the work of Christ, is one. In these different states—militant, suffering, triumphant—there is, all the same, but one Church. We can never realize this too keenly. We can differentiate better than many of our forebears between the temporal and the eternal, so that there is no longer any temptation to deny to the elect their essential blessedness. But if we take our stand, as we must, in the temporal order which is ours here below, we must surely affirm that the one and only Church will remain incomplete until the last day. We may conclude with Bossuet: "Jesus Christ will not be whole until the number of the saints is complete. Our gaze must ever be fixed on this consummation of God's work." [26]

NOTES TO CHAPTER IV

[1] Augustine, *in Galat. expositio*, n. 28 (P.L. xxxv, 2125).

[2] Augustine, *Confessions*, lib. 11, n. 3 (P.L. xxxii, 810).

[3] *In Ezech.*, lib. 2, hom. 1, n. 5 (P.L. lxxvi, 938).

[4] Baldwin of Canterbury, *Tractatus de vita coenobitica* (P.L. cciv, 550).

[5] *De civitate Dei*, lib. 10, c. 6 (P.L. xli, 284).

[6] Ildephonsus of Toledo, *De cognitione baptismi*, praef. (P.L. xcvi, 111). See Extract 19, p. 231.

[7] Augustine, *Confessions*, lib. 12, passim (n. 12, 20, 21, 24, etc., P.L. xxxii, 830 seq.).

[8] Gregory of Nyssa, *In Cant.*, hom. 15 (P.G. xliv, 1116-7).

[9] Hilary, *De Trinitate*, lib. 8, n. 7-11 and 15-19 (P.L. x, 241-50). See Extract 20, p. 231.

[10] *In Rom.*, lib. 4, n. 9 (P.G. xiv, 997).

[11] See Extracts 21 and 22, pp. 233 *seq*.

[12] *Protreptic*, c. 9.

[13] Augustine, *In Psalm*. 26, s. 2, n. 23 (P.L. xxxvi, 211).

[14] In Christian antiquity, it will be remembered, the porch or the atrium of churches was known as paradise, and often contained a reminder of Paradise in the shape of plants and a fountain. (Cf. *Revue d'histoire ecclésiastique*, 1939, p. 549).

[15] Amalarius, *De ecclesiasticis officiis*, lib. 4, cap. 31 (P.L. cv, 1221).

[16] *In Levit.*, hom. 7, n. 2. See Extracts 23 and 24, pp. 235 *seq*.

[17] Fr Mersch has noticed the disappearance in St Bernard of the doctrine of the Mystical Body. (Vol. ii, pp. 146-7).

[18] *In festo omnium sanctorum*, sermo 3 (Cf. *Apoc*. vi. 11); sermo 4, n. 2 (P.L. clxxxiii, 468-73).

[19] Sermo 122, n. 5 (P.L. xxxviii, 683). Cf. sermo 170, n. 9. (col. 931-2). A passage in the *Confessions*, lib. 9, c. 3, n. 6, shows Augustine's hesitation on this matter. He has just spoken of the death of his friend Nebridius: "Et nunc ille vivit in sinu Abraham, quidquid illud est, quod illo significatur sinu, ibi Nebridius meus vivit."

[20] "In aeterna beatitudine de eorum societate gaudere" (Collect

in the common of martyrs). "Cum omnibus sanctis tuis ad perpetuae beatitudinis consortium pervenire" (Mass for the Dead). "Perpetua sanctorum tuorum societate laetetur" (Leonian Sacramentary, Commemoration of St Sylvester).

[21] *Contra Gentes*, lib. 4, c. 50.

[22] *Contra Gentes*, lib. 4, c. 79.

[23] M. de la Taille, *Mysterium Fidei*, elucidatio 38.

[24] *In Joan.*, t. 10, c. 36.

[25] *Spes Christi* in *Nouvelle Revue théologique*, 1934, pp. 1020–1. Cf. *Ibid.*, 1937, pp. 1957–75.

[26] *Élévations sur les Mystères*, 18, 6. See Extracts 25 and 26, pp. 242 *seq*.

PART II

V

CHRISTIANITY AND HISTORY

Christianity, by those doctrinal aspects that we have just emphasized as well as by others, brought something absolutely new into the world. Its concept of salvation is not merely novel in comparison with that of those religions in existence at the time of its birth. It is a unique phenomenon in the religious history of mankind.

For what, in fact, do we witness outside Christianity whenever a religious movement rises above the domain of sense and effectively transcends the limit of nationality? In every case, though appearances may differ considerably, the basis is the same—an individualist doctrine of escape. It was this that inspired ancient mysticism, whether it sought to escape the vicissitudes of the sub-lunary world or to pass over the outer circle of the cosmos and to penetrate into the realm of intelligible Essences or even beyond. The Greek sage, though in a different sense from the saint, was a being apart. His contemplation was solitary. Flight, Escape: that in fact was Plato's dictum regarding the soul that acknowledges in itself a principle superior to the world. Plotinus, in his turn, recommended to his disciple the "flight of the alone to the Alone," and then Porphyry expatiates on the setting free and the *withdrawal* of the soul. The same terms may be encountered in the religious philosophies of India. The adepts of ancient Brahmanism purposed to flee by way of the gates of the moon and the sun in order to be united with the unfathomable Prajâpati. Though the six classical *darsana* rejected these childish imaginings, none the less they preserved an idea of salvation formed on the same pattern, and there is no essential difference from this point of view between Sâmkhya philosophers who hold the enduring plurality of liberated souls as of so many impenetrable monads and the thinkers of the Advaita—that absolute *reductio ad absurdum* of the world—who seek to set themselves free from the illusion of the cosmos so as to be absorbed in the unity of the Supreme Being. With the Buddhist, too, it is the same act of negation, whether he denies the existence of the world or believes in the reality of his present wretchedness; and he who practises charity to a degree that sometimes reaches the sublime in the last resort relinquishes even that. Asanga, the great mystical doctor of the Mahâyâna, when he starts to map out the path of his bodhisattva's ascent from "world" to "world" until he reaches the very highest state, which is that of Nirvâna, as a matter of course describes it as a whole series of evasions: *niryàna;* so much so that it has been said that Buddhism's only God is Escape.

Every adept has his method. For some it is initiation into secret rites, for others asceticism and ecstasy, for a few philosophy. Some consider that definitive escape is open only to that small number of privileged souls who alone are recipients of a particle of the divine Essence, whereas the "Hylics," the "Abhavya," and the "Agotraka" are condemned to languish for ever in their prison. Others, less exclusive, readily believe that all men, indeed all living creatures, can attain salvation either in the course of their life or by means of a whole series—longer or shorter—of reincarnations. Sometimes the escape that is sought will consist in a total rejection, a radical negation, and sometimes it will be a higher understanding. Sometimes it will be hoped for in a perfect form and at others "as far as possible." Some of the saved separate themselves disdainfully from all that is profane, others will be moved by pity. The moral value of the different systems varies very considerably. So does their spiritual depth; but in this connexion the achievements of Greek thought, though it reached a very high level, cannot be compared with the heights of Indian thought. Sometimes understanding is imprisoned in myth, and sometimes it is turned inwards in pure reflexion—or what seems to be. Yet running all through these many differences there is always agreement about the basis of the problem and its presuppositions: the world from which escape must be sought is meaningless, and the humanity that must be outstripped is without a history.

The "eternal return," from which nothing may be expected, in each of its phases—the Great Year, Mahâkalpa, Jubilee or whatever it is called—the end of one being the beginning of another, with never a forward movement, how overpoweringly monotonous it all is! "There will be another Socrates, another everybody, with the same friends and the same fellow citizens; and all this will occur not once, but frequently, or rather, all things will be eternally restored," and also eternally broken and destroyed, for after the period of growth comes the period of decline and the continuing series of rebirths that are also one continual death: "death made immortal," says St Maximus. The sage, thus staving off his hunger for eternity, may well be deluded for a space by the thought that he is master of the world rhythm—the rhythm of *yin* and *yang*, Brahmâ breathing in and out, the dance of Siva making and destroying worlds, endless alternation of enmity and amity—or that he captures it all in the net of his æsthetic contemplation. Yet in its toils the human mass threshes about vainly in the same unchanging state of servitude.

Amid this universal chorus Christianity alone continues to assert the transcendent destiny of man and the common destiny of mankind. The whole history of the world is a preparation for this destiny. From the first creation to the last end, through material opposition and the more serious opposition of created freedom, a divine plan is in operation, accomplishing its successive stages among which the Incarnation stands out as chief. So in close connexion with the social character of dogma there is another character, equally essential, and that is the historic. For if the salvation offered by God is in fact the salvation of the human race, since this human race lives and develops in time, any account of this salvation will naturally take a historical form —it will be the history of the penetration of humanity by Christ.

In the schemes we have set out above "the unfolding of time is a development without substance, in which nothing changes because everything changes." For Christianity, on the contrary, the course of history is indeed a reality. It is not mere barren dispersal but possesses, so to say, a certain ontological density and a fecundity. It is no longer, as in Platonism, merely "this moving image of unmoving eternity," "this eternal image without end" which is "unfolded in a circle following the law of numbers," this αἴδιον, a pale reflexion of the αἰώνιον. Development no longer seems a circular series comprising generation and corruption connected together according to that principle by which the "fact that generation is ever renewed is the nearest approach to eternal being." *Circuitus illi jam explosi sunt*: [1] that is the triumphant cry of the Christian to whom God the Creator and Saviour has been revealed. The infernal cycle is disrupted. Facts are no longer phenomena, but events, acts. Forthwith something new is wrought—birth, real growth; the whole universe grows to maturity. Creation is not merely maintained, but is continuous. The world has a purpose and consequently a meaning, that is to say, both direction and significance. The entire human race, the child of God, sustained through all the disconcerting variety of its activities—*ab Abel justo usque ad novissimum electum*—by those two hands of God, the Word and the Holy Spirit, that despite its mistakes have never entirely loosened their hold, in this one great movement sets forth to the Father. The divine Will, controlling all things, brings it infallibly into port. [2]

For there is a port, a definite terminus. The whole universe cries out for its delivery and it is sure to obtain it. Its groaning is begotten by hope. On that Christian tradition is unanimous, whatever the doctrinal differences—numerous and sometimes deep as they are—about the end of time or its beginnings, or even about the necessity for a temporal development of the human world at all. Such indeed is Origen's thought, in spite of a certain hesitation due rather to his overriding anxiety to preserve liberty of thought than to a too persistent Hellenism. He says: *In unum sane finem putamus quod bonitas Dei per Christum suum universam revocet creaturam*. [3] Just as God rested on the seventh day after he had created the world, so the world, having completed its course, will rest in God. "Then time shall be no more." [4] All things shall be renewed: *caelum novum, nova terra*. The resurrection, which shall indicate the passing of time into eternity, will be a definitive transformation of the universe: "a new earth will be created to contain the bodies that have been made new; that is to say, the whole nature of our earth will be transformed into a spiritual state, free, thenceforward, from any change." [5]

Consequently, if Christians continue to proclaim louder than all others the need to flee from the world, *fugiendum a saeculo,* it is with quite a different meaning and with another emphasis. If they insist on the vanity of earthly and temporal things it is on account of those who consider these things only as they are in appearance, making them the objects of their love in themselves, whereas whatever is real about them is a summons to look beyond them. Time is vanity only for one who, using it unnaturally, desires to establish himself in it—and to think of nothing but a "future" is to establish oneself in time. Of necessity we must find a foothold in time if we are to rise into eternity; we must use time. The Word of God submitted himself to this essential law: he came to deliver us from time, but by means of time —*propter te factus est temporalis, ut tu fias aeternus.*[6] That is the law of the Incarnation and it must undergo no Docetist mitigation. Following Christ's example, "loyally and with no cheating," every Christian must acquiesce in that state of engagement in time which gives him part and lot in all history, so that his connexion with eternity is not unrelated to a past that he knows is immense and a future the length of which is hidden from him.

Before it was reflected in formulæ and theories this belief found spontaneous expression through the selection of symbols and other usual representations. So it is that the old image of the ascent of the individual from sphere to sphere soon gives way to that of a collective progress from one age to another. We know the importance—real or symbolic—or cosmography in Hellenistic mysteries, in Pythagoreanism or neo-Platonism, and the place that the paths of the heavenly bodies, speculations about the planets and their approaches, the adornments of the soul, astral bodies and *media,* held in these systems. In India the mystic scheme is of a similar kind. The *bhûmika* of the Upanishad, the *bhûmi* of the Buddhist Mahâyâna are arranged in a series to be used as temporary mansions by the being that issues from the prison of our bodies. Each one of these dwellings is described with all its characteristics and many subtle distinctions.

In Gnosticism and later on in Manichæism all this is to be

found again, and in abundance. But authentic Christianity, though it did not at once give up all images of this sort, no longer attaches any importance to them. In Christian writers only traces of them continue to appear, and these are outside the stream of living thought. When they wish to symbolize the spiritual impulse their images are taken from scripture rather than from the stars and the planets: Jacob's ladder, the gates of the city of God described by Ezechiel, the new Jerusalem of the Apocalypse, the resting-places of the Jews in the desert. The resting-places to the number of forty-two were at first understood as the temporal sequence of the generations which led up to Christ, "the forty fathers according to the flesh by whom was brought about his descent to us," "as far as the Egypt that is this world"; even from such a figure, and one that was quite as obviously cosmographic as Jacob's ladder, teaching of a historical nature could be taken, by the method of analogy, thus revealing the mysteries of our Saviour's humanity.[7] Irenaeus, for example, just like his gnostic adversaries, can believe in the reality of the seven heavens that make up this world, and he seems to rejoice at the idea that Moses must have been thinking of this when he ordered the making of the seven-branched candlestick; nor has he any doubt that Isaias is alluding to it when he enumerates the "seven forms of worship." Origen, on the contrary, in his answer to Celsus is careful to specify that "this is mentioned nowhere in scripture." But none the less both of them are in agreement on the essential point, and all who come after them concur in this. How should they have need of intermediaries whom the one Mediator brings directly to the Father? And what do they want with seven gates since Christ is the one gate through which they pass from Egypt to the Promised Land? Moreover, they have all understood the warning given by the angel after Christ had disappeared into the heavens. There is always more commentary on Pentecost than on the Ascension—Pentecost is still the more solemn festival—and the Ascension itself is regarded in its relation to Pentecost according to Jesus's direction: *Expedit vobis ut ego vadam. . . . Si autem abiero, Spiritum mittam ad vos.* Contemplation of heaven will not distract the attention that must be given to the divine work which goes forward on earth, carried out with earthly materials but not for earthly purposes; a work that is accomplished in the Church wherein is prepared, and is already being realized in secret, the glory of him who humbled himself. And if the Master seems to have left his own for ever, yet we know that we must await, must hasten on, the time of his return: *unde missurus est Spiritum . . . unde venturus est. . . .*

Henceforward the stages of history are important: they are in reality stages of an essentially collective salvation. It is true, of course, that calculations of this sort have to be made, as Durandus of Mende remarks, *potius mystice quam chronice.* We must not expect too much precision. The system handed down by tradition was kept entire; only its subject-matter was changed. The number of stages—dispensations, laws, economies, testaments—was predetermined by the perfections, the "mysteries," to be found in certain numbers. Authors are not always in agreement as to their precise number, since the symbolic reasons or the circumstances that inspire their choice differ from one to another. But the differences are not contradictions and generally they are more apparent than real. Yet if one pressed details the complications would be extreme, for the Fathers' imagination found a great satisfaction in playing with combinations of numbers, whereby they exercised their ingenuity with subdivisions, additions and multiplications. We need only consider the principal systems, which, at first unrelated to one another, were afterwards harmonized by a differentiation between "times" and "ages." So we have on the one hand the system of four times, since four is a number that of its nature is universal—there are four elements, four seasons, four regions of the universe, the four pillars of the tabernacle, the four horses of Ezechiel's chariot, the four Gospels and the four rivers of Paradise. The four times may all be found in history or the fourth may be kept for the future life, according as the law received by Noe is added or not to the natural law, the law of Moses and the law of the Gospel. The first method of calculation was that used by St Irenaeus; the second, employed as early as St Gaudentius, prevailed from St Augustine onwards. On the other hand there is the system of the six ages or "centuries," which is extended to seven or sometimes even to eight, for these two last numbers are preeminently the perfect numbers and contain mysteries.

The combinations in this case are many, for each one

represents some "mystic reason." Thus it is that the seventh age, which according to the most usually accepted notion is the age of eternity, beginning at the end of time, may come to mean the period of the final struggle against anti-Christ, or even be added to the sixth age, from the time of our Saviour's Incarnation. As for the eighth age, which bears to the seven others the same relation as the Gospel does to the Law or as Sunday does to the Sabbath, it is the age of *Christus Oriens*, of the resurrection, and therefore of that full and final blessedness which follows the rest of the seventh day: *in octavo, resurrectionis est plenitudo.*[8] But these extensions apart, the division of human history into six ages, a practice of long standing in Judaism, was everywhere adopted in the Church. Does not the Bible teach that the world was created in six days? For each of these biblical days there is a corresponding age of the world. To each act of intervention required for the creation of the world there is the corresponding act which is necessary to lead it towards its end. The same number of ages go to its "perfecting" as there were days in its creation. Six days to make ready the mansion wherein Adam should reign, six ages to gather up this Adam again from the four quarters of the glove where he was scattered. This comparison, which the Fathers found useful in manifesting the truth of a single God who is both Creator and Saviour, shows just as clearly the corresponding truth about the world: nothing of the divine work shall be lost. The work of the Son completes and restores the work of the Father; the gifts of the Holy Spirit consecrate it. Whatever its weakness and its present state of wretchedness, this world is good and it will be saved.

It will be clearly seen that in this case there is no question of simple and more or less superficial theories. The contradiction that thus becomes manifest between Christianity and pagan thought is not just a difference between two sets of writers: it goes to the very foundation of religion. It is built into the doctrinal framework and finds eloquent expression in liturgical compositions. Of course there was no need for the Church to repudiate the harmony between the earth and the cosmos. Just as her doctors have preserved, often felicitously, many habits of thought and turns of phrase which are tainted in origin, so does the Church gather to her vast treasury riches rescued from all sides. She took the sumptuous setting of her worship from dying pagan-

ism, making a halo for the Sun of Justice out of the glory
of the *Sol Invictus,* adorning her cathedrals with the signs
of the zodiac, harmonizing her ceremonies with the rhythm of
the seasons. But it is neither the natural cycle nor some extra-
cosmic deliverance that is portrayed by her liturgical year:
it is the vast history of our redemption.

Compare it on this point, for example, with worship like
that of the Mithraic mysteries. Within the Mithraeum everything, though under the sign of the twelve regions of heaven
and the four elements, was at the same time under the sign
of the seven planets: furniture and ornament included seven
altars, seven knives, seven Phrygian caps, seven trees;
among the statues, seven busts of the Gods. Origen mentions
the scale of seven portals that was shown to the initiate, and
nowadays there may be seen at Ostia the seven-arched portals outlined on the pavement of a Mithraeum; on the banks
of the Rhine, whither soldiers of the Roman empire had
transported their cherished worship, miniature scales have
been found in many tombs. They were symbols of the seven
degrees of Mithraic initiation by which the heavenly ascent
of the worshipper was effected. Now in Christian liturgy
there is one privileged part of the year which is also under
the sign of the number seven. It is the season, with its imaginative rather than real divisions, which beginning on Septuagesima terminates on the Saturday *in Albis* or on Laetare
Sunday according as it is counted on the basis of seven
times ten days or seven consecutive Sundays. But the symbolism of this series of seven is quite different. In the Babylonian captivity we have a figure of the long captivity of
the whole human race from the time of its original sin down
to its being set free by Christ, and in the forty years from the
time of the exodus from Egypt to the entry into the promised
land is figured its long earthly pilgrimage, the long ascent
to its heavenly home. In practice, then, it is the whole of
human history. We have here our six ages of the world, the
six great stages of the redemption, with the addition of the
final age which begins with the resurrection, the definitive
sabbath, when Christ at last takes his rest, the seventh day
which shall know no decline. The scripture read in the brev-
iary at the beginning of this period is the account of the
creation, and the Gospel of the Mass is the parable of the labourers sent into the vineyard in whom tradition sees a
figure of the divine economy; this also is the burden of the

homily by St Gregory the Great read at Matins on that day. It is the history of salvation wrought by Christ, a single history with its components closely bound up together, wherein all the characters, labourers at an identical task, are mysteriously united, and where "escape" has no place.

This conception of the history of the world, like the social conception of salvation with which it is allied, has its roots in Judaism. Jahwe is the living God, the God who speaks to man's heart, but also the God of history. The Jews believe that their people was created by him on Sinai and was scattered by him at the overthrow of Jerusalem; on the first occasion his instrument was Moses, on the second Nabuchodonosor. Since it is he who made the past, he will rule the future and the destiny of his people is in his hands. As this little people came more in touch with its powerful neighbours and its intellectual bounds were widened, its faith also increased; and just as in the second part of the book of Isaias universalism reaches its zenith, so, a little later, there appears in the book of Daniel a philosophy of universal history.

Before this Jeremias had glimpsed that Juda of the prophets could not grow to maturity unless it were first uprooted, and since in his time the nation had no desire for reform he left it to rush to its downfall. He thought only of preparing for the nation to come which should rise from the ruin. Later, Ezechiel, able at that distance to view history in truer perspective, saw two periods in the development of God's kingdom; beyond the restoration of the nation, the first of Jahwe's victories over the world, he envisaged a definitive triumph. From the book of Daniel onwards this triumph appears as the end of human history, and it is allied with the physical transformation of the universe. Under the guise of four beasts—a lioness with eagle's wings, a bear, a leopard, and a horned beast terrible and wonderful—Daniel beheld four kingdoms which were symbols of the four empires, each one succeeded and absorbed by that which followed it, and together making up the empire of evil. This will be overcome by the empire of God wherein all the righteous, after their resurrection, shall have their part, all "the people of the saints of the most High whose kingdom is an everlasting kingdom."

Thus the idea of a divine work that the whole movement

of the world should bring to fruition, the idea of the progress of mankind in its entirety towards a determined end, finds vigorous expression in the Hebrew world. There has been some attempt to belittle the originality of this idea. Some twelve years ago M. René Berthelot wrote in this connexion:

> In the eschatological and already apocalyptic predictions that terminate the prophetic literature, the end of the world entails its re-beginning, with the return of the blessings of Eden, the garden of God. This, it should be noticed, is a result of that very conception of a moral and social cycle, linked with the great astronomical and biological cycles and with the "Great Years" in the life of the world, found in Chaldea as in China; but in Jewish apocalyptic literature the cycle comes to an end when it has reached, once and for all, its original starting-place.[9]

The clarity of this last remark excuses our dwelling on some other differences. A more serious objection to the originality of Israel comes from an examination of Mazdaism; at first sight it seems to bear a resemblance to Judaism that is all the more striking in that the history of religions can show no other such example.

According to the Gâthâs the world is proceeding to its end, and this end of the world is the "great event." Then when all things shall be revealed, man shall be judged by fire, which "will hurt the unrighteous and benefit the righteous." The faithful did not merely await this day of the "last crisis," they hasten on its advent and "make the world go forward" by their piety. By virtue of this they receive the title of benefactors, *saosyant*, a word which is not at all a proper name but a common title, just as Messias was for long with the Jews. They show the most intense interest in "the greatest event of all" in which they will take part—obviously through their resurrection. And then upon the earth, recast in the fire, the theocracy proclaimed by the Mazdean priests will become accomplished fact.

In the remainder of the Avesta, and the Pahlavi books, the part played by God (Ahura Mazda) at the end of the world, and the part of the faithful in its completion, will appear of lesser importance in comparison with the work accomplished by the principal Saosyant and his assistants. The whole of history simply is divided into four periods of 3,000 years each. The first period is that of a purely spiritual creation. During the second the material world is formed (myths of the primordial Man and the primordial Bull). The third starts with the beginnings of the human race and is filled with the struggle between Ahura Mazda, "the very wise Lord," and Aura Mainyu, the "Adversary." Lastly Zoroaster appears, and that is the fourth period; each of its thousand year divisions begins under one of the three sons of the prophet, born in their time from his seed which has been preserved miraculously in sacred milk. Right at the end comes the time of the supreme Saosyant; surrounded by his six assistants he "will make the power of evil disappear," "will complete the world" and "will raise up bodies."

The similarity with Jewish Messianism is evident, though it will have been noticed that Mazdaism is inclined to a greater optimism, a more activist conception of the world's growing to maturity, which is the work of each individual. But it does not seem right, fundamentally, to explain the similarity by the influence of one on the other.

Some of the details of the Pahlavi apocalypse, particularly the prominence of the figure of the Saosyant, could have come from the Bible, but everything seems to point to the Gâthâs being anterior to the meeting of Jews and Persians in Babylon; on the other hand, if the breadth of view of the book of Daniel and its imaginative expression betray some contact with Persia, it is none the less the result of an entirely Jewish line of thought. In reality we have to do with two lines of thought, the convergence of which careful examination will reveal to be more apparent than real.

In ancient Persia, as among many of the Indo-European peoples, there was a myth concerning the conflagration of the world. It was a nature-myth and does not seem to have involved at first any religious or moral significance. It was incorporated by the Zoroastrian reform, provided with a chronology and with a superimposed last judgement, and came finally to be the whole end of the evolution of the world and the human race. Memories or legends of the national epic were afterwards interpreted in this sense, and the primitive myth was gradually invested with certain notions of a supposedly historical nature. But the eschatology still remained entirely of "scientific" inspiration. With Israel the opposite occurred. Man and his destiny form the whole subject of the Bible; it is a drama, so to say, with two characters: Israel and Jahwe. Relations between them do not derive simply from the nature of things. Jahwe is not, like the other national Gods, physically bound to his people. If he is not served by them as he should be, in justice, not merely will he chastise them but he will abandon them for ever and raise up their destroyers. A historical fact lies at the origin of Israel, their choosing by Jahwe, followed by an alliance, a compact, *berit*. Israel is the people secured for himself by Jahwe. That is the concrete basis of the Decalogue: "I am the Lord thy God, who brought thee out of the land of Egypt, out of the house of bondage. Thou shalt not have strange Gods before me." Likewise the starting-point of Jewish eschatology is faith in Jahwe and his promises. It is the expectation of that day whereon all his power and faithfulness shall be made manifest. It is not the anticipation of some "natural" phenomena, but the hope—or fear—of an occurrence that will still be part of history, of a final judgement whereof past events are, so to say, an earnest.

In general the prophets spoke of God's action in history rather than of his action in nature. They lay greater stress upon Jahwe's part in the formation and leading of Israel than upon his making and governance of the world. After their threats against the unfaithful people they foretell the fall of the enemies of the holy people. The central purpose of their visions is not a cataclysm but the fall of empires—even though their faith finds expression in images borrowed freely from nature and from fragments of mythology. With Ezechiel and the second part of Isaias cosmic disturbances come to play an important part in the prophecies, though they appear as mere repercussions of human events, and if they are to be the concomitants of the last day and so prepare for the judgement they give no indication of when it will be. "No one knows the day or the hour. . . . The Son of man will come like a thief." However, when Israel, broadening its outlook, incorporated world history into its system, it took over also certain "scientific" ideas from its surroundings, so that the "Lord's day," as the second epistle of Peter bears witness, came to coincide in the end, though without losing its essential character, with world conflagration.

Mazdean eschatology is founded originally, then, on the myth of world conflagration, whereas the hope of Israel has its roots in history. This difference involves others which betoken it. In Mazdaism, although its calculations are small indeed as compared with Indian flights of fancy or indeed with the span of historic time, the end of the universe is primarily something afar off and, as it were, abstract; a belief without living connexion with actual existence. In Israel, on the contrary, and from the very beginning, national history was a divine drama leading up to its final act on the day of Jahwe. Of its very nature Mazdaism—and this second remark is no less important—insists in the first place on an individual judgement and salvation, whereas it is only at a very late period that Jewish theology took any interest in the individual. To sum up: the last ordeal according to Mazdaism remains a drama that is "essentially physical, arising from the fundamental structure of the cosmos"; but the Gospel, in which Jewish thought is fulfilled, deals with "a strictly moral drama in which man is . . . an intensely interested actor, and in which he has a keen realization of being personally involved." [10]

Thus it is not surprising that the "historicity" of Mazdaism has borne such fruit. It has not succeeded in grafting upon the human conscience the ideal that it perceived in the Gâthâs and in its relatively pure state was never a popular cult. Its earthbound prophesying, entirely lacking in mysticism, founders in a medley of undeveloped myth and artificial constructions which by their over-regular arrangement betray an outworn vein. To be sure it is not without interest to note that this religion, which has been described as the least pagan in the whole pagan world, should be the only one to show any resemblance, in such an important particular, with revealed religion. Yet what a gulf there is between the two! For Israel, history is the work of God in a sense that Mazdaism with its unresolved tendency to dualism could never achieve: "The Lord has done all this: he has prepared it from afar." "I made the earth and the men and the beasts that are upon the face of the earth, by my great power and by my stretched out arm: and I gave it to whom it seemed good in my eyes." So it is that the messianic hope of the Chosen People is not only proof against all disappointment, overcomes all obstacles: but rather engulfs them and draws from their substance the food of its irresistible strength and spreading scope. One thing is certain, whatever the precise method or moment of its coming. This hope is so consubstantial with Jewish thought that, far from declining in the face of the discoveries that follow the growth of civilization or growing feeble as a resultant of its maturity, it contrives to incorporate everything—universalist views, cosmic speculations, progress in the spiritual life or attempts to form a system of humanist knowledge. It endows everything with an historical form, it makes of everything the work of its God and the instrument of his plans, growing ever more eager in expectation of an event that is at the same time ever nearer and ever more awe-inspiring. "With a single glance, at one leap, at one stroke, heaven is joined to earth and they are ineffably bound together." [11] The Bible makes an extraordinary impression on the historian: the contrast between the humble beginnings of Israel and the potency of the seed, or rather the explosives, which it contains; its concrete shape shrouded from the outset in the loftiest beliefs; then its stately expansion, its confident though hidden progress to a boundless and unpredictable end: nowhere else can be found anything in the least like it. Nothing resembles the stupendous incoherence of its prophetic literature; only a transfiguration of the whole, glimpsed in sudden flashes, can prevent overwhelming and endless contradictions. The historical character of the religion of Israel can be understood in all its originality only through its consummation in the religion of Christ. We should never forget that the explanation of Judaism is not to be found within itself.

NOTES TO CHAPTER V

[1] Augustine, *De Civitate Dei,* lib. 12, c. 20, n. 4 (P.L. xli, 371).

[2] See Extract 27, p. 245.

[3] *Periarchon,* lib. 1, c. 6, n. 1; lib. 2, c. 3, n. 4–5 (Koetschau, pp. 79 and 119–20).

[4] *Apoc.* x. 6.

[5] Isidore of Seville, *De ordine creaturarum,* c. 11, n. 6 (P.L. lxxxiii, 943).

[6] Augustine, *In 1 Joan.,* tr. 2, n. 10 (P.L. xxxv, 1994).

[7] See Extract 28, p. 246.

[8] Ambrose, *In Lucam* (P.L. xv, 1745A).

⁹ *L'astrobiologie et la pensée de l'Asie* in *Revue de métaphysique et de morale*, 1935, pp. 194–5.

¹⁰ H. S. Nyberg, *Questions de cosmogonie et de cosmologie mazdéennes* in *Journal asiatique*, vol. 219, pp. 30–1.

¹¹ G. Cattaui, *Instances d'Israel* in *Les Juifs* (1937), p. 266.

VI

THE INTERPRETATION OF SCRIPTURE

God acts in history and reveals himself through history. Or rather, God inserts himself in history and so bestows on it a "religious consecration" which compels us to treat it with due respect. As a consequence historical realities possess a profound sense and are to be understood in a spiritual manner: ἱστορικὰ πνευματικῶς; conversely, spiritual realities appear in a constant state of flux and are to be understood historically: πνευματικὰ ἱστορικῶς. The Bible, which contains the revelation of salvation, contains too, in its own way, the history of the world. In order to understand it, it is not enough to take note of the factual details it recounts, but there must also be an awareness of its concern for universality, in spite of its partial, schematic and sometimes paradoxical mode of expression. It was in this way that the Bible was read by the Fathers of the Church. From Irenaeus to Augustine, by way of Clement of Alexandria and Eusebius, they all found in it a treatise on the history of the world. Had they known all the facts now in our possession doubtless the treatise would have been of far greater complexity, but the essential form would have been the same. For they would have been faithful, as we ought to be, to that fundamental principle they learnt from scripture: that if salvation is social in its essence it follows that history is the necessary interpreter between God and man.

This principle governs the whole of their exegesis; it divides off their method of interpretation very sharply from that of the allegorical philosophers, whose works they may have known, or even from Philo. There are two features in the allegorism of the philosophers that appear constantly whatever the text on which their work is based or the system

that they deduce from it; whatever purpose guides them or
the precise nature of the method they use. For on the
one hand they reject as myth what appears as an historical
account, and deny to its literal sense what they claim to reveal in its meaning as a mystery: their ὑπόνοια is, in the
strictest sense, an ἀλληγορία. "It does not mean that these
things ever happened," they all exclaim with Sallust, Julian
the Apostate's friend. On the other hand, if they "spiritualize"
in this way whatever purports to be historical, it is not for
the purpose of a deeper understanding of history. They do
not see mythical events as symbols of spiritual happenings;
but perceive beneath the historical veil scientific, moral or
metaphysical ideas: "It is not that these things ever happened—for they are thus from all eternity." The idea of a
spiritual Reality becoming incarnate in the realm of sense,
needing time for its accomplishment, that without prejudice
to its spiritual significance should be prepared, come to pass,
and mature socially in history—such a notion is entirely
alien to these philosophers. Confronted with it, they find it a
stumbling-block and foolishness.

Philo's exegesis, too, is very far removed, even in its form,
from what Christian exegesis was to be. Of course this orthodox Jew was very far from denying altogether the literal
meaning of the Bible story. He believes in the past greatness
of his people; he believes in its future and the coming of the
Messias. He is uncompromising, too, towards those of his fellow countrymen who excuse themselves from observing the
laws of Moses by pretending that they "are symbols of intelligible realities." Yet even Philo in trying to derive a spiritual
teaching from the Bible denudes it somewhat of its historical significance. Facts interpreted in this way, whether
they are real or not, are of no interest save through what
they symbolize: this is true more especially of the structure
of the human soul—which is still only the object of a
"physic"—or its experiences in search of God. The student
of the scriptures thus abandons the religious plane for that
of abstract speculation—this is especially true of Philo's *Allegory of the Laws*—or at least strays into an individualistic
mysticism.

It is quite otherwise with the Fathers. Far from diminishing the historical and social character of Jewish religion,
their mysticism strengthens it by discovering its depths. Of
course there are more or less superficial similarities to be

found between them and the writers who preceded them—similarities of vocabulary in the first place: did not St Paul use that ambiguous word *allegory*? Some of their exegetical methods they inherit from the Greeks, their explanation of this or that passage is borrowed from the Jews, this or that point of their "symbolist" doctrine is a part of the common heritage of their century and environment, or some other feature is to be found also in Hinduism, Buddhism, or wherever there are men who ponder a sacred text. Such comparisons are not without their interest, here as with so many of the ideas, rites and institutions of primitive Christianity, and an investigation of this kind may well yield a rich reward. But it would be entirely wrong to suppose that such a method will account for the spiritual interpretation which Christianity gives to the Bible. We shall make no distinction between the Greek and Latin Fathers or between those of Antioch and Alexandria and the Augustinian school; such distinctions have in the past been pushed too far. For is not what the Fathers of Antioch, together with Diodorus of Tarsus and Theodore of Mopsuestia, call θεωρία, using the more platonic, less traditional term, the same thing that Origen, closely following St Paul, calls ἀλληγορία? They all mean "to understand the spirit of history without impairing historical reality." For "there is a spiritual force in history" (it is a Greek, one of those least interested in a purely "historical" approach, who tells us this); by reason of their finality the very facts have an inner significance; although in time, they are yet pregnant with an eternal value. On the other hand, the reality which is typified in the Old—and even the New—Testament is not merely spiritual, it is incarnate; it is not merely spiritual but historical as well. For the Word was made flesh and set up his tabernacle among us. The spiritual meaning, then, is to be found on all sides, not only or more especially in a book but first and foremost *in reality itself*: *In ipso facto, non solum in dicto, mysterium requirere debemus.*[1] Indeed what we call nowadays the Old and New Testaments is not primarily a book. It is a twofold event, a twofold "covenant," a twofold dispensation which unfolds its development through the ages, and which is fixed, one might suppose, by no written account. When the Fathers said that God was its author—the one and only author of the Old and New Testaments—they did not liken him merely, nor indeed primarily, to a writer, but saw in him the founder, the lawgiver, the institutor of these two "instruments" of salvation, these two economies, two dispensations which are described in the scriptures and which divide between them the history of the world. "There is only one same God of both," they said, "one same Father." And did not St Paul mention the two covenants or testaments before our New Testament was written? Convinced that all therein was full of deep and mysterious meaning, the Fathers bent over the inspired pages in which they could trace through its successive stages the covenant of God with the human race; they felt that, rather than giving a commentary on a text or solving a verbal puzzle, they were interpreting a history. History, just like nature, or to an even greater degree, was a language to them. It was the word of God. Now throughout this history they encountered a mystery which was to be fulfilled, to be *accomplished* historically and socially, though always in a spiritual manner: the mystery of Christ and his Church.

As this mystery is in process of fulfilment and will not be completed until the very end of time, the New Testament does not contain, any more than the Old, a complete meaning in its literal sense. Both contain, then, a spiritual meaning, and equally in both this spiritual meaning is prophetic. Yet from the expositor's point of view their position is very different. For truth itself is present in the New Testament, though it can be perceived only as a reflexion, and to such effect that if the Christian Passover is a transition, yet this necessary and continual transition from the Gospel in time to the Gospel in eternity never goes beyond the Gospel. If Christ is beyond all figures of him, the Spirit of Christ cannot lead further than Christ. The New Testament will never date; it is of its very nature the "Testament that never grows old," the last Testament, *novissimum Testamentum*. It should therefore be interpreted—as far as is possible while we are still in this world—in accordance with those principles that are laid down in it; whereas the Old Testament, beyond the facts and events which the literal meaning of the text teaches us, designates also "something else" the very reality of which (not merely the manifestation of it) is to come. In consequence it is true to say that its symbols are prophetic ones, προφητικὰ σύμβολα: a declaration, a foreshadowing, προτύπωσεις, as well as a preparation, *Praeparatoria figu-*

rativa, said St Thomas Aquinas.[2] "The Law," says the Epistle to the Hebrews, repeating an expression which occurs, with differences of meaning negligible for present purposes, in the Epistle to the Romans and the Epistle to the Colossians, "The Law" was a "shadow of the good things to come." [3]

Do we realize how daring such an expression is? And do we understand how it involves the complete reversal of the accepted notions of the old exemplarism and of common thought? For see how the body follows its shadow, the exemplar its "type": Τύπος τοῦ μελλόντος, σκιὰ τῶν μελλόντων. The rough sketch is the preparation for the archetype, the imitation (μίμημα) comes before the model. The μελλόντα are the πρωτότυπα. The figure is what comes first, and the dawn is a reflexion of the day that it heralds. This is the truth that is to come and will arise one day on earth: *futura Veritas, secutura Veritas—Veritas de terra orta.* Unheard of paradox! Was not Truth before all ages? Is it not that divine Logos which Philo said was the eldest of God's sons? "Never does the shadow exist before the body," says Tertullian, "nor does the copy come before the original." Yet that is the disconcerting reality of the Christian fact; it is both the substance and the model, the truth that is foreshadowed and reflected in the Jewish history that went before it, *Umbra Evangelii et Ecclesiae congregationis in Lege.* The whole Christian fact is summed up in Christ—as the Messias who was to come: ὁ Μέλλων—who had to be prepared for in history, just as a masterpiece is preceded by a series of rough sketches; but as the "image of the Invisible God" and the "first born of all creation" he is the universal Exemplar.[4] The Son of David, he who is desired of all nations, is at the same time that mysterious mountain on which Moses beheld the ideal forms of all he was to establish for the formation of God's people. Christ, in so far as transcendent and existing before all things, is anterior to his figures, yet as a historical being, coming in the flesh, he appears after them. The whole Law spoke the words of John the Baptist: "He who comes after me was made before me." But this living synthesis of the eternal and temporal is one in its duality: Christ existing before all things cannot be separated from Christ born of the woman, who died and rose again. *Nascitur Veritas de terra Christus Dei virtus, Christus Dei sapientia de carne humana, Deus Dei Filius de Virgine*

Maria.[5] He who was sent by the Father "last of all in these days" is the very same "by whom also he made the world."[6] Late in historic time, but prior in priority to all time, Christ appears to us preceded by the shadows and the figures which he himself had cast on Jewish history.

It is tempting to say that it was the peculiar genius of the first Christians thus to graft the new religion on to the old, establishing the unique cohesion of the two interwoven parts which we call the two Testaments. "What conception of God and the world enabled men not only to place the Old and New Testaments side by side, but even to understand one in the light of the other?"[7] But the question of genius does not arise here, and in this conception of the world we are confronted with a consequence and not a cause. We have not to do with some wonderful creation, some scheme invented by an intellectual, the vision of some contemplative. Rather was it the consequence of the fact of the Incarnation on the conscience of some few Jews. In the end what was originally known by intuition was developed into a skilfully constructed theory capable of withstanding Jewish attacks on the one hand and those of the Gnostics on the other, at the same time providing the means for preserving the scriptures and using them as a basis, while yet freeing itself from Judaism: *gladius bis acutus* like the scriptures themselves. In the vast field thus opened to him the perspicacity of the investigator had ample scope; he could wander at will and uncover many different shades of meaning by a process of textual comparison, whereas the philosopher had all that he needed to construct a system of universal symbolism. But right from the beginning the essential was there, the synthesis was made, in the dazzling and confused light of revelation. *Novum testamentum in Vetere latebat: Vetus nunc in Novo patet.*[8] This well-known axiom is no echo of an individual point of view. Very early, of course, separate traditions in the interpretation of scripture were established, different schools arose, some restrained, others exuberant; differing habits of mind came into conflict. But the same fundamental principle compelled the recognition of all. From the beginning "the harmonious agreement of the Law and the Prophets with the Testament delivered by the Lord" was the "rule of the Church." In the conjunction of the two Testaments was woven a single vesture for the Word; together they formed one body, and to rend this body by rejecting the Jewish books was no less a sacrilege than to rend the body of the Church by schism. If indeed the coming of Christ determined the "end of the Law," τέλος, the Law itself bore witness that its end was Christ, σκοπός. History and the Holy Ghost had met at last, and with the abandonment of an outworn literalism scripture was made new in the everlasting newness of the Spirit.

If the Old Testament was to be understood in its "true," "absolute" meaning, it was imperative that the time should be accomplished and that Christ should come. For he alone could "break the mysterious silence, provide the clue to the riddles of the prophets"; he alone could open the book sealed with seven seals. He alone, the one corner-stone, could join the two arms of the arch of history, as he was, too, the junction of the two peoples. For a Christian to understand the Bible means to understand it in the light of the Gospel. "No one can understand the Old Testament without the teaching of the New, since the spiritual meaning of the Old Testament is nothing else than the New." If in scripture we perceive, so to say, a body and a soul, we can assert—and it amounts to the same thing—that this body and this soul are the literal meaning and the spiritual meaning, or that they are the Old and New Testaments. The former requires the latter, else is it no more than a vain shadow, the "letter which kills." Or, as Origen remarked: "We who belong to the Catholic Church do not despise the Law of Moses, but accept it, so long as it is Jesus who interprets it for us. Only thus shall we understand it aright." [9] But it should be added that this interpretation is not a mere commentary. For there is no comparison of Jesus's relation to scripture with that of Chrysippus or Proclus to Homer or the Orphic myths. He comes not to explain it intellectually but to fulfil it in deed: *operante Christo, in Novum Testamentum observatio vetusta transfunditur*. [10] That is the victory of the Lion of Juda. If theology, according to a much-used equivalent expression perpetuated by St Thomas at the beginning of the *Summa*, is the science of the scriptures, then in truth it may be said that the whole of theology is *Theologia Crucis*, that is *Theologia a Cruce*. For it is the Cross which disperses the cloud which until then was hiding the truth. "Behold the page between the two Testaments all set in vivid red." [11] At the very moment that Christ, having finished his work, gave up the ghost, the veil of the Temple was rent: a symbol with a double meaning like the reality which it signified. For it signified at the same time the downfall of the letter of Jewish worship and the manifestation of the mystery foretold in figure by this worship.

Yet the act of redemption is not a key which by unlocking the Old Testament reveals a meaning already present in it. This act in some sort creates the meaning. It is only for God, from the eternal point of view, that the Old Testament contains the New already in a mystery: *semel locutus est Deus et plura audita sunt.* The entire Bible contains no other Logos than him whom we adore in the flesh; so that if, to suppose an impossibility, Christ had not come, no man confronted with the sacred text would have the right to go beyond its literal meaning; "the Lord is the Spirit." By their rejection of Christ the Jews were deprived of this right. Moses and Elias are transfigured only in the glory of Thabor, and the two Testaments, like the two angels in white garments at the tomb of Christ, appear as identical only in the bright light of Easter day. If therefore it should happen that on some point of detail the same "spiritual" interpretation is found in a Jewish and a Christian exegete, such a coincidence, even when it arises through a borrowing by the one from the other, does not alter the fact that their fundamental principles of interpretation are entirely different. In some sort Christ took scripture into his own hands, and he has filled it with himself through the mysteries of his Incarnation, Passion and Resurrection. The value that Christianity accords to time, that is, to the *act* that is registered in time, is here revealed in its full meaning:

> Before the coming of Christ, writes Origen, the Law and the prophets were not yet, one may say, the announcement of what came to pass in the Gospel, since he who was to make their mysteries clear had not yet come. But when the Saviour had come to us and had given a body to the Gospel, then, by means of the Gospel, he effected that the whole (of the scriptures) should be like the Gospel.[12]

A miraculous transformation this, on a par with, and fundamentally identical with, the miracle of our adoption as sons. A mystery which tradition, following Origen once again, has seen symbolized in that water of Mara which was bitter and turned to sweetness when Moses cast into it the tree that the Lord had shown him, for "by the wood of the Cross

the bitterness of the Law is changed into the sweetness of
spiritual understanding, and the people of God can quench
its thirst." A mystery that we are taught, too, by the same
sort of symbolism in the miracle of Cana: "For in truth
scripture was the water: but since the coming of Jesus it has
been turned for us into wine." [13]

The social character of the most spiritual Christian exegesis
is just as noteworthy as the historical. The latter chiefly concerns the principles of interpretation; the former is manifest
in the subject matter.

For the whole of the Old Testament is habitually seen by
the Fathers as one comprehensive and extensive prophecy, and
the subject of the prophecy is no less than the mystery of
Christ, which would not be complete were it not also the
mystery of the Church. Thus, to quote for the moment a
single example, Job in his trials is at the same time Jesus
crucified and his persecuted Church. "From the beginning of
the world this mystery of the Catholic Church is ceaselessly
proclaimed through the books of scripture." Everywhere the
Church appears in figure, in the whole fabric of the history
of God's people—*ipsum regnum judaïcum prophetia fuit*—
or in particular events. The Church is the starry firmament;
she is Paradise in the midst of which Christ, the tree of
life, is planted, whence spring the four rivers of the Gospel.
She is Noe's ark: if the ark had double walls it was because
the Church was made up of Jew and Gentile; if in certain
places those walls were in three thicknesses it was because
she is formed from the descendants of three sons of Noe.
She is Mount Sion. She is the Holy Place whereon Jacob or
Moses trod. She is to be seen in the tabernacle, the bow in
the clouds, the golden candlestick. She is also that garment
washed in wine by the son of Juda, and Rahab's house in
Jericho where the strip of scarlet, symbol of the Passion, is
ever shining. She is the dwelling place of Abimelech, the
city of David, the temple of Solomon, the vestment of the
true high priest. She is the great tree that Nabuchodonosor
saw in a dream. . . . Very often these symbols are connected
together to make a composite figure; thus in the seventy
thousand who went forth with David to seek the Ark of the
Covenant and to bring it into the city can be seen the
seventy tongues of the different peoples, who by Christ are
made into the one people with which he fills his Church.

From one end of the Bible to the other there is scarcely a
woman of prominence who is not in some way a figure of
that Church. The ingenuity of the first commentators, encouraged by the speculations of the rabbis, saw her in Lot's wife;
following Paul, they recognized her in Sara; she it was, too,
that they found in Rachel and Rebecca, in Debora and in
Samuel's mother Anne, in the widow of Sarepta and in Esther.
And do not all those wells by which Moses and the patriarchs
made their covenants teach us that it is in the waters of
baptism that Christ will find his bride?

The foreigners, the slaves, the harlots delineate an especially striking figure of the *Ecclesia ex gentibus*. There is the
pagan Jahel, who held the victory in her hands; there is the
Ethiopian, the Cushite woman whom Moses took to wife;
the thought of his union leads naturally to the thought of
the union that was to come one day between his Law and
the Gentiles, or to the engrafted branch of wild olive. Then
there is that curious group of four women which St Matthew
carefully picks out—he mentions no others—in his genealogy
of Jesus: Thamar, Rahab herself, Ruth, and the fourth,
Bethsabee, whom he names only by allusion as "her that had
been the wife of Urias." Ruth was a beggar woman: yet
Christ did not scorn her, and her poor humanity bestowed
on him a royal line. On the other hand, there is the queen of
Saba "casting aside her ceremonies and her ways of error to
come to Jerusalem for the wisdom of Christ, the King of
Peace, to offer to him the gold of her wisdom and the precious
stones of her virtues." [14] There is her rival, Pharaoh's daughter, the wife of Solomon: the daughter of the devil whom
the "true" Solomon could draw to his palace. And finally
there is the harlot whom the prophet Osee was commanded
to marry: "for what Osee did in figure Christ accomplished
in reality." [15]

This last type of symbol, one of the most constantly elabo-
rated, is at the same time one of the most important, for it
reminds us of what the Church was in the thought of the
Fathers and of the breadth of their vision. In the privileged
history of the patriarchs and the faithful people they saw
the long betrothal of Christ with his Church which preceded
the mystic marriage of Nazareth and Calvary. But among
the Gentiles as among the Jews, however far their gaze
travelled, they could discern the *Corpus Ecclesiae* already in
process of formation. For them, in fact, in a certain sense

the Church was nothing else than the human race itself, in all the phases of its history, in so far as it was to lead to Christ and be quickened by his Spirit. It was the *omnis humana conditio*. They never lost sight of this vast mass of humanity so long in exile, "without God," with no hope in the world, wasting itself in apparently vain effort; it was this humanity which Christ came to tear from its idols, which he loves with a gratuitous love in that miserable nakedness which is the result of its sin, which he undertakes to cleanse, to make holy, which he changes from darkness into light, which at the last he makes his bride *sine ruga neque macula*. At the very beginning of scripture, right on the threshold of history, that is the mystery which they see in the story of Adam and Eve. And it is the same mystery that is proffered again at the end of the scriptures in the "woman clothed with the sun" of the Apocalypse.[16]

It is clear, then, that we have not here just one symbol among many others, characterized merely by the frequency with which it occurs and its preponderant interest. All the others are more or less directly related to it. It is the central symbol, the guiding spirit, as it were, of the whole interpretation of the Old Testament. This interpretation occurs in a threefold but indivisible sense: spiritual, historical and social; and it is merely to give it these attributes all together if we say that its subject-matter is, in one word, the Church. *Prophetia semper figuris variantibus loquitur, sed res una in omnibus invenitur*. That is what the terms used by St Hilary teach us, though they are not used with that express intention. Just as in Hilary's mouth the meaning of the *praefigurationis significantia* that he discerns on every page of Holy Writ is equivalent to the *spiritualis praeformatio*, so this second expression alternates with a third: *Ecclesiae praeformatio*. Our twofold equivalent has cropped up again: the spiritual meaning, essentially prophetic, is no less essentially an "ecclesiastical" meaning:

> "The wings of the dove are covered with silver," says the Psalm, "and the hinder parts of her back with the paleness of gold." This dove is scripture. By the silver wings, outwardly shining, should be understood the sacred words in their literal meaning. As for the paleness of gold, it refers to the precious mysteries of Christ which shine with an inner radiance.[17]

Just as the Church is in figure throughout the precepts of the Old Law and the events of sacred history, so is she continually foretold in the visions of the prophets, more clearly indeed, according to St Augustine, than Christ himself: *obscurius dixerunt Prophetae de Christo, quam de Ecclesia*. Christian writers, aiming at systematic classifications, divide the prophecies into two categories: those which deal directly with Christ as Head and those which deal with his Body. This is the line taken by Junilius and Isidore of Seville. And it is Tertullian's. But there is one book especially rich in mysteries wherein these two aspects are closely bound up with another. Continually in the Psalms it is Christ who speaks, and continually he is speaking of us, by us, in us, while we speak in him. "He would not speak separately because he would not be separated." From one sentence to another, and even in the same sentence, there is, so to say, a constant intermingling: sometimes Christ speaks in his own name as Saviour, born of a virgin; sometimes he identifies himself with his members, and it is then that Holy Church appears, though it is always the same "I" that speaks in the double rôle. What is to be found in the Psalms occurs in other prophecies. The Lamentations of Jeremias, for example, deal with "the sufferings of Christ and the tribulations of the Church." The mysterious servant of Jahwe, who in certain passages stands out so clearly as a person, in others suggests a collectivity. We should not be surprised, but should remember here again that "to understand the scripture it is absolutely necessary to think of the whole, complete Christ." [18]

A similar principle governs the interpretation of several Gospel texts: there is "communication of idioms" between the Head and the members of the one Body of Christ, just as we saw there is between this Mystical Body and the visible Church. And, as we found in that case also, there are excesses in the application of the principle, excesses which amount to an abuse. This method of interpretation was too readily employed in the first place by the followers of Athanasius against the Arians, and later against the Nestorians —to bolster up a Christology tainted, moreover, with Docetism —in order to evade certain texts that seemed difficult. Such were those concerning ignorance of the last day, the announcement of the approaching coming of the Son of Man, the account of the agony in the garden or the cry of our Lord on the Cross. But this abuse was only possible on the basis of the doctrinal principle which lay behind it. Origen, explaining St Matthew, sees without hesitation the *ut quid dereliquisti me?* as a complaint of our Saviour to his Father against the humiliating straits to which he was reduced; yet in his explanation of the Psalms the same commentator acknowledges that this very cry is the "voice of humanity proclaiming its distressful state through the mouth of its head and representative." And has it not been said that St Augustine, in repeatedly returning to this subject, on no occasion does so "as a controversialist or apologist but rather as exegete and theologian?" At Gethsemane, on Calvary, Jesus spoke in his own name; yet none the less he spoke at the same time on behalf of humanity. *Sive caput loquatur, sive membra, unus Christus loquitur. Et capitis proprium est loqui etiam in persona membrorum.*[19]

It is not merely certain passages of this kind but the Gospels as a whole which lend themselves, like the Old Testament, to such spiritual exegesis, from which there emerges a predominant concern for the great mystery of the whole Body. What great ingenuity is brought into play to find in so many episodes a figure of the two peoples that divide the world between them—of the difference in their destinies and in their attitudes to Christ, and of their final union in one same Church! Nazareth, of course, is taken to represent the unbelieving Jews, and Capharnaum the motley crowd of Gentiles. Before they were seen as symbols of action and contemplation Martha and Mary were the synagogue and the Church. The ass on which Jesus rode into Jerusalem represents the Jewish converts, and the colt running beside him those from the Gentiles. The two thieves are the Jews and the "Greeks" whose sins are crucified with Christ. The two blind men of Jericho also are the two peoples who are to be enlightened and reconciled in Christ, unless perhaps they are Israel and Juda, or, on the other hand, both of them are Gentiles, one a figure of the descendants of Cham, the other of Japhet's. Zacchaeus again represents the Gentiles, so also the Canaanite woman or her daughter. Mary Magdalen, the Samaritan woman, the woman taken in adultery, are in their conversion each in her own way the *Ecclesia exgentibus*, as is the woman who touches the hem of Jesus's garment, whereas Simon Peter's mother-in-law is a figure of the *Ecclesia ex circumcisione*. The man of Siloe who was born blind is a symbol of the whole human race that our Redeemer

snatches from judgement: its eyes of wondrous beauty wherein
divinity was reflected had been darkened by looking on the
Prince of Darkness; now they receive their light once more.
If Jesus is born in Bethlehem, the house of Bread, it is because there is only one house where the true bread of heaven
may be found. His calming of the storm is his coming to the
help of his Church tossed by the cross-currents of the world,
buffeted by the winds of unclean spirits, that he may lead
her to the peaceful haven of heaven. When Peter in the
name of Jesus of Nazareth raises the lame man "who was
laid . . . at the gate of the temple called Beautiful" he is
healing the Church herself—and that means, always, the
human race—erring in idolatry, and by the gate Beautiful
which is Jesus he leads her to knowledge of the true God.

The parables especially are interpreted in this way. We
have already noticed this with the lost sheep and the labourers
sent into the vineyard. But it holds good also for the guests
at the wedding feast, Lazarus and the rich man, the pharisees and the publican, the rebellious husbandmen. Moreover,
in some cases it was, almost in detail, the obvious interpretation. Even those allegorical treatments which are the
least objective are revealing in this connexion. They show
the spontaneous tendency of the "analogy of faith."

In the fifteenth chapter of St Luke's Gospel the accounts
of the lost groat and the prodigal son, together with that of
the lost sheep, make up the wonderful sequence of the "parables of forgiveness." We need not be surprised that they
have been often commented on as a group and in the same
sense. For what better symbol of the human race could be
imagined than that paltry groat "bearing a royal effigy"? It
does not matter that it is a woman who seeks it; for she is
divine Wisdom—*incarnata Sapientia*—that is, the Word. Her
whole wealth consists of ten coins, for in addition to the
human race there are the nine choirs of angels. Finally she
calls together her neighbours that they may share her joy;
and does not Christ bid the heavenly host celebrate with
him the salvation of mankind? The prodigal son also in the
eyes of many stood for sinful humanity; while in his elder
brother, who stayed at home, they believed they could see
the angels that had remained faithful. This last inference,
obviously a little strained, was not for long without its adversaries. Cyril of Alexandria mentions it only to reject it.

By this time Luke's narrative had received another interpretation, this also giving it a collective sense, which for long remained the tradition of the Latin commentators. When it was proposed to compare the prodigal son to repentant sinners in the Church, Tertullian protested: it was his rigorist spirit that rebelled against this; but he could, it seems, base his objections on this other interpretation—already classical—which saw in the unhappy son's return to his father's house the conversion of the pagan nations; as for the elder son, he stood for the Jews, "not indeed because they were without sin and obedient to God, but because they who had never strayed from their Father's house were jealous of the salvation of other nations." [20]

It was surely obvious that those two sons whom their father sent to work in the vineyard, the first refusing at the outset but afterwards obeying, the other full of assurances yet not going, should be taken to represent the Jews and the Gentiles. In spite of the objections to it, this interpretation was adopted. The Gentiles were mentioned first, either because they went back to Noe, whereas the Jewish line began only with Abraham, or because in the divine plan they were chosen first and destined to believe before Israel.[21] They had abandoned the worship of idols, and had finally answered the Gospel summons; while the Jews, with their materialist interpretations of the Law that they professed to keep, had prepared the way for their present hardness of heart. The really obedient son was the people that, having given up hope of the Messias, had shown a change of heart when at last he came, not the people who professed to await him but would not receive him. Surely the woman who hid her leaven in three measures of meal was the Church which through the leaven of the Gospel joins together the descendants of the sons of Noe, or the men of the three periods that divide history before Christ's coming, so causing the whole dough of humanity to be raised.

The Fathers, with a wonderful discernment, which can be explained only by their habit of envisaging the religious life in historical terms, also noticed that the six parables of the thirteenth chapter of St Matthew followed each other just like the six ages of the world. Thus the teaching of the parables taken all together was in its fashion a sacred history. Those who had "ears to hear" witnessed the fate of the divine Seed entrusted to our race from the time of the earthly paradise down to the great day of judgement. The sower of cockle played his sorry part with Adam and with Cain. The grain of mustard seed was sown after the flood to grow into the towering tree of all races. The leaven of Abraham's faith, accepted in the first place by the synagogue, was one day to spread throughout the world. From the time of David onwards there was a great treasure hidden in the field of prophecy. The pearl of great price that the best among the Jews, deprived of their riches since the exile, had come to desire, was to be found at Christ's birth. Thereafter all those who proclaim the Gospel are like that householder who is continually giving out "things new and old." The net of the kingdom of heaven begins to fill, and when all things are completed the angels will accomplish the triumph of the righteous.

Far more simply, the one parable of the Good Samaritan lends itself to a full statement of our collective history. Consequently it found particular favour in tradition. Every feature of it had its allegorical explanation, so that with an accuracy that reminds one of the canvasses of the Dutch masters it presented an epitome of the whole mystery of our redemption. It was an interpretation adopted by all, and it must have been current by the end of the second century, since Origen, quoting it before he adds his own commentary, considers it "reasonable and beautiful," and attributes it to one of those "elders" whose opinions he so readily quotes:

The man means Adam with the life he originally led and with the fall caused by disobedience. Jerusalem means paradise, or the Jerusalem on high. Jericho is the world, the robbers are the opposing powers, whether devils or false teachers, who profess to come in the name of Christ. The wounds are disobedience and sins. Man is stripped of his clothing, that is, he loses incorruptibility and immortality, he is despoiled of every virtue. He is left half dead because death has seized a half of our human nature. The priest is the Law. The Levite represents the prophets. The Samaritan is Christ who took on human flesh through Mary. The beast of burden is the Body of Christ.

The wine is the word of teaching and correction, the oil is the word of philanthropy, compassion or encouragement. The inn is the Church. The innkeeper is the college of apostles and their successors, bishops and teachers of the churches, or else the angels who are set over the Church. The two pennies are the two Testaments, the Old and the New, or love of God and one's neighbour, or knowledge of the Father and the Son. The return from Samaria is the second coming of Christ.[22]

In spite of all this the realities of the interior life, the "spiritual life," are not forgotten. This social exegesis, which sees on all sides the human race in its relation to the Saviour, which seems almost obsessed by the antagonism between the Church and the synagogue, is none the less concerned with the individual soul. But these are not two separate subjects, and the order in which they are treated—the order of teaching and practice—has its significance. For, if all that happens to Christ happens also to his Church, "whatever happens to the Church happens also to each individual soul." In this well-known maxim in the letter to Mlle de Roannez, Pascal sums up the unanimous tradition. The soul in question is the soul of the believer, *anima in Ecclesia*. Since it is through its prophecies of the mystery of Christ and of the Church that the Old Testament acquires the right, so to say, of intimating eternal verities—no man can journey from the earthly to the heavenly Jerusalem save in the train of him who came down therefrom—so is it only on condition that we see in both Testaments this single but twofold mystery, that we have the right to elucidate its spiritual sense. For there is no authentic spiritual life which does not depend on the historic fact of Christ and the Church's collective life. Nothing exceeds the scope of this twofold but single mediation, and "of his fullness we have all received."

Tradition, whether it deals with the Old Testament or the Gospel, and especially when it deals with the parables, preserves both these aspects of the mystical meaning—one has in view the collective destiny of man, the other the interior life of the soul. Thus all that we are taught by scripture finds its fulfilment in each one of us. *Quidquid illic gestum historialiter legitur, totum in nobis per mysterium spiritualis intellectus impletur.*[23] "And as the eighth (? beatitude) is the perfection of our hope, so also is it the sum of all virtues."[24] Paradise, which is the Church together with all her saints, is at the same time the inner life of these saints to-

gether with their virtues. Within every man there is a Church
and a synagogue—an Abel and a Cain, an Esau and a Jacob,
an Agar and a Sara—two warring peoples of whom one must
overcome the other. The two thieves crucified with Jesus,
types of the two peoples, are types also of the two spiritual
states. The tears shed in Babylon by the captive daughter of
Sion are at once those of the future Church and those of
every human soul, and the calls to repentance that the Lord
addresses to her are addressed equally to them. The oint-
ment poured out over the feet of Jesus at the meal in the
house of Simon the Pharisee is a symbol of every sincere
conversion: the continual conversion of every Christian, in
whom the pagan is never entirely dead, as well as the conversion of the Gentiles: *conversam gentilitatem designat
. . ., nos ergo, nos illa mulier expressit.*[25] As Christ, the
new Isaac, has come to dig again the wells of scripture
that had been filled up by the Philistines, so every day does
he dig again the well which is the soul of his faithful. The
long Paschal vigil recalls the crossing of the Red Sea by
the Hebrews and commemorates the risen Christ's definitive
transition from death to life: firstly there is signified the transition of the whole world to the "dignity of Israel," and then
also every convert's transition to divine life through baptism.
Christ's tomb, which is the universe, is also the heart of each
one of his faithful. The four rivers of Paradise, which are
the four Gospels, are also the four virtues of the soul; but
whether Gospels or virtues they all issue from the same
source, the wounded side of our Saviour. The wall of partition between the two peoples is also that which creates a
division in the life of every righteous man through the war
between the spirit and the flesh, and the peace which is
made between the powers of heaven and earth is the very
same that grace effects in his heart. When such symbols as
the tabernacle, the house, and the city have been applied
to the Church, they are likewise applied to the soul. For
the soul too is a Jerusalem which must praise the Lord,
"and, speaking generally, whatever in scripture fits the Church,
can also be applied to the soul." *Unumquemibet ex Ecclesia, tanquam Ecclesiam Christus alloquitur.*[26]

So it is that the widespread speculations of antiquity on
the subject of the microcosm and the macrocosm become,
by a double transposition, a doctrine both of social (historical) and of individual salvation. There is a correspondence

between the spiritual growth of the world and that of the individual soul, for both are caused by the same divine light. The soul is the microcosm of that great universe, the Church, and all the stages traversed by the Church in her long pilgrimage are to be found in the vicissitudes of the spiritual life. Just as there is a correspondence in the body of Christ between head and members, so is there between each of these members and the whole body. St Bonaventure mapped out his spiritual *Itinerarium* on the plan of the six biblical epochs. St Augustine, following St Paul, uses his profound psychological insight in a description of the four states, those four essential moments of consciousness which are at the same time the four successive states of humanity: *natura, lex, gratia, patria*, spiritual growth and temporal development, thus becoming symbols of one another. Mystical ontogenesis is only a reflexion of phylogenesis.

The exegesis of the Canticle of Canticles is a good example of this use of two registers. Fundamentally, the Bride of the Canticles is the Church. In the beginning she wanders abroad, seeking the beloved foretold by the prophets; at last she finds him and receives many gifts from him; and then her beauty is perfect, "without wrinkle or blemish." The two Testaments are her two fruitful breasts at which her children draw a nourishment which surpasses wine. But the Church is here the prototype of the soul. The first two commentators on the Canticle, Hippolytus and Origen, tell us of this. Hippolytus sees the Bride as the Church in so far as she is the successor to the synagogue, but he sees her also as the soul dwelling in this Church as in a garden. Origen establishes a constant parallelism between the soul and the Church. Although he applies the text sometimes to one and sometimes to the other in no apparent order, his thought is quite clear: what he says about the soul is attributed to it as a member of the Church. He is fond, also, of comparing souls to the band of maidens who follow the Bride; and so he can speak of them in the plural, at the same time emphasizing their dependent state. Or, again, in that one Beloved, pure and without blemish, he sees simultaneously the whole company of holy souls "who make up the body of the Church." With a precision of language which he is obviously at pains to maintain, he shows that while the Church is united to Christ the soul cleaves to the Logos; that is, the law of the Incarnation, which is both individual and social, governs the whole spiritual life. It is only through the flesh of the Logos that the soul feeds on his divinity. The soul is taught by the Logos and becomes his bride only in the house that he himself has built; for the Master within is revealed to those only who receive Christ's word transmitted by the Church's preaching. On the subject of that verse in which the Bridegroom looks through the lattices of the windows, Origen again explains to us that Christ, before the fullness of time, looked on his Church across the Law and the Prophets; now the Bridegroom and the Bride see each other clearly in the full light of the Gospel, the transition from the letter to the spirit is accomplished, the Bride rejoins her Bridegroom; although the Logos will keep himself until the end of time half hidden behind the lattice-work of creatures; for however perfect a soul may become, she cannot contemplate the invisible in the present life save through figures and enigmas.

We have emphasized Origen because he is of capital importance not only on this head but on many others like it. As an interpreter of scripture this great leader of souls, who was also a great churchman, is by no means the innovator suggested by the writings of Porphyry and Photius or the unfair attacks of his enemies, or even by some of his own declarations, as in those chapters of the *Contra Celsum* where he uses an *argumentum ad hominem* in a comparison of Christian exegesis with the methods used in the writings of the pagans. He is the great master. His influence went far beyond what is generally known as the Alexandrian school. In particular the twofold interpretation of the Canticle employed by Hippolytus as well as by himself is to be found in varying degrees in most of their many successors, both Latin and Greek. Even in the twelfth century, the golden age of commentaries on the Canticle, the same line is taken by St Bernard, Gilbert of Hoyland, William of St Thierry, Honorius of Autun and Richard of St Victor. It is used again by St Thomas Aquinas in the thirteenth century.

It is true, of course, that it is not always clearly brought out what is the connexion between the social meaning and the spiritual meaning, the collective and the individual, the allegorical and the moral, the *sacramentum* and the *exemplum*. Nor is the natural order always followed. All our commentators are not like St Gregory the Great, who says: *Hoc quod generaliter de cuncta Ecclesia diximus*, nunc *specialiter de unaquaque anima sentiamus.*[27] Nor are all so careful as he is in his commentary on Job "to distinguish the allegorical meaning in the first place from what is historical," so as to "give the allegorical meaning its proper moral application." The two lines of interpretation are rarely to be found so harmoniously interwoven as they are in Origen, where they tend to merge and culminate in the simple consideration of the perfect soul. As the normal differences between "theologians" and "spirituals" evolve in the course of the centuries it often happens that in their meditations on scripture the latter do not mention the Church's rôle as the link between the "letter" of scripture and its "spirit." They may even forget about it altogether. From this standpoint it would be interesting to compare St Gregory with another great mystical doctor, St John of the Cross, who also draws inspiration from the Canticle. Or, earlier still, St Cyril of Alexandria and St Nilus—or those two very different works, both of them largely indebted to Origen, by St Gregory of Nyssa and Theodoret. Whereas in Theodoret the collective meaning predominates throughout, the emphasis in Gregory is on the individual soul. Yet Theodoret does not neglect an immediate spiritual application, nor does Gregory fail to keep in mind the basis which he always presupposes: at the end of his admirable homilies the Bride is revealed in the fullness of her mystery—"the only one, the dove, the perfect, the chosen one," appears as the very unity of all Christ's members, the *Corpus Christi* spoken of by St Paul. Moreover, why need one go back each time to those fundamental truths which teach all the faithful to find throughout the Bible what St Ambrose called the *processus animae*? Yet these must not be despised if we would avoid peculiar interpretations or the unfruitful products of pious imaginings. In the interpretation of the Old Testament the aspect of historical fulfilment and that of the social community, two aspects that practically coincide, are of prime importance. They govern, explicitly or implicitly, all that concerns the hope of heavenly things, all the realities of the spiritual life. The law of "spiritual intelligence" is the very law of all spirituality, which is never authentic and trustworthy save only as it is not an individualist way, but a spiritualization of the liturgy—an application, that is, to the life of the soul of the Church's life-rhythm. For one and the same essential mystery permeates the whole of scripture and liturgy, apart from which there is no participation in the mystery of God. Here again must we say with St Epiphanius: "At the beginning of all things is the holy Catholic Church." [28]

NOTES TO CHAPTER VI

[1] Augustine, *In Psalmum* 68, s. 2, n. 6 (P.L. xxxvi, 858).

[2] 3*a*, q. 70, a. 1.

[3] *Hebr.* x. 1; cf. viii. 5; *Rom.* v. 14; *Coloss.* ii. 17.

[4] *Coloss.* i. 15; *II Cor.* iv. 4; *Hebr.* i. 3.

[5] Richard of St Victor, *Quomodo Christus ponitur in signum populorum* (P.L. cxcvi. 525).

[6] *Hebr.* i. 2; *Micheas* v. 1; *Apoc.* xxii. 13.

[7] Karl Barth, *Parole de Dieu et Parole humaine*, French trans., p. 100.

[8] Augustine, *Q. in Heptat.*, lib. 2, q. 73 (P.L. xxxiv, 623).

[9] *In Jesu Nave*, hom. 9, n. 8 (Baehrens, p. 353).

[10] Pseudo-Augustine, s. 90, n. 4 (P.L. xxxix, 1919).

[11] Paul Claudel, *L'épée et le miroir*, p. 74.

[12] Origen, *In Joannem*, t. i, n. 8 (Pr., p. 11).

[13] Origen, *In Exod.*, h. 7, n. 1 (Baehrens, pp. 204–6).

[14] Paulinus of Nola, *Epist.* 5, n. 2 (P.L. lxi, 168).

[15] Irenaeus, *Adversus Haereses*, 4, 20, 12 (P.G. vii, 1042).

[16] See Extract 33, p. 252.

[17] Rupert, *In Gen.*, lib. 6, c. 43 (P.L. clxvii, 441–2).

[18] Augustine, *In Psalm.* 30, enarr. 2, n. 4: "In Christo loquitur Ecclesia et in Ecclesia loquitur Christus; et corpus in capite, et caput in corpore." (P.L. xxxvi, 231–2). See Extract 34, p. 254.

[19] Augustine, *In Psalm.* 140, n. 3 (P.L. xxxvii, 1817).

[20] Jerome, *Epist.* 21.

[21] I realize that these verses in *Matthew* xxi (28–32) provide a problem in textual criticism: which of the two sons was mentioned first by the primitive text? I shall not take sides in a question about which the experts are still disagreed, but it can be pointed out that the solution that seems to emerge from an examination of the manuscript tradition is the same as that furnished by the ancient commentaries.

[22] Origen, *In Luc.*, hom. 34 (Rauer, pp. 200–2) and *In Cant.*, prolog. (Baehrens, p. 70). See Extract 35, p. 255.

[23] Peter Damian, *Opusculum* 32, n. 2 (P.L. cxlv, 546 D).

[24] Ambrose, *In Lucam*, lib. 5, c. 49 (P.L. xv, 1649 C).

[25] Origen, *In Gen.*, hom. 10, n. 5 (Baehrens, 99–100).

[26] Augustine, *Sermon* 46, n. 37 (P.L. xxxviii, 292).

[27] *In Cant.*, c. i, n. 3 (P.L. lxxix, 479).

[28] *Panarion*, lib. 1, t. 1, c. 5 (P.G. xli, 181). Had it been possible to lengthen an already overlong chapter I should have liked to show how, according to tradition, in addition to the Church and the soul, which are everywhere present in the Scripture, and more especially in the Canticle, there is a third "person," Mary,

who is the bond of their unity. Consult at least the beautiful excerpt from Isaac de Stella (Extract 37, p. 259). Cf. Guerric, *In Assumptione,* sermo 3, n. 3: "Si quis tamen curiose inquirere velit, cujus potissimum vox illa sit, 'in omnibus requiem quaesivi,' vox est utique Sapientiae, vox est Ecclesiae, vox est Mariae, vox est cujuslibet sapientis animae." There is a systematic treatment in Denis the Carthusian, *Enarratio in Cant. cantic.* (Opera omnia, t. 7, pp. 293–447). See also A.-M. Henry, O.P.: *Ève, l'Église et Marie,* Cahiers de la Vie Spirituelle, *La Sainte Vierge figure de l'Église,* 1946, pp. 96–136.

VII

SALVATION THROUGH THE CHURCH

Thus we always come back to the Church without ever being able to consider her mystic reality apart from her visible existence in time. She is both at the beginning and at the end, and all that lies between is full of her foreshadowings and her expansion. Seen by the eye of faith the whole religious history of mankind stands out illuminated, its several parts fall naturally into place, and what many were tempted to consider the irremediable conflict between belief in a world-wide call to salvation and belief in the Church as necessary for this same salvation is seen to be resolved.

The problem of the "salvation of unbelievers" has confronted the Christian conscience in tragic guise as a consequence of successive discoveries in geography, history and pre-history which, while they immeasurably increase the sum of human achievement, seem to diminish in proportion the achievement of Christ. But gradually this problem has been solved by most theologians in the only true Catholic sense. "Not one single drop of grace falls on the pagans," exclaimed Saint-Cyran with a sort of holy enthusiasm. Such a narrow solution has been rejected and condemned, like that of certain Jansenists who, with their idea of a God like to the meanest of men, feared that the "grace of God would be degraded if it were used lavishly." [1] So too has been rejected, as quite inadequate, the solution that has recourse to miracles, for it is of the nature of a miracle that it should be of rare occurrence. How can it be believed that God, contrary to the designs of his providence, will multiply private revelations? So, lastly, has been rejected the expedient of a natural salvation by which the greater part of humanity, though all of it is made in the image of God, should be cast into the twilight of Limbo. This thesis, which was taught in the seventeenth century by Trithemius and Archbishop Claude Seyssel, was taken up again by many apologists in the eighteenth and nineteenth centuries to meet the objections of Jean-Jacques Rousseau; but it was too much opposed to be best-established tradition to have any chance of prevailing.[2] Without closing our eyes to the miserable state of many who are "in the shadow of death," we consider, nevertheless, with St Irenaeus, that the Son, from the very beginning and in every part of the world, gives a more or less obscure revelation of the Father to every creature, and that he can be the "Salvation of those who are born outside the Way." We believe, with St Cyprian, St Hilary and St Ambrose, that the divine Sun of Justice shines on all and for all. We teach, with St John Chrysostom, that grace is diffused everywhere and that there is no soul that cannot feel its attraction. With Origen, St Jerome and St Cyril of Alexandria we refuse to assert that any man is born without Christ. And, lastly, we willingly allow, with St Augustine, the strictest of the Fathers, that divine mercy was always at work among all peoples, and that even the pagans have had their "hidden saints" and their prophets. In spite of differing explanations of detail and with degrees of optimism or pessimism according to the variations of individual temperament, experience or theological tendencies, it is generally agreed nowadays, following the lead of the Fathers and the principles of St Thomas, that the grace of Christ is of universal application, and that no soul of good will lacks the concrete means of salvation, in the fullest sense of the word. There is no man, no "unbeliever," whose supernatural conversion to God is not possible from the dawn of reason onwards.[3]

But this solution gives rise at once to another problem, and it is important to understand its terms. Christ, in fact, did not confine himself to the accomplishment of the redemptive sacrifice and, in addition, to the proclamation of the good news for the anticipated consolation of a small number. He preached a law, he founded a society. He commanded his Apostles to propagate both. He declared that faith in his person and membership of his Church were necessary to salvation. Now if every man can be saved, in principle at least and at whatever hazard, what reason is there for this Church? Is it merely for the purpose of obtaining a better, more certain salvation for a small number of privileged souls?

Or if it be supposed that her presence in the world is necessary in order that grace, which reposes by right in her alone, should be poured out all around her and attain in mysterious fashion the souls even of those who know her not, how can we account for the demand that has been reiterated for the past two thousand years calling for her expansion as the most urgent of all tasks? In any case, how can it still be claimed that the Church is a vital necessity?

On the practical side also the problem is no less acute. Since salvation is made accessible to those who are called (no longer with good reason) "unbelievers," is not the necessity for their belonging to the visible Church diminished to such an extent that it vanishes altogether? By what right henceforward is any obligation of entering the Church imposed upon them? It is not sufficient answer to say: the obligation devolves only on one who encounters the Church. For it might well be asked on what this positive command is founded. And here again it is not enough to reply that between the "unbeliever" and the Catholic the difference as regards the conditions of salvation is considerable. For if this difference, which no one calls in doubt, is only a matter of "more" or "less," how is it to be understood that, though strictly speaking the "less" suffices, yet the "more" should be required? Of course it is always unwise not to choose the most favourable conditions and it is foolish to neglect the means to a fuller life; but it can never be a crime. In a well-known work Fr Faber remarked (not without some exaggeration) that if we were not blinded by the light all around us the so-called darkness of paganism would seem to us a real light illuminating every man coming into the world. In any case we cannot but admire the attempts of so many missionaries to show us, by dint of human and divine sympathy, the elements of real religion which ennoble the cults even of the most inferior peoples. But if these elements, though mingled with others, are found on all sides, if the darkness, in certain cases at least, is so full of light, where is the obligation to seek the additional light that the Church bestows on her children? If an implicit Christianity is sufficient for the salvation of one who knows no other, why should we go in quest of an explicit one? In short, if every man can be saved through a religion that he unwittingly possesses, how can we require him to acknowledge this religion explicitly by professing Christianity and submitting to the Catholic Church?

Of course, the Church militant has no need to be furnished with a systematic answer to all the questions she raises before she can function to capacity. It is enough to know that "she is by divine intention and Christ's institution the only normal way of salvation." [4] And that should be enough for our faith, just as belief in the *Tu es Petrus* suffices for submission to Christ's vicar without looking any further. But as Fr Charles remarks in this connexion, "a command, even a divine command, is never the final justification of anything . . . the final justification of the precept is not the precept itself but harmony." [5] And does not the work of theology consist to a great extent in humble search after this harmony? So there is nothing to forbid our trying to explain the assertion of faith on which the missionary activity of the Church is based, and it may be useful at the same time to show how the complementary and the no less certain affirmation of the possibility of salvation for the "pagans" is in agreement with it. Is not this the only way to assure definitive theological recognition for the teaching in their regard which happily is winning acceptance in our time? For it is certainly important not to leave the smallest opening for that accusation formerly made by the Jansenists against the Jesuits (generally unjustly) of having brought the century to unbelief through their false maxims about the possibility of salvation for men of all religions. [6]

Surely we can find the required explanation, at least in embryo, in the traditional principles that the preceding chapters have tried to reproduce. The human race is one. By our fundamental nature and still more in virtue of our common destiny we are members of the same body. Now the life of the members comes from the life of the body. How, then, can there be salvation for the members if, *per impossibile*, the body itself were not saved? But salvation for this body, for humanity, consists in its receiving the form of Christ, and that is possible only through the Catholic Church. For is she not the only complete, authoritative interpreter of Christian revelation? Is it not through her that the practice of the evangelical virtues is spread throughout the world? And, lastly, is she not responsible for realizing the spiritual unity of men in so far as they will lend themselves to it? Thus this Church, which as the invisible Body of Christ is identified with final salvation, as a visible and historical institution is the providential means of this salvation. "In her alone mankind is re-fashioned and re-created." [7]

Outside Christianity humanity can doubtless be raised in an exceptional manner to certain spiritual heights, and it is our duty—one that is perhaps too often neglected—to explore these heights that we may give praise to the God of mercies for them: Christian pity for unbelievers, which is never the fruit of scorn, can sometimes be born of admiration. But the topmost summit is never reached, and there is risk of being the farther off from it by mistaking for it some other outlying peak. This is a fact noticed by many missionaries. It is often more difficult—though in the last resort more worthwhile—to bring to the fullness of truth souls whom a relatively more developed religion has stamped with its mark, though there is no necessity to accuse them on that account of pride and perversion. A critical judgement, not of individual souls—for their precise situation in relation to the Kingdom is never known save to God alone—but of objective systems as found in a society and as offering material for rational examination, shows that there is some essential factor missing from every religious "invention" that is not a following of Christ. There is something lacking, for example, in Buddhist charity: it is not Christian charity. Something is lacking in the spirituality of the great Hindu mystics: it is not the spirituality of St John of the Cross. And yet those are privileged cases. Outside Christianity all is not necessarily corrupt; far from it, and the facts do not support that supposed law of degeneration in which an explanation was sought for the whole religious development of mankind left, so it was thought, to its own devices. All is not corrupt, but what does not remain puerile is always in peril of going astray, or, however high it climbs, of ultimate collapse. Outside Christianity nothing attains its end, that only end, towards which, unknowingly, all human desires, all human endeavours, are in movement: the embrace of God in Christ. The most admirable, the most vigorous of these endeavours needs—absolutely—to be impregnated with Christianity if it is to bear its eternal fruit, and as long as Christianity is lacking, in spite of appearances to the contrary, they only increase that great void in humanity whence arises the cry to the one and only Plenitude, and only make more obvious that slavery from which it stretches out its arms towards its Liberator.

Outside Christianity, again, humanity tries to collect its members together into unity. Throughout the centuries a powerful instinct compels it through an apparent chaos of dispersal and conflict, collisions and strivings, social integration and disintegration, towards a "common life," an outward expression of that unity which is obscurely felt within. But humanity, as we see only too clearly, can never overcome all the opposing forces which are everywhere at work, forces which it contains within itself and is always producing or re-awakening. Cities expand yet are always closed societies, they combine together but only to fight more bitterly with one another, and beneath their outward unity there is always the personal enmity of the souls within them. But here is that divine house built upon the rock *in qua*, according to that marvellous formula of the Vatican Council,[8] *veluti in domo Dei viventis, fideles omnes unius fidei et caritatis vinculo continerentur.* Here is the marriage house in which heaven is joined to earth. Here is the household in which all are gathered together to eat of the Lamb; here is the place of true sacrifice. Only that Ideal which Christ gave to his Church is pure enough and strong enough— for it did not issue from the brain of man, but is living and is called the Spirit of Christ—to inspire men to work for their own spiritual unity, as only the sacrifice of his Blood can bring their labour to fruition. It is only through the leavening of the Gospel within the Catholic community and by the aid of the Holy Spirit that this "divine Humanity" can be established, *unica dilecta Dei*.

If God had willed to save us without our own co-operation, Christ's sacrifice by itself would have sufficed. But does not the very existence of our Saviour presuppose a lengthy period of collaboration on man's part? Moreover, salvation on such terms would not have been worthy of the persons that God willed us to be. God did not desire to save mankind as a wreck is salvaged; he meant to raise up within it a life, his own life. The law of redemption is here a reproduction of the law of creation: man's co-operation was always necessary if his exalted destiny was to be reached, and his co-operation is necessary now for his redemption. Christ did not come to take our place—or rather this aspect of substitution refers only to the first stage of his work—but to enable us to raise ourselves through him to God. He came not to win for us an external pardon—that fundamentally was ours from all eternity and is presupposed by the Incarnation itself; for redemption is a mystery of love and mercy—but to change us inwardly. Thenceforward humanity was to co-operate actively in its own salvation, and that is why to the act of his Sacrifice Christ joined the objective revelation of his Person and the foundation of his Church. To sum up, revelation and redemption are bound up together, and the Church is their only Tabernacle.

But if the Church—the historic, visible, hierarchic Church —is thus necessary to transform and complete human endeavour, she herself is by no means complete. She has not even begun her work in some parts of the world. It is a matter of urgency, then, that she should increase, and primarily that her extension should be conterminous with that of the human race. We do not know, of course, what the future has in store for us in this respect, though we may realize fully that our exercise of freedom is continually thwarting God's plans: that ignorance and that knowledge save us from so many illusions. But we cannot doubt that just as of old the mission of Providence in time was to prepare for the first coming of Christ, so now is it to extend the Church everywhere that the Kingdom of God may have more powerful sway in every soul.

As long as the Church has not covered the whole earth and bound all souls together, to increase is a very necessity of her nature. The history of her "missions" is the history of her own growth, is her own history. Her advance is often slow and sometimes it is checked by reverses, such as occurred in the seventh century in face of the overwhelming progress of Islam, or in the eighteenth when Christianity was overthrown in the Far East. The mistaken impression of having already attained to the ends of the inhabited world together with an anticipation of the early approach of the last day combined at times to weaken her effort. Did not St Gregory the Great himself, the organizer of the English mission, confess that he thought the Church was in her old age and that he had hardly anything left to hope for save the final conversion of Israel? According to him nothing more remained but to retire within oneself and, while rejoicing over victories won, to strengthen one's soul against the attacks of anti-Christ. . . . Yet the Church has ever acknowledged her responsibility for all the human race, that human race which the Middle Ages summarized in the threefold posterity of Noe spread out over three continents, but united in their trial and in praise of the Lord like the three children in the fiery furnace; from this humanity they would exclude neither the "Pygmies," the fabulous long-eared Scythians, nor the grotesque "dog-headed ones." From the very first she has always kept her objective before her. A Christian age which deliberately turned away from it would be worse than an age of heresy—is it not, indeed, one of the signs of the true Church of Christ, the indefectible guardian of the faith, that at no time in her history has she ever repudiated this aim?[9] It would amount to a denial of her very being, what Newman would have called her "Idea." Her Catholicity is both her strength and at the same time a continual demand upon her. She knows "that she was born for nothing else than the propagation everywhere of the Reign of Christ, so as to bring all men to take part in his saving redemption," and that therein lies not the isolated task of some few specialized workers but the "principal office" of her pastors.[10] She cannot forget the prophecies that have always guided her progress and nourished her hope. So long as the Church does not extend and penetrate to the whole of humanity, so as to give to it the form of Christ, she cannot rest.

The Church is a growing body, a building in course of construction. Both metaphors suggest that her completion is not the work of one day. Even supposing in man a complete correspondence with the plans of the divine Architect, the work is long and exacting, and the laying of the foundation stone, that "corner stone" which is no other than Christ, "the first born among many brethren," required, as we know, vast preparations beforehand.

Every created being, in fact, is subject in this world to the law of development. If salvation, which is God himself, is free from it, humanity in order to receive this salvation is not so free. Just as for intelligence to dawn in a corporeal organism and shine at last in human eyes it is first necessary that life should arise in the body and that it should discover ever-improving means of communication with the outside world, though its rôle is solely to prepare itself for receiving this intelligence which is of a higher order and which it receives like a grace—the comparison is enlightening, although its details must not be pressed—so did it need thousands of years of preparation for Christ's revelation to be *received* of men, and for the divine Likeness in all its splendour to shine in the eyes of his saints; and this is true not only of the Jewish revelation, that incomparable stream of light and of enigmas stretching from Abraham to Jesus, but also of all those other, obscurer, more external preparations which went before it or were contemporary with it among the pagans, and of the whole gradual raising up, social, intellectual and material, of fallen man.

Now this wonderful spectacle of divine "economies" cannot be represented as a straightforward development. Spiritual life, like all life, takes shape in a suitable organism only after much hesitation. Outbursts of sudden energy are followed by long barren periods, and not every promise of progress is followed by fulfilment. For every concentration of fruitful effort there is a whole heap of material which seems wasted. One success comes after hundreds of more or less abortive efforts and involves a certain number of miscarriages. And since nature had to produce an unbelievably extravagant profusion of living species so that in the end the human body could appear, we must not be astonished at the strange multiplicity of the forms of religion, before or outside Christianity, shown to us in history.

We must not be astonished, but we must draw the necessary inference and so find the key to our problem. For since a necessary function in the history of our salvation was fulfilled by so great a mass of "unbelievers"—not indeed in that they were in formal error or in a state of degradation, but in that there is to be found in their beliefs and consciences a certain groping after the truth, its painful preparation or its partial anticipation, discoveries of the natural reason and tentative solutions—so these unbelievers have an inevitable place in our humanity, a humanity such as the fall and the promise of a Redeemer have made it.

There is no comparison between their rôle and that of the scaffolding which, necessary as it is in the construction of a building, is discarded once the building is complete without further thought of what will become of it. For if the heavenly Jerusalem is built of living stones,[11] it is also living beings that go to make its scaffolding. In other words, humanity is made up of persons who have all the same one eternal destiny, in whatever category or century their birth has placed them; their relationships cannot be envisaged, then, as just external ones, as if some existed only to prepare suitable conditions for the development of others, as in Renan's paradox of the coming of a superman. In spite of great differences of understanding and of function, all members of the human race enjoy the same essential equality before God.

As "unbelievers" are, in the design of providence, indispensable for building the Body of Christ, they must in their own way profit from their vital connexion with this same Body. By an extension of the dogma of the communion of saints, it seems right to think that though they themselves are not in the normal way of salvation, they will be able nevertheless to obtain this salvation by virtue of those mysterious bonds which unite them to the faithful. In short, they can be saved because they are an integral part of that humanity which is to be saved.

People speak sometimes of a "supplying"; what we have just described seems in the last analysis the only possible "supplying," one that gives their value to all others for those who have not received the fullness of light. Although in certain cases the "less" seems to suffice—to return to the terms in which our original objection was formulated—the "more" exists and supplies what is lacking that this "less" can suffice, that the "insufficient can be sufficient." More precisely still, there is presupposed not only the restricted precarious presence of this "more" somewhere in the world, but its unrestricted growth and its definitive completion, though in a form that to us remains mysterious. In short there is presupposed both the existence of the Church and the success of her mission. When a missionary proclaims Christ to a people that does not yet know him, it is not only those men or their descendants that hear his preaching, who are concerned with the success of his mission. It is also, it can be said in more than one sense, their ancestors. Indirectly but really it is the whole nameless mass of those who, from the beginnings of our race, have done their best in that darkness or half light that was their lot. And so it is that God, desiring that all men should be saved, but not allowing in practice that all should be visibly in the Church, wills nevertheless that all those who answer his call should in the last resort be saved through his Church. *Sola Ecclesiae gratia, qua redimimur.*

We are now in a position to understand the full force of that rigorous and at the same time comforting axiom which,

from Origen and Cyprian right down to Pius XI's encyclical
Mortalium animos, has ever been the expression of orthodox
doctrine on the subject we are treating: outside the Church,
no salvation. Obviously it cannot mean that no one is ever
saved who does not belong exteriorly to the Church, and it
is significant that the texts in which it occurs, when they
are not addressed simply to schismatics, contain also the immediate qualifying statement which we should expect, ex-
cepting the case of invincible ignorance in pagans of good
will.[12] But the explanation for which a formula has been
found during the last few centuries in the distinction between the body and soul of the Church is neither sufficient
nor entirely exact; for the axiom refers, more often than
not, not to the soul but to the body of the Church, her social
visible body. Following Innocent III's example Pius IX is
still more explicit: he speaks of the Roman Church.[13] The
explanation taken from Suarez also appears to us incomplete:
according to this in order to be saved it is necessary to belong, at least in heart and by implicit desire, to the Catholic
communion, *voto saltem ac desiderio.* Whereas these explanations take on again their true force and can be used
without danger once it is recognized, by interpreting them
collectively, that, for humanity taken as a whole, there can
be no salvation outside the Church, that this is an absolute
necessity, and a necessary means to which there can be no
exception.

In this way the problem of the "salvation of unbelievers"
receives a solution on the widest scale and at the same time
no opening is left for compromising laxity. There is no encouragement to indifference. We see now how the Church
can, in the words of a theologian,[14] "be merciful to paganism without diminishing her proper character of being the
only vehicle of salvation for souls"; and if it is thought that
in spite of all these considerations the formula "outside the
Church, no salvation" has still an ugly sound, there is no
reason why it should not be put in a positive form and read,
appealing to all men of good will, not "outside the Church
you are damned," but "it is by the Church and by the Church
alone that you will be saved." For it is through the Church
that salvation will come, that it is already coming to mankind.

Of course the method of this salvation will differ according to whether the unbeliever has or has not encountered the

Church. In the second case the only condition on which his salvation is possible is that he should be already a Catholic as it were by anticipation, since the Church is the "natural place" to which a soul amenable to the suggestions of grace spontaneously tends. The "less" is then sufficient—to employ the expression for the last time—not in itself, of its own worth, but in so far as it aspires to the "more," in so far as it is ready to be lost in this "more" directly the exterior obstacles which hide the "more" from it are removed. Far different is the case of the unbeliever who comes in contact with the Church—as long as she is shown to him in her true likeness, he has a strict obligation actually to enter her fold. For if in truth, by the very logic of his correspondence with grace, he already aspires to her in secret, he would deceive himself if he shirked answering her summons. Those who do not know the Church are saved by her, therefore, in such a way that they incur the obligation of belonging to her even outwardly directly they come to know her.

Since the solution that has just been sketched is founded on principles laid down by the Fathers, it also allows us to harmonize their testimony to the Church as the sole means of salvation with their testimony quoted at the beginning of this chapter to the universal action of our Saviour. Indeed it is very noticeable that when the Fathers allow the pagan world something of the light of Christ they generally set this light in a prophetic relationship with the full light of the Gospel, and that they see the Church that is to come in the lives both of the holy people of the Gentile world as well as of the righteous under the Old Law. So, for St Irenaeus, it must be said without exception of all the saints who lived before the time of the Gospel that, in a sense, "they heralded Christ's coming and obeyed his Law." According to Clement of Alexandria: "Just as God sent prophets to the Jews, so did he raise up in the midst of Greece the most virtuous of her sons and set them as prophets amidst their nation." When St Augustine in connexion with Job the Idumean speaks of a vast "spiritual Jerusalem," he does not use this term in any sort of opposition to the visible Church, as the soul of the Church might be opposed to its body, but only to the material city of which it was a figure. And when St Leo lays down that from "most ancient times the mystery of man's salvation has known no interruption," he thereby emphasizes very strongly that unity which binds together the innumerable means of salvation and wonders at their providential variety. The visible tangible link between the Old and New Testaments admits of no doubt, historical continuity being presupposed by the very transformation: so that of all the Gentiles that are saved it will be said, as of the Jews themselves, that they were "in the Old Testament," that they were "saints of the Old Testament." It matters little whether scripture mentions them or not: we know that many are not mentioned there. Moreover, certain pages are eloquent for those who can read them aright: for example, does not scripture give a part to Gentile as to Jew in the genealogy of Christ? The emphasis laid on this detail shows that the Fathers saw in it the sign of a more fundamental collaboration between the two peoples. Indeed, did not Jews and Gentiles down through the six ages of the world replenish with the same water, that water one day to be changed by Christ into wine, the waterpots of humanity? Jews and Gentiles were all related to the same Christ, waited for him and—especially in their sufferings, those sufferings which never spare the righteous—prefigured him. Thus all prepared for the universal Church; and she does not hesitate now to recognize them as her members.

We can therefore conclude: as Jews or Gentiles, although they lived before the visible coming of Christ, must be described as saved by Christ and not merely by the Word, so, though they lived before the appearance of the visible Church among them, they are saved not by belonging in a purely spiritual, intemporal manner to the soul of the Church, but by means of a very real though indirect and more often hidden bond with her body.

It becomes increasingly clear that in such a doctrinal context the Christian's watchword can no longer be "escape" but "collaboration." He must co-operate with God and men in God's work in the world and among humanity. There is but one end: and it is on condition that he aims at it together with all men that he will be allowed a share of the final triumph, that he will find a place in the common salvation: *in redemptione communi*. The city of the elect does not welcome "profiteers."

Hence arises the Christian's responsibility with regard to his "unbelieving" brethren. All grace is *gratia gratis data*, that is, in the old meaning of the expression, given for the

sake of others. The grace of Catholicism was not given to us
for ourselves alone, but for those who do not possess it, just
as the grace of the contemplative life, as St Teresa understood so well, is bestowed on chosen souls for the benefit of
those who undertake the labours of the active life. Fidelity to
that grace by which we are members of the Church makes
two demands upon us: we must co-operate in the collective
salvation of the world by taking part, each in accordance
with his own vocation, in the construction of that great
building of which we must be at once the workmen and the
stones; at the same time we must co-operate, by the impact
of our whole Christian life, in the individual salvation of
those who remain apparently "unbelievers." Two duties these
that are inter-related: two ways, if we can so speak, of bringing redemption to maturity.

In the first place, we must work, as far as we can, for the
increase of the Church. "The Church," writes Fr Charles,

> is to-day like a child: no organ is missing, but she has still
> to grow four or five times her present size. This law
> of growth, inherent in a child's body, hidden but working
> in the grain of mustard seed, is also a compelling neces-
> sity in the body of the Church, and the Sovereign Pontiffs
> who recall this to us with such insistence are but lending
> their voice to the silent clamour of the Church which
> *must* increase. And when a living organism begins to grow,
> it grows all over. Its growth is not confined to one organ,
> it is not the monopoly of one limb . . . all must work
> together in harmony, observing the same measured rhythm.

It can be truthfully said that missionary work is the duty
of all, normally no doubt the least determined of all duties,
but the strictest and the most universal; "we are not to look
for our mandate" to work at this capital extension of the
Kingdom of God "in the tables of the Law; it is in our
baptized souls that we find this demand laid upon us." [15]

In the next place we must strive to earn merit by intensive
use of the use of the Church's spiritual treasury on behalf
of those, less fortunate, who are far from this treasure, for
those who have died or will die without having the Good
News preached to them. Meditation on this inspiring but
formidable duty tempts one to ask whether it is quite certain
that within the Church, according to an expression that is

all too common, salvation is more easily found. That does not mean that we would belittle the value of the means of grace normally at the disposal of every one of the faithful. But would not this truth be the pretext for a great abuse if it were made an excuse for indolence, as if the fact of being *in Ecclesia* entailed automatically being *de Ecclesia?* A natural tendency exposes the believer to this dangerous feeling of security, and it is one that has sometimes led explicitly to formal error. St Augustine and St Caesarius of Arles had to fight hard against it. In any case, he on whom more is bestowed incurs the greater risk: the more numerous the talents, the greater the fear of leaving them unproductive; *quibus plus dedit, plus ab eis exacturus.* The rest of the world is bound up with us, and it cannot be saved without us. This being so, are not our personal responsibilities tremendously increased? *Paucis humanum vivit genus;* the old axiom is profoundly true. It is the law of nature, and the Christian does not repudiate it. But he completes it, reversing the medal, by the law of grace. For it is not for these chosen few, for whose coming the hidden labour of the whole mass was in travail, to enjoy, proud and isolated, their precarious superiority. They do not belong to themselves but owe service to all men. "Let him who is the greatest among you be as he who serves": Christ's great lesson is aimed not only at those who hold some authority; it is a commandment envisaging all who enjoy greatness of any kind. Those who, by receiving Christ, have received all, have been raised up for the salvation of those who could not know him. Their privilege constitutes a mission. There is no other way for them to keep their riches, for in the spiritual order "only that is possessed which is given away," and so they will keep them only if they give them away; no one will be more empty handed at the last day than the waster who believed himself to be well provided. *Vide hunc vacuum, qui sibi abundare omnibus videbatur!*

Judgement will be given to the privileged, according to what their privileges have yielded for the common good in favour of those who had been excluded. The adjustment to a single level, mistakenly required by the Syncretist systems for the unification of doctrines, will be effected at the last Judgement in the judicial weighing-up of responsibility.[16]

"It is for us to avail ourselves of the remedy that Jesus Christ provided," Bossuet wrote one day to Sister Cornuau,

and not to torment ourselves about those who, for some reason or other, do not make use of it; just as a patient in a large hospital would be mad if he saw the doctor approaching with an infallible remedy, and tortured himself by wondering what was going to become of the other patients instead of accepting it himself.

That was perhaps sensible counsel to put an end to an anguished soul's distress, to calm "the intensity of a mind which was losing itself in its own thoughts." [17] Monsieur Albert Bayet, who quotes this letter, was a little hasty in his indignation about it. But if these words were taken in a doctrinal sense, as giving a theoretical definition of our attitude to the problem of salvation, they would be anti-Christian. No one has the right to say with Cain: "Am I my brother's keeper?" No one is a Christian for himself alone.

Muros Ecclesiae nostrae aedificare debemus.[18] There were great saints in the Middle Ages who understood it very well; at a time when Christianity had periodically to draw itself together, as it were to retire within itself, against the assault of Islam, they helped to keep alive the pure ideal of Catholicity: Mechtilde of Magdeburg, who would take on herself the fears and the hopes, the sorrows and the joys of the whole of humanity, who composed a "universal prayer for salvation;" a little later Angela of Foligno saying in prayer over and over again, "May your Love embrace all nations"; or, at the time of the Great Schism, Catherine of Siena declaring that her only concern was the salvation of the world, and after having worked without respite for the peace and union of Christians, offering her life "for the Mystical Body of holy Church." So did they carry out Christ's last wish. So did they unite themselves with the prayer of those priests and monks who in the office of matins, the symbol of the sixth age of the world, thought of the innumerable peoples who in this last age would be gathered together from all the countries of the world before the Church should enter at last into peace. So did they make their own those words of Methodius of Olympus: "The Church is in the pains of childbirth until all peoples shall have entered into her." [19]

NOTES TO CHAPTER VII

¹ Frémont's censure of Fénelon. On Dec. 7, 1690, Alexander VIII condemned the following proposition: "Pagani, Judaei, haeretici aliique hujus generis, nullum omnino influxum a Jesu Christo accipiunt."

² Cardinal Billot's revived form of it did not meet with much support.

³ Fr Hugueny, *Le scandale édifiant d'une exposition missionnaire* (1933), p. 56.—The author adds: "There is a great difference between the possibility of its happening and the frequency with which, in fact, it occurs," which is incontestable; and also, on p. 60: "In general (unbelievers) do not make use of the restricted enlightenment" that is granted to them. For my part, I prefer to say that we know nothing at all about it. In any case, the solution that I have just referred to is in no way prejudicial to the solution of the entirely different question about the number of the elect. We are concerned here, as in all that follows, with the possibility of salvation, and not with its actual realization; with the divine summons and not with the human answer to it.

⁴ *Bulletin des Missions*, mars-juin 1934, p. 60.

⁵ *Christi Vicarius*, in *Nouvelle Revue théologique*, 1929, p. 454.

⁶ *Nouvelles ecclésiastiques*, 17 février, 1768.

⁷ Augustine, *Epist*. 118, n. 33: "Totum culmen auctoritatis lumenque rationis in illo uno salutari nomine atque in una ejus Ecclesia, recreando atque reformando humano generi constitutum est." (P.L. xxxiii, 448).

⁸ *Constitutio dogmatica de Ecclesia Christi*, init.

⁹ It is acknowledged that in their beginnings the Protestant churches had not this missionary consciousness. On this both Catholic and Protestant historians are agreed. "I cannot forgive the English and the Dutch their neglect," wrote Leibniz, Oct. 1, 1697. Cf. Fénelon, *Sermon for the Epiphany* (1685), first point: "This fruitfulness of our mother in all parts of the world, this apostolic zeal which shines in our pastors alone, which those of the new sects have not even tried to imitate, is an embarrassment to the most famous of the defenders of schism. I have read it in their latest books. They are unable to hide it. I have known the most sensible and upright people in this party confess that this radiance, in spite of all the subtleties employed to obscure it, strikes their very heart and attracts them to us."

It may be remembered, also, that the missionary zeal of the Roman Church compared with the feebler expansive vitality of the Orthodox communions was one of the reasons that influenced the Anglican William Palmer, Newman's friend, towards Catholicism. "Primarily he saw it only as a very estimable exterior mark, the Eastern Church possessing, as he then thought, the mark of doctrinal orthodoxy; but gradually from the outward Catholicity of the Roman Church he deduced her inward Catholicity, and perceived in her the very fullness of the Church" (P. Baron, *Al.-St. Khomiakov, son ecclésiologie,* stencilled thesis, p. 215). Cf. W. Palmer, *Dissertations* . . . (1853), d. 2: "Of the present apparent conflict between 'Orthodoxy' and 'Catholicism'" (pp. 9–31). In his correspondence with Palmer, Khomiakov was unable to hide his difficulties on this point (Baron, *op. cit.,* pp. 212–5; C. Tyzskiewicz, *La Mission de William Palmer, in Études,* vol. 136, pp. 190–4).

[10] Pius XI, *Rerum Ecclesiae, A.A.S.,* 1926, p. 65.

[11] *I Peter* ii. 5: Λίθοι ζῶντες.

[12] Vatican Council, *Constitutio de fide catholica,* c. 3.

[13] Alloc. consist. *Singulari quadam,* Dec. 9, 1854. Profession of faith for the Vaudois, Dec. 18, 1208. Cf. Encyclical *Quanto conficiamur,* Aug. 10, 1853. Maximus of Turin spoke in the same way of "The Church of Peter," *Sermon* 114, (P.L. lvii, 722).

The expression itself, "the soul of the Church," after being very popular for a certain time, is generally criticized at the present day. The preparatory dogmatic commission at the Vatican Council rejected it "utpote scolasticam et novam omnino in modo loquendi conciliorum" (Mansi, vol. 49, pp. 624–5).

[14] Stiefelhagen, quoted in Capéran, *Essai historique,* 2nd edn., p. 475.

[15] P. Charles, *La Prière apostolique,* in *Xaveriana,* Dec. 1928. M. Ledrus in *Nouvelle Revue théologique,* 1929, p. 485.

[16] L. Massignon, *Les trois prières d'Abraham,* ii (1935), p. 47.

[17] Bossuet, July 3, 1695 (*Correspondance,* t. 7, p. 155).

[18] Durandus of Mende, *Rationale,* lib. I, c. i, n. 8 (p. 5).

[19] *Banquet,* orat. 8, c. 5.

VIII

PREDESTINATION OF THE CHURCH

These pains have gone on for the last two thousand years, and their end cannot yet be seen. But our faith is unmoved, for we remember how much longer was the time required to prepare for the birth of the Church herself. And our faith can draw the proper inferences from that social, historical view of the world that Christianity gives us.

It was this that minds faithful to the old pagan ways of thought could not do. They were scandalized by Christianity's novelty in time because they had not assimilated Christian teaching about time. So we see these defenders of the old religions always coming back to the same supposedly unanswerable objection. If Christ is the only Saviour, as his faithful people claim, why did he come so recently, leaving up till then so many men to be lost? "In the previous centuries where was the solicitude of so great a Providence?" If the Christian religion is the only perfect one, God must be very evil, very weak, or else very lacking in foresight to have remedied so late the imperfection of his first work. That was how Celsus argued, and Porphyry and afterwards, doubtless, Symmachus. So, too, many others down the centuries and even in our own day, all of them more or less conscious heirs of that principle, called by Monsieur J. Bidez "platonic immobilism," which Julian the Apostate in his treatise against "the Galileans" expressed thus:

> God is eternal, so it is fitting that his commands should be eternal too. Now these commands are the very nature of things or are in conformity with the nature of things: and how could nature offer resistance to the commands of God? [1]

In their answer to such an objection Christians were not obliged to say merely that God's plans are impenetrable. They had only to draw their inspiration from St Paul, for he had by implication provided an answer in advance when he laid down the principle of the "dispensation of the grace of God" [2] and recalled the stages of the natural law and the law of Moses, both of them necessary preliminaries for the coming of the fullness of time. On these Pauline themes Irenaeus had developed his wide optimistic views, teaching that Christ came in reality for all men, of every country and of all times, since he came, after a long preparation, to lead humanity to its final end.

If anyone says to you: "Could not God have caused the perfect man to appear at the very beginning?" let him know that God is certainly almighty, but that the creature, by the very fact of its creation, can only be imperfect. God will bring it gradually to perfection, like a mother who at first gives suck to her new-born child, and then as he grows bigger gives him the food that he needs. God acted in this way, and so did the incarnate Word. . . . By this gradual education created man is formed little by little to the image and likeness of the uncreated God. The Father is well pleased in this and ordains it, the Son effects and creates, the Holy Spirit nourishes and causes its growth, and gently man makes progress and is raised to perfection. He alone who is not created is perfect at once, and he is God. So it was necessary for man to be created, and then for him to grow, to attain maturity, to multiply, become strong, and then to arrive at glory and see his Master. . . . Therefore, they are entirely unreasonable who, without waiting for the period of development, attribute to God the infirmity of their own nature. They know neither God nor themselves. Insatiable and ungrateful, they do not wish to be for a start what they are by the fact of their creation: men, subject to passions; but, exceeding the law of their nature, before becoming men they would be already like to God, their Creator. . . . More insensate than the animals, they upbraid God for not having made them Gods from the outset. [3]

No doubt in this passage, as in many another, Irenaeus's

treatment of the subject is inspired by the need to refute Marcion. In Adam's creation Marcion saw only the work of a lower demiurge; in the history of God's people only the action of this demiurge, revengeful and cruel in his justice; in the Incarnation finally only the unforeseen appearance of the good God in an unwonted sphere. In opposition to Marcion it had to be established that it was one and the same God who had created man in the beginning, had then watched over his gradual development and lastly had appeared to him in the reality of the flesh to guide him to his fulfilment, the divine Likeness. But this answer to Marcionism goes beyond the controversy that provoked it. It is not merely the profound unity of the two Testaments that is brought to light, it is the whole divine plan of the world, a work not only of infinite patience but also of mighty and infallible wisdom. For Irenaeus had no thought of diminishing God's almighty power by his insistence on the necessity of humble beginnings; he taught that everything was possible with God, but that, through the intrinsic infirmity of the creature, a limit was set to the reception of God's gifts; an initial gift is necessary to make him capable of receiving a second and a third . . . Christianity, a perfect religion, could come therefore only when it was time.

Thus it was that the defence of the Old Testament against Gnosticism was a preparation for the defence of the New against pagan thought. Irenaeus's teaching was worked out in opposition to those who rejected the Mosaic revelation as unworthy, but it was a good deal more than just an apologetic expedient. Consequently it did not fall into oblivion when the danger that evoked it was averted. Tertullian, who made use of it in his turn against the same danger, actually contrived an argument out of it when he turned Montanist, against the tradition of the Church, in favour of the "new prophecy"; but this abuse was not enough to discredit it. Afterwards, even those who would not go all the way with Irenaeus in his "supernatural evolutionism" often adopted the essentials of his point of view. Thus Origen, in the first place, who taught that man was unable to receive straightway "the precepts of liberty"; thus Gregory of Nyssa, speaking of those χρονικὰ διαστήματα that even divine Power must respect to establish man in good; thus too Basil, marvelling at "that great mystery of our salvation" and declaring that those who repudiate it "betray mental immaturity."

In religion, as in human learning, we need a gradual introduction, beginning by the more easily learned matters and the first elements. The Creator comes to our aid so that our eyes, accustomed to darkness, may be gradually opened to the full light of truth. He has arranged all things in view of our weakness; he trains us first to perceive the shadow of objects and the sun's reflexion in the water so that we are not blinded by direct contact with its rays: the Mosaic law was the shadow of things to come, and the teaching of the prophets was the truth in a form which was still obscure.[4]

In the same way, and in terms that are very near Irenaeus's, Theodoret answers those who "with vain curiosity and as if they could measure with their reason the abyss of divine mysteries" dare to ask why the Christian dispensation was not given to the world from the beginning. He says that Adam received a precept fitted to his age—the age of humanity that began with him—because God bestows on each period what is suitable for it, measuring out his teaching in proportion as man can bear it. Then Theodoret, with the complacency of an apologist, gives a detailed exposition of those providential stratagems which from the time of Abraham made the chosen people God's intermediary and collaborator in his work of teaching the Gentiles. And so was prepared the fullness of time when the Gospel could at last be proclaimed. It is therefore true, Theodoret concludes, that the God of the universe has never ceased, in his gradual preparation of this final revelation, to make provision for the salvation of all. Ambrose too, in his answer to Symmachus, takes his expressions from Tertullian, and makes a comparison between Christian fertility and the harvest which cannot ripen before its hour:

Those who complain (that faith was not bestowed earlier) might as well blame the harvest because it ripens late; or the grape-gathering because it takes place at the fall of the year, or the olive because it is the last fruit to ripen.[5]

Truth must mature: so Felix Minutius had said; Augustine's idea is little different when he writes: *in Adventu Domini matura messis inventa est*; or in his commentary on the Apostle's teaching about the "elements of the world." If he often compares the members of his two cities to two men, the old and the new Adam, beneath the actual dualism he can discern the unity of the divine call: like a vast tapestry he unrolls before our eyes the history of the human race advancing towards its salvation in the form of the history of a single man, and against Porphyry's objections he holds up to our admiration this man's progressive education by an all-wise Providence which raises him up step by step "from time to eternity and from the visible to the invisible." [6]

It is especially among the Jews that this gradual education of man takes place, as Basil has just reminded us. Not that the law of Moses was held superior from all points of view to the "natural law" which went before it. Quite the contrary: in one section of its prescriptions, the *servitutis praecepta*, it showed, rather, a deterioration. But the idolatry into which man had fallen made it necessary, as a sort of mentor, first to raise him up, then to protect him and guide him, and finally to lead him to the threshold of evangelical perfection. It was because the wine of the natural law had run out as a consequence of the guests' extravagance that they were reduced to the water of the written law. In itself it may be held to be inferior to the natural law, but its chief value was, as we have seen, figurative or prophetic: it was one day to be changed into the wine of the law of grace, a wine of higher quality than that of the natural law. Meanwhile we are not to be astonished that the "blessed Patriarchs, scarcely delivered from the habits of idolatry and the error of polytheism," should on many points give evidence of "quite imperfect ideas." Their immediate descendants "who had grown up among the Egyptians" had also maintained their "barbarous ways." Moses—that is, God who dictated his law to him—was obliged to adapt himself to this situation. How could he have spoken right at the outset of eternal life, for example, and of sanctions beyond the tomb, since he "was dealing still with children, with beings whose minds were servile, who laughed at all remote punishments and were afraid only of the retribution hanging over their heads. We must not suppose that God was pleased with the sacrifices of oxen, sheep or goats; he granted them only on account of the Jews' fondness for them, for they "ceased not to yearn after altars and victims," and "to turn them away from pagan superstitions like a good father who, unwilling that his son should play in the street, yet allows him, so as to avoid the temptation, to play in the house." Many of the Fathers say this in so many words: many other ceremonies inaugurated by Moses "also originate in the grossness of the Gentiles"; he was obliged "to be content with bringing them a little way to perfection in order to raise men imperceptibly to higher ideas." His legislation about purity is aimed especially at bodily purity: it was the necessary indirect approach, leading up eventually to the conception of purity of mind. "One who had to avoid defiling his body in the end perhaps would come to shun also stains of soul, learning it by himself, and to keep aloof from the works of death." Thus it is that Christ, like a good teacher, arouses in man the train of thought which turns him from exterior to interior things and raises him up from the sensual to the spiritual. Like a good doctor he adjusts his medicines to the patient's condition, and his treatment is given in wisely ordered stages.

Moreover, it is not advisable to judge the past by the standards of the present. Elias was right to call down fire from heaven on the guilty, for such severity was required to strike the imagination of a people that was still immature; but James and John, wishing to imitate the prophet, were blamed for it by our Saviour. Some things were fitting *pro tempore prophetiae* which to-day are fitting no longer. Polygamy would be an evil to-day, but it was not so in the days of the Patriarchs. The whole of the Mosaic law should be appraised not only in the light of the circumstances of its promulgation but also in respect of what it brought about and prepared for:

> Do not ask, now that they have been abolished, how the precepts of the Old Testament could be good. Ask how they were good at the time for which they were made. Or rather see how their real value is to show us in what they were deficient; for if they had not formed us so that we are now able to receive better ones we should never have seen what was missing in them.[7]

The whole of the Old Testament, in all its long duration, was not too long to prepare for the great day of the New. A παιδαγωγία, a necessary preliminary to the φιλοσοφία. Had not "the shadow to come first so that the truth might be believed"? And ought we not to admire "how God when he wishes to accomplish a wondrous work sends forth first shades and figures so that by this means the Truth finds more ready acceptance"? [8]

Lest we misjudge the thought of the first Christian centuries we should remember that their outlook was on the whole by no means intellectual. Except in rare cases, of which Gregory Nazianzen is an obvious example,[9] the Fathers of the Church do not compute the stages and measure the progress of objective "revelation." Without believing that for the generality of the people the figures had unveiled their mystery before their time, they tend to credit the "ancient Father," the "saints" under both Laws, or at least the greatest of them, with an abundance of prophetical illumination about the truths of the Gospel: so lively is their desire to refute the synagogue, so great is their anxiety to affirm the unity of the God who gave the two Testaments, or the continuity of his Church stretching from those who of old desired the coming of Christ down to those who now await his return. But they know, too, that the religious problem concerns all mankind, and that it is not purely a problem of objective knowledge. What they paid greatest attention to was not the propagation of an abstract doctrine but the actual meeting of man with God, the familiarization of human nature with the divinity, the transformation of man by the action of God's grace, the bursting forth of the "Divine Energy" and of the "Strength of the Holy Spirit." It is this whose various conditions they study, whose history they narrate, whose stages they mark off, whose vicissitudes they portray. For this they all affirm—in spite of their differences of opinion—that the passage of time was necessary: *non pauci gradus qui adducunt hominem ad Deum.*

The optimism of Irenaeus is not shared by all the Fathers; no more, certainly, did they all share the broad humanism of the greatest among them, Alexandrians, Cappadocians, Antiochians, and among the Latins, of Augustine himself. Here again we must avoid misconceptions. In many of them there may still be discerned traces of that ancient pessimism for which the history of the human race was but a series of declensions; they show us every beneficent intervention followed by a greater downfall, necessitating on God's part an increasingly drastic remedy, better adapted to the patient's accumulated disorders. Thus Philaster sees the Incarnation of the Word as the most efficacious but also as the lowliest of divine manifestations. And even this view is not without its depth of meaning. Whereas some set out the series of "economies" in an ascending scale, others describe them, very anthropomorphically, as so many repetitions of the divine Plan, so many methods devised in succession as a remedy for an ever-recurring evil. Methodius of Olympus is an example of this treatment in his comparison of the four successive laws with the fig tree, the vine, the olive tree and the thorn bush. . . . But at the basis of these very dissimilar explanations the same fundamental idea—and it is that which alone directly concerns us here—is presupposed by all: the unity of the human race in its temporal development. Whence there follows that behind a relative discontinuity there is a real continuity: if God makes, as it were, fresh starts in his work and devises fresh methods to bring it to a successful conclusion, it is by no means a fresh work that he undertakes. It is always the same city that the Lord seeks to build. It is always the same sheep that the Good Shepherd seeks to bring back to the fold.

In accounting for the protracted history of paganism, for that apparent long desertion of the world by God, the same tendencies are apparent. Some of the Fathers insist especially on the fact that human understanding had to make much progress so as to be able to receive the object of revelation. They say for example with Eusebius: "Why was not the Word of God proclaimed of old to all men, in all nations, as it is to-day? For this reason. The human race, in olden times, was not able yet to receive the teaching of Christ, the perfection of wisdom and virtue." It was necessary in the first place that from the Patriarchs and Moses onwards "the seeds of religion" should be spread abroad throughout the world like "a wind burdened with scents" until "all the nations of the earth should be thus made ready to conceive the idea of the Father that was to be imparted to them . . . then the Word appeared in person, in a human body. . . . This took place at the beginning of the Empire." [10] According to others, under the guidance of a more deeply religious intuition, humanity "left to its own devices" had to undergo a long and varied experience of its own wretchedness, and in some sort to plumb the depths, the better to acknowledge that it stood in need of a saviour and to be ready thus to welcome him. This explanation was valid in the case of both peoples, for if among the pagans moral corruption wrought greater havoc, among the Jews the law of Moses, in all the rigour of its ordinances, was a wonderful means of making man acknowledge himself a sinner: that was its secondary function under Providence, as St Augustine too brings out, following St Paul: *Quid dubitamus ad hoc datam esse Legem, ut inveniret se homo? Invenit ergo se, in malis invenit se. . . .*[11] Moreover, these two modes of explanation are not contradictory, since they belong to different categories. Several of the Fathers adopt both of them, and Marius Victorinus in his commentary on the Epistle to the Galatians contrived to combine them:

> As there is a fullness in things there is one also in time; for each order has its fullness. The perfection and fullness of things is Christ. The fullness of time brings the achievement of our deliverance. Now, just as Christ, that he may be the final perfect fullness, gathers together the scattered members . . . so, in the same way, the fullness of time comes to pass when, all men having grown to maturity, ready to receive the faith, and with the mass of sins now reaching its apex, a remedy was needed against universal death. Then Christ comes, and the fullness of time is accomplished.[12]

In any case, whatever each one's favourite explanation and whatever the precise opponent he is refuting, all are agreed in enunciating the same principle: *nihil sine aetate, omnia tempus exspectant.*[13] They even go further: in addition to realizing that the delay in Christ's coming was a real necessity, they admire its very fitness. Those slow "maturations" fill them with wonder. *Nihil immaturum, nihil non ordinatum. Nihil non dispositum. Nihil repentinum aut inopinatum.*[14] Without being blind in the slightest degree to the defects of paganism or the narrowness of the Mosaic law, they could not avoid referring to the providential harmony of history— *Deo pulchre omnia moderante*—that admiration which their pagan contemporaries continued to bestow on the harmony of the spheres. That well-ordered sequence of laws, adjusted to each period, seemed to them, in one of St Augustine's phrases, *velut magnum carmen cujusdam ineffabilis modulatoris,*[15] and now no longer do they see the world as an immense seven-stringed lyre, but as a great Book from which the Holy Spirit himself, the sevenfold Spirit, proclaims God's deeds. The octave of the eight spheres becomes for

them the octave of the eight ages. Christ is the "Master of the
Choir" around whom the whole of history is disposed, just
as the cosmic lyre answered in all its range to Apollo's
plectrum. The old and the new harmonize together, since
both issue from the same Author, and form in the variety
of their contrast a single melody, *ex multis et contrariis
sonis subsistens*. Moreover, the "revolutions" caused by
successive revelations did not bring in their train sudden
and complete upheaval, for God willed that man should be
subject not to violence but to persuasion. If the adhesion required of man, whatever his cultural level and the degree of
natural or supernatural light proffered to him, always calls
for his total conversion, that is, a turning away from evil
to good and from darkness to light, it is no less true that
the invasion or rather the investment of human nature by
the divinity takes place gradually, starting with the first
dawn of natural light and continuing to the broad daylight of eternity. After having appeared and spoken on many
occasions and in many ways, God came himself in his Christ
to accomplish the last stage along with us, *Dispositionis
antiquae munus explevit*. Christ, then, was long awaited; he
came *late,* but he did not *tarry*. It was in the natural order
of things that he should come late. The Incarnation took place
at its proper time: at the beginning of the sixth hour, in the
evening of the world, so that the true Lamb should be offered,
as was the paschal lamb, in the evening of day; at the time
when humanity, like Sara, was growing old; not right at the
end, no doubt, but towards the end, *in ultimis temporibus*.
For this is the beginning of a period of time as much as or
perhaps more than the end of one. As man, created on the
sixth day, was creation's masterpiece, the Incarnation is re-
creation's masterpiece. It is the beginning of consummation.
After the vicissitudes of battle it opens the era of victory.
After the long betrothal comes the marriage feast. After the
Incarnation the human race at last attains to the divine likeness, the end for which it was created.

Here we have another of those complete reversals, of which
we have already seen examples. Taken literally, the explanation seems exaggerated, and it is difficult to reconcile such a
concept of complete maturity or of failing life saved only at
the last moment with the impression of freshness and youth-
ful joy that radiates from the early Christian writers, or the
fervour and impetuosity of which we catch the glimpses in

the great succession of Christian conquests.[16] Upwards of a century after the Gospel period these latter characteristics are still to be found in the apologetic of Clement—that keenly intellectual Greek, heir to ancient culture, astonishingly learned and an Alexandrian by adoption into the bargain. We must not look for logical coherence in all this; rather should we marvel at the incomprehensible: Christianity, for those who lived in its first period, was at one and the same time both spring and autumn. *Complexio oppositorum*. It was both an achievement and a hope. In the evening of the world the Cross was the consummation of all things, but on Easter morning a new day was born for mankind: *Sacrificium vespertinum pependit in ligno, et beneficium matutinum surgens praebuit e sepulcro.*[17] The soul that turned to Christ entered into Paradise with him, and there found once more the springtide of the earth.

"What is old has passed away, behold all is now made new." "Christ has turned the setting into the rising sun." The old man has been overcome, and now the new Man arises. "Oldness" is a sin, henceforward sin itself; it is evil, it is night, error, the essential error, want of faith in the complete newness of Christ. *Omnem novitatem attulit—Quomodo vespera ubi Christus est?* The eternal day has dawned at last and no night shall ever follow it. The necessary preparations were of long duration, wisely spaced out in stages; but the bright light of the Word made flesh shone forth all at once, for it was the sudden beginning of a stupendous revolution.

No doubt the Fathers' thought could be regarded at the outset as a relic of the Jewish idea about the end of time, which was to coincide with the one advent of the Messias. The harvest and the grape-gathering were traditional symbols of the judgement. And did not St Paul call Christ "the last Adam," that is, Adam of the last days?[18] Does not the Epistle to the Hebrews show him offering his sacrifice at the end of the ages?[19] The distinction always made by Christian thought between his coming in the flesh and his coming in glory did not at once reveal its implications. The line of reasoning to which we have referred may be explained also by the Fathers' desire to humiliate the Jews without forgoing the advantages of their tradition, and to reconcile the newness of Christianity in its definitive form with the "majestic antiquity" that they claimed for it. We may think that some of them, such as Theodoret, set about it with an ingenuity that was too self-satisfied. But it remains true, all the same, that in his answers to the objections of a Celsus or Prophyry the leading idea is no temporary expedient or factitious subtlety. It was an intellectual reflexion, so far as the historical and exegetical resources of the period allowed, of the living consciousness of the Christian community. It presupposed an entirely new concept of the world, of man, and of their relations with God. Now this concept is of the very essence of Christianity. *O Christum et in novis veterem—et in veteribus novum!* Still for us all to-day the coming of Christ in the person of his Church is at the same time both autumn and spring.

Now, like the coming of Christ, this coming of his Church is twofold. There is in the first place the visible coming, the preaching of the Gospel and the setting up of the hierarchy. But when the Church is established on all sides it will be by no means the end. The body of the elect will not have completed its growth, that growth by which "Christ builds himself up, increases his stature by joining the saved to himself." In a mysterious hidden fashion and whatever the record of apparent triumphs or apostasies, it must go forward until the time that is without end: the definitive autumn and spring, dawn and harvest time of eternity. Then when the six ages of the world have been accomplished, will dawn the seventh day, *sabbatum sine vespere,* the Lord's day, whereat of old Isaias rejoiced, in a prophecy wholly spiritual in emphasis, that must be interpreted more spiritually still:

> In that day there shall be a way from Egypt to the Assyrians, and the Assyrian shall enter into Egypt, and the Egyptian to the Assyrians, and the Egyptians shall serve the Assyrian. In that day shall Israel be the third to the Egyptian and the Assyrian: a blessing in the midst of the land, which the Lord of hosts hath blessed, saying: Blessed be my people of Egypt, and the work of my hands to the Assyrian: but Israel is my inheritance.[20]

Peace upon the world, unity of all peoples in the service and praise of Jahwe! That is no dream, it is the word of God. No afflictions and disappointments can ever make us doubt it. The Church realizes full well that she will never triumph completely over evil, that is, disunion. She knows that "the state of war," since its principle is in the hearts of all of us, will be to the end the state of our earthly condition. That great city built up by Cain's sins will never be overthrown as long as time shall last. The "world," in the pejorative sense, flows in again unceasingly to the very midst of these islands which have been won from its expanse of miry waters. As she expands the Church discovers the world within herself, a subtler threat. She is fully aware of it. She knows, too, that man's most certain and glorious triumphs always contain an equivocal element from which evil may profit. The "mystery of iniquity" has not yet wrought its greatest destruction, and the Church, as in all ages of her history, perhaps more than ever to-day, can see its formidable shadow growing larger. So it is that, despite the ever-recurring illusions of those won for her cause but incompletely imbued with her Spirit, she awaits no other triumph than that of her Bridegroom who reigned from the Cross—but there is a "beyond" to her Cross in time itself. Her establishment on earth, a source of temptation for so many of her sons, can never be for her anything but a semblance, for she knows that after all she, like the Truth itself, is only a stranger on earth, *scit se peregrinam in terris agere.* Her outlook remains, as it was in her early days, essentially eschatological. Nevertheless, here on earth she is tireless in attempting the impossible. That is why men go out to establish her in hostile and far-off countries, according to that fine definition of their work furnished by Fr Manuel Diaz, Visitor of the Jesuits of Macao, a disciple of the famous Ricci. On June 26, 1639, when disagreements about method had begun to appear among the missionaries in China, but had not yet reached that frenzied condition that makes the history of the whole quarrel about "Chinese Rites" so painful a subject to every Catholic heart, Diaz wrote to the Dominican Provincial of Manila to state his Order's point of view. "We have come from Europe," he said, "to this end of the world to join ourselves with the Chinese Gentiles and to make up with them one Christian body." [21] Sustained by the divine promises, this missionary was working, then, to transform the prophet's vision into actuality. But the universal establishment of Christendom, even supposing that so unlooked for an event had taken place, could never be more than a pale and remote prefiguration of the final unity. *Nondum apparuit quid erimus.* "We hope for that which we see not, for what we cannot everywhere glimpse, but we wait for it with patience." The Holy Spirit who spoke by the mouth of the prophets found a fresh interpreter in Paul; he ascribes to the Church, in her world-wide mission, the rôle that was Israel's in regard to the neighbouring peoples, while keeping for Israel according to the flesh a place in the reconciliation, the final integration. The whole world taken up by man and made one with his destiny—man in his turn, in the whole stupendous complexity of his history, taken up by the Church; the world made spiritual by man, and man consecrated by the Church; the Church in fine, holy, spiritual, world-wide, like an immense ship laden with all the fruits of the earth, will enter upon eternity.

Spes non confundit. The Church, and that means every man and the whole world in her, is predestinate. That is St Paul's assertion at the climax of his great doctrinal work.[22] This text of the Epistle to the Romans on predestination has given rise to many disturbing comments and many heated arguments. Many, paying insufficient attention to its context,[23] have thought that he teaches therein the inevitable glorification of those whom God has chosen, and, as a consequence, a positive reprobation of all others. This interpretation of the eighth chapter of the Epistle has sometimes influenced that of the eleventh. In the exclamation *O altitudo* terror rather than trust has been discerned. The habit has formed of uttering it only with awe. In it an answer has been sought— an *effugium* rather—for the insoluble questions about efficacious and sufficient grace. In reality the problem that calls for this sublime exclamation had but a remote connexion with such questions. As for the uneasiness that it shows, it is simply that which arises in every creature who draws near to the sacred Mystery. It is the dizziness that sweeps over the mind faced by the "depths of God." As St Hilary well understood, it is a disturbance that is not incompatible with peace, a dizziness that does not banish confidence. Origen and Cyril of Alexandria have well shown that if St Paul emphasizes the sovereignty of the Lord whose judgements are impenetrable, it is yet the treasures of his goodness that he marvels at in the first place. The Apostle's thought is concerned more with the astounding ways through which God leads us than with their ultimate issue. What causes his

exclamation, a rapturous, exulting exclamation, is the ingenuity of the universal mercy that could bring the Jews
themselves back to the unity of ultimate salvation after
having made use of their blindness for the conversion of
the Gentiles. "For God repents neither of his gifts nor his
summons . . . he has enclosed all men in disobedience so
that he may be merciful to all." Likewise in the eighth chapter
Paul, lost in wonder, proclaims his faith in the success of the
divine plan, in the completion of the Body of Christ. He
echoes Jesus's promise for his Church, "The gates of hell shall
not prevail against her," and guarantees in a solemn manner
what he had himself written to his children of Corinth:
"God will be all in all." [24]

He knows well that no man can be saved in spite of himself, that after having lived by the Spirit, it is possible to fall
again under the dominion of the flesh, and he does not fail
to say so. He preaches exertion and watchfulness; he desires
all men to "work out (their) salvation." Sometimes even he
trembles when he thinks not of God who is faithful but of him
self. He has some frightening words for those who, having
received the "goodness of God," wild branches ingrafted on
the olive-tree, give themselves up to pride; they will be "cut
off." [25] It is this remark that Clement of Alexandria repeats on the subject of idolaters:

> God placed the stars above their heads as a path to lead
> them to him. But far from keeping to these luminous
> bodies they turned away again from the heavens to kneel
> before wood and stone . . . and thenceforward, found
> unfit for salvation, like the straw that is snatched from
> the millstone, the drop of water that falls from the vessel,
> they are cut off from the body. [26]

But this figure of the limb cut off—lost, dead—makes the
salvation of the body as such stand out more precisely. Directly afterwards Paul adds: "the fullness of the Gentiles
(shall) come in"—τὸ πλήρωμα τῶν ἐθνῶν; "all Israel (shall)
be saved," πᾶς Ἰσραὴλ. Israel, the Gentiles: within the compass of these two peoples is contained, we know, the whole
human race.

In a few pregnant accurate phrases St. Irenaeus comments
on this teaching. The salvation of the world is confided to
the Church: *hoc enim Ecclesiae creditum est Dei munus.*
Now this is no arbitrary divine edict. For definitively the

Church is nothing else than humanity itself, enlivened, unified by the Spirit of Christ. She was willed by God "in order to give life to creation." Woe, then, to him who separates himself from her. If schism is the sin that leads to death, it is because death itself, damnation, is a schism: the greatest schism, complete "estrangement," definitive cutting off—which may happen to those who to all appearances are the most zealous for unity: for if "many are inside who seem to be outside," some may be outside who pose as keepers of the gate. *Novit Dominus qui sunt ejus.* Whatever is revealed on this subject at the Last Day one thing is certain: the Church will not enter maimed into the Kingdom. According to the Jewish legend, when Lot's wife had been turned into a pillar of salt one or other of her limbs was continually being torn away, but by some marvel of instantaneous reparation she yet remained whole. So it is with the Church, "the salt of the earth," often maimed but at once finding her members afresh. So it is with humanity itself: no falling away will leave any gap in it. It is as nothing in the face of her fullness. As in our fleshly body the limbs are all interdependent, involved by one another, so will humanity share in the destiny of him who has taken it for his body. Since the head has triumphed, the whole body, the "Pleroma," will be saved.

NOTES TO CHAPTER VIII

[1] "Against the Galilaeans," fr. 143 and 178.

[2] *Eph.* iii. 1.

[3] *Adversus Haereses,* 4, 38 (P.G. vii, 1105–9). See Extract 38, p. 260.

[4] *On the Holy Spirit,* c. 14, n. 33 (P.G. xxxii, 125–7).

[5] *Epist.* 18, n. 27 (P.L. xvi, 979–80).

[6] *Epist.* 102, *ad Deogratias,* q. 2 (P.L. xxxiii, 373–6). The philosophy of history that emerges from the *City of God,* and the importance assigned to history in many of Augustine's other works are the more significant because they were in no way due to the education that he had received: "St Augustine's philosophical formation," notes H. I. Marrou, "is distinctly antihistorical" (*Saint Augustin et la fine de la culture antique,* p. 235, n. 2). In the *De doctrina christiana,* speaking academically of history, if it can be put thus, he sees it almost as mere chronology: lib. 2, c. 28, n. 42–4 (P.L. xxxiv, 55–6). See Extract 39, p. 261.

[7] Chrysostom, *In Mat.,* hom. 17, n. 5–6 (P.G. lvii, 260–2).

[8] Chrysostom, *In II Cor.*, hom. 2, n. 3 (P.G. lxi, 284).

[9] *Orat.* 31, c. 25–7 (P.G. xxxvi, 160–4). See Extract 40, p. 262.

[10] H. E., lib. 1, c. 2, n. 16 and n. 21–3 (Grapin, t. 1, pp. 23 and 25–9). See Extract 41, p. 264.

[11] *Sermo* 154, n. 1 (P.L. xxxviii, 833).

[12] *In Galat.*, lib. 2 (P.L. viii, 1176).

[13] Tertullian, *De virginibus velandis*, c. 1 (P.L. ii, 890).

[14] Tertullian, *Adversus Marcionem*, lib. 3, c. 2 (Kr. n. 378).

[15] *Epist.* 138, n. 5 (P.L. xxxiii, 627).

[16] "The young community was uplifted . . . by a joy of a fundamentally spiritual nature (ἀγαλλίασις). This joy came from the Holy Spirit, the eagerness of their souls, their certitude of belonging to a new world, etc." L. Cerfaux, *La première communauté chrétienne à Jérusalem,* in *Ephemerides theologicae lovanienses,* 1939, p. 30. Cf. Clement, *Paedag.*, lib. 5, c. 5, n. 20–1.

[17] Mozarabic Missal, Holy Saturday, *Oratio ad Pacem* (P.L. lxxxv, 474).

[18] *I Cor.* xv. 45.

[19] *Hebr.* ix. 26.

[20] *Isaias* xix. 23–5.

[21] *Lettres de M. l'abbé de Lionne* (1700), p. 36.

[22] *Rom.* viii. 18–39. Cf. *I Tim.* iii. 15–16 and Augustine's commentary, *Epist.* 199, c. 12, n. 50 (P.L. xxxiii, 924).

[23] Indeed, the whole doctrine of justification is envisaged by St Paul from the social standpoint: cf. Cerfaux, *La théologie de l'Église suivant saint Paul,* pp. 183–4.

[24] *I Cor.* xv. 28; cf. *Eph.* i and *Gal.* iii. 22. See Lagrange, *L'Épître aux Romains,* p. 217 and pp. 289–90; P. C. Boylan, *St Paul's Epistle to the Romans,* pp. 188–9; Joseph Huby, *L'Épître aux Romains,* p. 305. St Augustine expresses the same fundamental hope when he says that the devil will never be able "seducere Ecclesiam," *De civitate Dei,* lib. 20, c. 8, n. 1.

[25] *Rom.* xi. 17–24.

[26] *Strom.* 6, c. 14 (St., t. 2, p. 487). Cf. *Isaias* xl. 15.

IX

CATHOLICISM

If the manner of the second coming of the Church is the subject of our faith and certain hope, such is by no means the case with her first coming, her advance over the face of the earth. For the Church also, which has been in the sight of man for 2,000 years, undergoes in a very real manner a spring and an autumn. How does this spring develop, this autumn come to maturity? Its essential features are unpredictable, it is entirely a free gift and there is no history of what is eternal. But since the law that directs the outpourings of charity is a law of the Incarnation, can we not, by gathering together once again the Fathers' teaching and the Apostles' example, seek a definition, at least on general lines, of the Church's attitude to this many-sided humanity that she besets with such patience? In that we shall be led to see again, in a more concrete way, what she herself has taught us about her wonderful name of "Catholic."

Ever since the day when, full of the strength and the promises of the Holy Spirit, the Church issued from the Cenacle to overrun the earth, she has encountered everywhere in her progress countries that are already, in the religious sense, occupied. Now the religions with which she comes in conflict are by no means, for their respective peoples, just like a cloak that they have merely to put off. Customs, traditions, social and intellectual life, morality, all bear their imprint. Sometimes everything has been formed by them, or at least they have impregnated everything and absorbed it. Must everything be jettisoned to give place to the Gospel? There have never been wanting those who claimed that it was so. Everything in false religions, they asserted, is bad, for they are lies and perversions of the truth. They must be

151

destroyed. We see before us the city of Satan; it must be razed to the ground. We must change and refashion everything, put everything down and build afresh. This was Tatian's reasoning, more or less, on the subject of the old Greco-Roman world; so also Marcion's—not even Israel was excepted from his severity. That, too, nearer our own day, was the reasoning of the extreme Jansenists who refused to believe that anything but corruption could come from the Gentiles.

Such an attitude is unfair. It is not possible that what has lasted so long as the life-blood of whole races should not be worthy of respect from some point of view. And such an attitude is based on an illusion. Nowhere within our world is there any absolute beginning of any kind, and if, *per impossibile,* everything could be destroyed it would be impossible to create all afresh. So we can leave to Nicodemus his way of understanding Christian renewal, and ask of the Church herself, of her history, of her teaching, what is her own attitude.

Human nature, she tells us at the outset, is certainly sick, infirm, but it is not totally depraved. Human reason is weak and wavering, but it is not entirely doomed to error, and it is not possible for the divinity to be entirely hidden from it. "The seed of the Word is innate in the whole human race." The divine likeness in it may be dimmed, veiled, disfigured, but it is always there. *Etsi avertis, Domine, faciem tuam a nobis, tamen signatum est in nobis lumen vultus tui, Domine.*[1] False religions, therefore, are religions that stray from the truth or become engulfed in error, rather than religions whose whole direction is misleading and whose principles are wholly false. They are based on childish ideas more often than on evil ones. Is that not what we are increasingly shown nowadays by the origins of myth and the study of "magical" thought control? The Creator and the Redeemer, the Church adds, are one and the same God; therefore there can be no conflict between their works, and it is to stray from the true path to believe the second can be magnified at the expense of the first. The Word that became incarnate to renew and complete all things is also he who "enlighteneth every man that cometh into this world." *Dominus naturalia legis non dissolvit, sed extendit et implevit.*[2] Just as he did, his messengers come not to destroy but to accomplish; not to lay waste, but to raise up, transform, make holy. And even the moral decay that they encounter requires not rejection but rectification. *Sana quod est saucium, rege quod est devium.*

Long before theology had codified these principles the Church was living them. They are the foundation of her constant practice, and when the "reformers," not content with attacking abuses that were only too real, took it on themselves to expose on all sides what they called the pagan infiltrations into the Roman Church, they were obliged in order to indicate their source to go back farther and farther to the very beginnings of Christianity. Scripture itself seemed contaminated.

The work of the Creator, however spoilt by man, yet remains the natural and necessary preparation for the work of the Redeemer, and the better the history of Christian origins becomes known the more we realize it. "How marvellous it is," Pascal exclaimed, "to see with the eyes of faith Darius and Cyrus, Alexander, the Romans, Pompey, Herod working unwittingly for the triumph of the Gospel." And to-day our wonder can go farther still. How marvellous it is to see the "elements of the world" slowly forming, growing to maturity, evolving—no man knowing—to provide a body for the Christianity of the future!

Christianity transformed the old world by absorbing it. Can St Paul's thought be imagined cut off from the numberless roots which bound it to Tarsus and Jerusalem, to Greek civilization, Eastern mysticism and the Roman Empire? These ties are necessary to it, the more so because of its profound transcendence. "Supernatural" does not mean "superficial," in spite of a dangerous verbal similarity. Thus we saw that the Fathers agree in making the most of the Pauline idea of the fullness of time, just as they bring out clearly the "preparations of the Gospel." However keenly we may appreciate the novelty of the Christian miracle, the fact remains that they were careful, none the less, to avoid giving it the appearance of a "sudden improvisation," and they would not allow that Christ arose on the earth "like a strange star." If indeed Christianity is divine, entirely divine, it is in one sense human, the more human for being the more divine, and by penetrating into the very fabric of human history —yet without rending it—it has come to transform mankind and to renew the face of the earth.

Jesus, our Saviour, took the elements of his body from

our race. Being born of a woman his human nature is not like to ours only in an ideal way; it is our own nature. *Aperiatur terra et germinet Salvatorem*. The Docetist heresy, even in a mitigated form, by destroying his humanity destroys our salvation. "For if he had not received of man the substance of his flesh, if he was not *homo ex homine*, he would not be truly man." So Jesus, the gift of God, is no less the flower of Jesse. Though he came from heaven he is also the fruit of the earth. *Dominus dabit benignitatem, et terra nostra dabit fructum suum*. In like manner his Church: it is humanity that provides it with a body.

Now with the growth of the Church this human contribution must increase. That is an extension of the same truth, and most of the Fathers do not hesitate to recognize it. Strong in their conviction of Christianity's divine origin— they knew it by its fruits—which from the very first set it in a category apart, they were fond of emphasizing, sometimes to excess, the points of similarity between Christian beliefs and the teachings of the philosophers, so paving the way for the facile arguments of modern rationalists. Although they were hard enough on the philosophers' proud claims and made sport of their inability to reach final truth, yet these Fathers had no hesitation in following their teaching and in considering Christian belief in the light of their ideas. These Fathers never understood the "purity of Christianity" in the wholly negative sense adopted by some of their defenders. And although they were firmly convinced of the diabolic origin of idolatrous creeds, Porphyry's, Julian's or Faustus's irate and ironical protests about the gradual introduction of "pagan" customs into Christian life failed to disturb them. Newman, heir to their way of thought, puts it admirably:

> To the objection "these things are in heathenism, therefore they are not Christian," we, on the contrary, prefer to say, "these things are in Christianity, therefore they are not heathen. . . ."

He adds:

> We are not distressed to be told that the doctrine of the angelic host came from Babylon, while we know that they did sing at the Nativity; nor that the vision of a Mediator is in Philo, if in very deed he died for us on Calvary.[3]

As long as growth is spontaneous and centres of Christianity gradually increase in number, spreading out like an oil stain, these human contributions, with their local differences, appear of themselves, spontaneously, as a matter of course; it is, too, a spontaneous reaction that eliminates whatever is unwholesome in them. Without serious risk of wrong emphasis attention can be wholly concentrated on the combating of error and evil. But directly the apostolate is turned to a more distant field and appeals to alien peoples it becomes more clearly conscious of the rules that govern it and reproduces them in its method of work. We can see this in St Gregory the Great, for example, when he gave instructions to the monks whom he sent to set up the Church in England, or in John of Montecorvino, in the thirteenth century, when he began his work by translating the New Testament and the Psalter into the language of the Mongols.[4] But the principle appears most clearly in the missionaries of the modern period: Matthew Ricci, who without playing the oriental "educated himself so cleverly and so wholeheartedly that he had the sentiments and the appearance of an oriental;"[5] his follower in India, Robert de Nobili, who made himself a Brahmin among the Brahmins:[6] the very diversity of their methods bears witness to the unity and purity of the Catholic spirit by which they were inspired, even as it is still to-day the inspiration of their successors. In the eighteenth century the same spirit is shown all through the Instructions of Propaganda to the bishops sent to China, and it may be found again in the formal teaching of recent popes, *Maximum illud* of Benedict XV (1919), *Rerum Ecclesiae* of Pius XI (1926).

This twofold desire willingly to entertain whatever can be assimilated and to prescribe nothing that is not of faith, although it is acknowledged and systematically employed, is by no means the calculated plan of cunning men in search of a successful method, as has been sometimes suggested. It is governed by doctrinal considerations. It is true all the same, as experience proves, that it is the only fully effective way. But it can only be done at the cost of a systematic, persevering effort that love alone makes possible. For it requires of the apostle not only a continual adaptation of self, like St Paul who, becoming all things to all men, did not speak before the Areopagus as he spoke to his fellow-countrymen. Much more than a mere outward adaptation is required: a whole inner transformation, a real exodus from the secret places of the soul: "leave your country, your family and your father's house, to go to the place that I shall show you." Such a method demands also an enduring patience, for it is impossible without a deep study of the peoples who are to be converted, their customs, morals and beliefs. Without coming to terms with error it avoids unfruitful controversy, and seeks rather those toothing stones that Providence has placed on all sides for the building up of truth. It knows that there are two ways of being strict: one that is unjust, and arises from lack of understanding, and the other that is a requirement of love itself; the first increases the evil, the second produces good where there was none before, and is at pains to show in every field how revealed truth, because it is Catholic, makes its own and completes all man's genuine thinking, which of itself is always fragmentary and mean in some degree.

Such a method has its own risks, since it calls in question so many things that long habit has made sacred, some of them seeming almost bound up with dogma. It can also beget some illusions. When Ricci treated Confucius as Ambrose treated Seneca or Cyril Plato, he was on the right path; his followers, who in their enthusiasm to search like him into "the long advent of Chinese thought" saw in the old philosopher "an epitome of all that philosophers had recognized to be soundest in morality" and even "as it were a ray or shadow of Christianity," [7] were far from being entirely wrong; with even better justification they might have extolled the moral teaching of Mo-tseu; but several of them went strangely astray afterwards in their interpretation of the old canonical books. . . . Yet these risks, these illusions or possible extremes cannot obscure the necessity of a method which the logic of faith prescribes, and without which the Church would be paralysed. If, for example, the efforts made to convert the Mohammedans have remained so long fruitless, to such a degree that Islam has gained a reputation, still far too widespread, of being beyond hope of conversion, have not the difficulties arisen from the fact that for long Christians have been unable to make that indispensable effort at comprehension? Many, terrified at their danger as a result of the conquering fervour of Agar's posterity, had no other thought than to carry out their leader's orders: *Ejice ancillam hanc et filium ejus,* and forgot that they must find some way to accomplish that other saying: *Benedicentur in semine tuo omnes gentes terrae*.[8] The most absurd fables about the law of Islam and its founder were circulated by the Crusaders, and collected in controversial works. St Thomas Aquinas, following St Raymund of Pennafort, complained of this at the beginning of his *Contra Gentiles* and took the occasion to recall the exact knowledge that the ancient Fathers generally possessed of the teaching which they had to oppose, and to praise the method of discussion which they approved: *ut ex his quae dicunt (errantes) possimus rationes assumere ad eorum errores destruendos.* "Truth," said Severus of Antioch, "must endue each individual on the basis of his own thoughts." From a far-off continent, centuries ago, a missionary gave utterance to that same fundamental law. "Hinduism," wrote Fr Wallace, repeating a remark that had been made to him, "is a tree which will never fall as long as the handle of the axe that is cutting it is not made of its own wood."[9] And that is exactly what another Indian missionary, Père Calmette, said in the eighteenth century in his announcement to learned circles in Europe of his recent discovery of the Veda:

> It is by no means pure gold, but like gold as it comes from the mines; the brilliance shed by certain ideas and passages shows that there is really gold in it. . . . We have already obtained from it great benefit for the advancement of religion, for we can find in it arms with which to fight the teachers of idolatry, arms which inflict the deepest wounds on them.[10]

That is a method of immanence, the most traditional of all, and its application is not confined to discussion and books. When it is genuine, loving, straightforward—a single word or gesture can bring it to light. An unobtrusive work of art can epitomize much patient negotiation. It is this method that can be seen at work in that humble chapel at El-Abiodh, continuing among the Mohammedans Charles de Foucauld's silent vigil. From the flat roof the Angelus gives the call to prayer, and in the chapel an extra station in the Way of the Cross, a recess pointing towards Jerusalem, as the mihrab of the mosques points towards Mecca, reminds all Abraham's children of the love shown by Christ in agony.

How pressing is the need for such an effort at understanding when it concerns those features of a civilization whose chief fault is merely that they are unfamiliar to us! Missionary history shows many a good example of this, and the lessons to be drawn from them are by no means exhausted. But what a difference in this respect between the age of Louis XIV and the last century! The latter, the age of Europe's expansion, was also and only too often a century of barbarous blindness; and never more than at that time was there current among us "that common prejudice that the sun illuminates the West with its full strength and lets fall on the rest of the world only the reflexion of its rays." [11] The founders of our scientific civilization did not share the disdainful perversity of those who gathered its fruits. We can beat our breasts now at the pride in our machines and in our arms that has made us so unjust towards other races, at the narrowness of an education which, claiming to furnish us with a unique human culture, has shut us off from understanding the beautiful things that man has made in other parts of the world. But the Church, which is not tarnished by our sins, is also not straitened by our artificial boundaries nor paralysed by our prejudices. Her ambition is to gather the whole human family together, and she has nothing in common with our cheap pretensions. As charity's ambassador she lays no claim to cultural imperialism. In spite of the intermingling of races that is taking place nowadays all over the earth she understands that civilizations are original—like human beings—and essentially varied. All countries can fit themselves out with European goods. The processes of industrialism, like Western political systems, may be disseminated on all sides. But this apparent unification is no obstacle to the continued existence of certain outstanding varieties of spiritual experience, in the broadest sense of the word, which are logically irreducible.[12] Now it is the Church's mission to purify and give fresh life to each of them, to deepen them and bring them to a successful issue by means of the supernatural revelation that she holds in deposit. The Church cannot forgo this pre-eminently world-wide mission so as to be in the exclusive service of one or other form of civilization.

For her it is not merely a matter of justice. For she knows that, apart from the fact that no human achievement has been promised eternity, all races, all centuries, all centres

of culture have something to contribute to the proper use
of the divine treasure which she holds in trust: *ex toto
mundo totus mundus eligitur*. A sort of treasure house "giving forth things old and new, casting the gold of fresh tributaries into her refiner's fire. . . ." [13] She is mindful of those
providential harmonies which prepared the resources of
Greece and Rome for her first expansion, and she well knows
that in this conjunction of events something definitive was
accomplished, yet she does not share the illusion of some
of her children for whom there now remains no more to do;
since the miracle of the past must continue, she believes in
fresh providential harmonies for her further expansion. At
periods of fearful conflict she still has hope, though it be
in her humblest members, and a fresh assimilation is prepared in the silence of prayer and study. The story of a few
Dominicans kidnapping Aristotle (though to some it appeared that it was Aristotle who kidnapped the Dominicans)
is not an isolated case. Moreover, the past history of the
Church provides her with examples of an opposite type, and
she is too painfully conscious of the impoverishment caused
by the great schisms not to seek compensating factors. Why
should she desire to change flexible and vigorous structural
unity for a drab uniformity? Why should she wish "to make
the rising sun show the colours of sunset"? As she is the
only ark of salvation, within her immense nave she must
give shelter to all varieties of humanity. She is the only
banqueting hall, and the dishes she serves are the product
of the whole of creation. She is Christ's seamless coat, but
she is too—and it is the same thing—Joseph's coat of many
colours. "She is the bond of indissoluble concord and perfect cohesion" and she will bind her abundant harvest into
well-packed sheaves. She knows that the various customs hal-
lowed by her "confirm the unanimity of her faith," that this
visible catholicity is the normal expression of her inner riches,
and that her beauty is resplendent in its variety: *circumdata
varietate*.[14]

She is the Catholic Church: neither Latin nor Greek, but
universal.[15] Heir to the *Catholica bonitas* of God himself
she ever proclaims, as in St Augustine's time: *Ego in omnibus linguis sum; mea est graeca, mea est syra, mea est
hebraea, mea est omnium gentium, quia in unitate sum
omnium gentium*.[16] Nothing authentically human, whatever
its origin, can be alien to her. "The heritage of all peoples

is her inalienable dowry." In her, man's desires and God's have their meeting-place, and by teaching all men their obligations she wishes at the same time to satisfy and more than satisfy the yearnings of each soul and of every age; to gather in everything for its salvation and sanctification. "Said the chapel to the meadow: 'None of your good qualities prevents your accepting my help.'" *A fortiori*, then, there is nothing good which Catholicism cannot claim for its own. To see in Catholicism one religion among others, one system among others, even if it be added that it is the only true religion, the only system that works, is to mistake its very nature, or at least to stop at the threshold. Catholicism is religion itself. It is the form that humanity must put on in order finally to be itself. It is the only reality which involves by its existence no opposition. It is therefore the very opposite of a "closed society." Like its Founder it is eternal and sure of itself, and the very intransigence in matters of principle which prevents its ever being ensnared by transitory things secures for it a flexibility of infinite comprehensiveness, the very opposite of the harsh exclusiveness which characterizes the sectarian spirit. *Omnis gens secundum suam patriam in Ecclesia psallit Auctori.*[17] The Church is at home everywhere, and everyone should be able to feel himself at home in the Church. Thus the risen Christ, when he shows himself to his friends, takes on the countenance of all races and each hears him in his own tongue.

Such is the Church and such is its real attitude. Nowadays it is more than ever important to make this clear, because the temptation to interpret it otherwise has become stronger, and quite a different notion of it is tending to prevail among many witnesses outside. After a period of triumphant optimism which linked the destiny of Europe to that of Christianity it has now come about that a mood of disillusion links the destiny of Christianity to that of a Europe supposedly in a decline. To the belief that the East could easily be westernized has now succeeded the opinion that any project of making it Christian is chimerical and must be abandoned:

In the long run, we are told, Christianity must recognize that there are certain great religions which it cannot penetrate. All over the world spheres of influence have been allotted, definite positions taken up. . . . To leave one system of belief in order to enter another is a change of civilization rather than of religion. Ultimately Christianity will have to accept this proof that it is linked with a culture and ways of thought that are not universal.[18]

That is a disastrous, a fatal idea, encouraged by all too many failures in the past and by all too many suggestions in the present. It is an idea which finds among us too much covert agreement, and which only a great spiritual asceticism will overcome.

The Church, trusting in the Holy Spirit that leads her, trusts also all the peoples that she comes to free. That is no sign of *naïveté* on her part. She realizes that all races are not at the same cultural level, that not all afford the same possibilities. But she knows, too, that all men are one in community of their divine origin and destiny; and that suffices to give her confidence in face of all the theories engendered by pride and egoism. It has often been said that the Church, by the Council of the Vatican and the Encyclical *Pascendi*, upheld the rights of human reason. To-day it can be said that she upholds the nobility and unity of human nature. Her motherly prudence does not prevent her from making at critical times one of those bold gestures that our cautiousness and circumspection would delay indefinitely. Besides, does not the only efficacious way to bring out the hidden truth and to avoid extinguishing the good that would break forth lie in a systematic desire to study sympathetically those forms of thought that are most remote from us, and in this study to pay particular attention to privileged cases, however rare they may be? It is at its highest reaches that humanity must be understood; the plains—or the depressions —will always be explored soon enough.

The Church's method is not syncretist any more than it is naïve. Syncretism is artificial, generally the work of rulers or literary men, and presupposes declining faith. It is an insult to the living God. In the energetic language of the prophets, syncretism is fornication. In the spiritual order it is barren, like the political system or the philosophy from which it springs.[19] It lowers and vulgarizes all the elements it combines—like the "pidgin" language of the great Mediterranean ports. But here again the history of the Church can teach us. Christianity rejected Gnosticism, a representative of the syncretist system; but such an uncompromising boldness has not hindered her in carrying out her work of assimilation with a breadth of vision that is more clearly manifest every day.

Finally it is equally unfitting to speak of liberalism, of tolerating error, or of making the salt of the Gospel savourless. For if Christianity must be shown with all its exigencies, it must also stand out in all its purity. It would be wrong to obscure the gentle severity of the Gospel, but it is not lawful either to load it with additional burdens: the first Council declared this.[20] And if it is once understood that the work of conversion consists, fundamentally, not in adapting supernatural truth, in bringing it down to human level, but, on the contrary, in adapting man to it, raising him up to the truth that rules and judges him, we must especially beware, as of blasphemy, of confusing ourselves, its servants, with it—ourselves, our tastes, our habits, our prejudices, our passions, our narrow-mindedness and our weaknesses with the divine religion with which we are so little imbued. We must give souls to God, not conquer them for ourselves. If this is to be thought liberalism, it is, in any case, none other than the liberalism of charity. *Da mihi amantem et scit quid dicam.*

St Paul's great example is the most fitting of all to secure us against the mistakes to which we are liable in this connexion. No man has been less ashamed to flaunt the scandal of the Cross or been in greater dread of deadening its force. No man has so unreservedly proclaimed the necessity of breaking with error and sin and of dying to oneself, to live a renewed life in Christ: "Purge out the old leaven, that you may be a new paste." But Paul refuses to allow the demands of the Judaizing party, and he even attacks those who were cowed by their audacity. Was it only, in his own words, "lest we should cause any hindrance to the Gospel" and to "gain to Christ a great number" of Gentiles? This anxiety is not the complete explanation of his conduct. It was not primarily concern for propaganda that guided the Apostle; it was the logic of his faith. His opponents charged him with lightening the yoke of the Lord from motives of policy, jettisoning the Law; he replied that it was not to make himself well received among men that he acted in this way, but to deserve well of God. Preaching the Gospel of God he would by no means preach it "according to man."

Far from compromising doctrine by opportunist opinions, Paul upholds its real character in the face of Peter's imprudent concessions; he refuses to change the Gospel to please other men, because then he would be unfaithful to Christ.[21]

The Holy Spirit who guided the Apostle is the same who still guides the Church, and speaks by the voice of the modern Popes. The path to which it commits us is the only safe one. To follow it is neither *naïveté*, nor syncretism, nor liberalism; it is simply Catholicism.

NOTES TO CHAPTER IX

[1] Cf. Ambrose, *In Psalm.* 43, n. 88 (P.L. xiv, 1131).

[2] Irenaeus, *Adv. Haereses,* 4, 12, 1 (P.G. vii, 1004).

[3] See Extract 47, p. 270.

[4] It may be noted that the Nestorian missionaries were able to adapt themselves to the Chinese language and method of thought, without, it appears, any injury to orthodoxy, and to express the essentials of dogma in terms taken from Taoism and Buddhism.

[5] E. Duperray, *L'Église et la civilisation chinoise,* in the *Bulletin des Missions,* 1937, p. 251. See Ricci's letter to the Emperor, June 28, 1601 (Couvreur, *Choix de documents,* 1898, pp. 81–5). In his *Lettre à Mgr le Duc du Maine sur les cérémonies de la Chine,* Fr Le Comte gave this justification of his colleagues: "They were sufficiently aware, on the one hand, that when it was a question of converting the whole earth it would be a dreadful sacrilege to introduce the smallest error into the Church of Jesus Christ. . . . They had read in the sacred Scriptures that the Lord could have nothing in common with Belial. But they reflected, too, that it was not right lightly to condemn the customs of so ancient and so prudent an Empire as the Chinese because they were not in agreement with our ideas. . . ." (1700.) On Ricci's apostolate and missionary method see Fr Henri Bernard's important work: *Le Père Matthieu Ricci et la société chinoise de son tempts,* B vols. (Tientsin, 1937).

[6] Nobili, *Apologie de* 1610 (French translation by Dahmen, 1931). To justify his conduct the missionary relied on the definitions of superstition given by St Augustine, and by St Thomas, IIa, IIae, q. 94, a. 1.

[7] *Lettre sur la morale de Confucius,* p. 2. And p. 58: ". . . If from this last saying of Confucius it seems that the Decalogue was not unknown to him, when his teaching on charity has been shown, it will seem more likely still that he knew the Gospel maxims."

[8] *Genesis* xxi. 10, and xxii. 18.

[9] *De l'Évangélisme au Catholicisme par la route des Indes* (1921), p. 196. In the *Éclaircissements* that Fr Le Comte fur-

nished on the subject of his *Nouveaux Mémoires de la Chine* he wrote: "If the Jesuits applied themselves to discover in Chinese history some trace of the religion professed by Noe . . . ought they not to be thanked for it rather than accused of it as a crime? Did not St. Paul endeavour to extract from the writings of the pagans, and from the very midst of idolatry, some enlightenment that he might utilize to disperse their darkness; and following his example did not the holy Fathers do likewise?" (p. 16).

[10] 1732 and 1733. The complete text of the first letter may be found in the *Revue d'histoire des missions*, March 1934.

[11] Ko, S. J., *Essai sur l'antiquité des Chinois*, in *Mémoires concernant les Chinois*, t. 1, 1776, pp. 149–51.

[12] J. Monchanin has endeavoured to bring out their chief characteristics: *Santé, sagesse, sainteté* (in *Médecine et Éducation*, pp. 214–7). By the same author: *L'Inde et la contemplation* in *Dieu Vivant*, number 3; *L'Hindouisme*, in *Bulletin des Facultés catholiques de Lyon*, December 1946; *Islam et Christianisme* in the *Bulletin des Missions*, 1938, p. 10–23; *Islam* in *En Terre d'Islam*, 1938, pp. 107–23.

[13] Newman, *Critical and Historical Essays*, 1871, vol. ii, p. 231. See Extract 47, p. 270.

[14] Benedict XV, allocution to the Consistory of March 10, 1919: "Nec solum (nostri decessores) orientalium mores et instituta, seorsum a latinis, conservanda, sed etiam eorum ritus, nobiles certe ac splendidos, incorrupte et integre retinendos curarunt, quo scilicet Sponsa Christi in vestitu deaurato circumdata varietate suam melius pulchritudinem ostenderet." *A.A.S.*, 1919, p. 98.

[15] Benedict XV's *Motu proprio* of May 1, 1917, setting up the Sacred Congregation for the Eastern Church: ". . . cum vel ex hac re sit manifestum, in Ecclesia Jesu Christi, ut quae non latina sit, non graeca, non slavonica, sed catholica . . ." *A.A.S.*, 1917, p. 530. Cf. Encyclical on St Ephraem (*ibid.*, 1920, p. 466). *Apoc.* vii. 9. See also Benedict XIV's encyclical *Allatae sunt* (July 25, 1755) in which are enumerated at length a whole series of documents and facts testifying to the attitude of the Roman Church towards the different rites. The Apostolic See, concludes the Pope, ardently desires "ut omnes Catholici sint, non ut omnes Latini fiant." *Bullarium*, vol. 3, Prati, 1846, pp. 249–72.

[16] Augustine, *In Psalm.* 147, n. 19 (P.L. xxxvii, 1929).

[17] Rhabanus Maurus, *De Universo*, lib. 22, c. 3 (P.L. cxi, 598).

[18] J. Schlumberger, *Sur les frontières religieuses*, 22 (1935). Cf. P.-L. Couchoud, *Jésus le dieu fait homme* (1937), conclusion.

[19] Manichaeism is sometimes quoted as an example of a successful syncretist religion. That is not quite accurate. For if it is true that Mani deliberately made an arbitrary choice of doctrines, it was to the advantage of one of them, Persian dualism, which remained fundamentally intact and vigorous; and what was arti-

ficially introduced into the new religion explains perhaps why it did not succeed better. "Manichaeism," observes H. Lietzmann, "was incapable of development; it became fossilized and continued to exist on the fringe of universal history for about a thousand years, keeping its form but losing its spirit" (*Histoire de l'Église ancienne*, French trans. vol. ii, 1937, p. 279). See A. Christensen, *L'Iran sous les Sassanides*, chap. 4: *Le prophète Mani et sa religion*.

[20] *Acts* xv. 28: "For it hath seemed good to the Holy Ghost and to us, to lay no further burden upon you than these necessary things."

[21] *I Cor.* i. 17; v. 7; ix. 12 and 19–22. *Gal.* i 10–11; ii. 11.

PART III

X

THE PRESENT SITUATION

"A religion made for the interior consolation of a few chosen souls": so Renan defined the Christianity of the first two centuries at the end of the great work in which he had taken it upon himself to comment on its fundamental texts.[1] It may be asked how he could have read these texts so as to come to such a conclusion. Of course he was unable to take the *Didache* into account, for it was discovered only two years after the publication of his *Marc-Aurèle*.[2] But the *Didache,* convincing though its emphasis is, would have provided him with nothing essentially new. How did Renan read the epistle to the Romans, to the Ephesians, or I Timothy?[3] And how did he explain to himself, leaving out of account all question of its authenticity, the command that ends St Matthew's Gospel, "Teach ye all nations"?[4] Did he never stumble on a certain page of the Acts[5] or on the verse of the Apocalypse: "After this I saw a great multitude which no man could number, of all nations, and tribes and peoples and tongues . . ."?[6] Did he not know that great prayer in Clement of Rome's letter?[7] Was he not struck by the all-embracing solicitude manifested by certain pages of Hermas himself or St Justin? And, lastly, how did he read St Irenaeus, whose broad-minded teaching admittedly was not developed in a single day?

It remains true, of course, that in Renan's day the echo of that broad-minded teaching was all but silenced. If it has never been repudiated, there has not been the same readiness in all the Christian centuries to drink at the springs from

which it is so unfailingly given forth. It is only honest to
acknowledge this. Certainly the great traditional views that
we have recalled were not to be accepted uncritically. They
carried with them, sometimes, a certain arbitrariness, and
they were not always expressed in the most careful terms.
There was a twofold illusion to be avoided: the illusion of a
social pseudo-mysticism and that of a new millenarianism,
which a superficial interpretation might have suggested. Thus
many precisions and many distinctions were required. Fidelity to a tradition, moreover, is never servile repetition. A
twofold task, of restatement and adaptation, was therefore
needed—and theology has successfully accomplished it more
than once. Unfortunately this indispensable task sometimes
lost sight of the end in view, which was not to obscure or
discard the doctrine, but to strengthen and clarify it. Into
some of our present-day teaching there has crept, particularly
in certain of its current applications—less indeed by formal
assertion than by regrettable omissions; less through positive
deviation than through a certain lack of the Catholic mentality; and less again in the teaching of the Pastors than in
the theses of the schools—a fairly strong, sometimes a very
strong, admixture of individualism. Fortunately, some effort
is being made nowadays, almost everywhere, to eliminate it.

In this connexion the combined influence of Aristotelian
logic and Roman law on the formulation of theology during
the Middle Ages has been pointed out more than once. These
two excellent instruments of precision, which should have
been the instruments of progress, were not in the event without their dangers. For in the second was inherent the danger
of a legal outlook in expounding the mysteries—an outlook
entirely foreign to their nature; and the first showed itself un-
suited to those organic, unitary ideas which had formerly,
in some respects, found an ally in the Platonic mentality. It
is certain, speaking more generally, that logical intelligence
—that of *homo faber* rather than that of *homo sapiens*—
begins by separating, "defining," isolating objects in order
afterwards to connect them again artificially; and it is no
less certain that its desire for analytical clarity makes it impatient of any idea of mystery . . . a condition of science
which carries with it its own penalty. Also it is right to add,
no doubt, that the theology of history which occupied so
large a place in the Fathers' thought never found—or was
never provided with—its essential groundwork, a more or

less systematic philosophy of history; I mean a philosophy
of history as such, a philosophy of humanity in time.[8] The
suggestions made by Gregory of Nyssa or Augustine were
only the beginnings and were insufficient to bring out and
compel recognition for the idea of a spiritual continuity, essential for each individual and common to all, within which
all our acts are registered in a concrete order. Medieval
thought, with that overriding anxiety for rationality which
is one of the causes of its greatness, was inevitably bound to
disregard one aspect of a teaching which at that time appeared so obscurely.

Yet we must be careful not to exaggerate, and must not
judge by later and by no means inevitable abuses. What was
lost on one side was recovered on the other. We know, for example, what resources were to be found in the social moral
science, properly adapted, of the Nicomachean Ethics. Thus
the activity of secondary causes now seems more important
still, though it is more diffuse and less easily apprehended.
The individualist aberrations of recent centuries were due
not so much to some special conception, to the use of some
special philosophical system or mode of thought, but to a
general development of individualism. They are just one
aspect of it among a hundred others. We are dealing with a
universal phenomenon which, moreover, defies definition in a
single formula, just as it cannot be condemned without re-
servation or limited to certain dates, although it appears to
coincide with the gradual dissolution of medieval Christianity. Common to all schools, it was bound to leave its
mark on theology. For however unsusceptible to outside in-
fluences the theological world would sometimes like to be,
it cannot always remain untouched by the trend of thought
in the world, and it is not always when it thinks itself particularly well-shielded that it offers the most effectual resistance.
These trends may sometimes penetrate it to its advantage; it
may also happen that they do so to its disadvantage, more
especially when they are unperceived and it is unable to control them. "If in modern times," writes Père Philippe de
Régis,

   individualism seems to have assumed an excessively predominant rôle in ascetics, preaching and even theology
   and liturgy, that especial sanctuary of collective life, at the
   expense of a point of view which is nevertheless in the

foreground of Christ's mind and the Church's, we must simply conclude that something is not altogether in order.

And the same writer adds, thus hinting at the wide bearing of such a theological issue: "Perhaps Marxism and Leninism would not have arisen and been propagated with such terrible results if the place that belongs to collectivity in the natural as well as in the supernatural order had always been given to it." [9]

On the two essential questions of the Church and the Eucharist another enemy which has been very properly denounced is controversy. For a heavy tribute has been paid to its requirements. "It is a great misfortune," it has been said, "to have learnt the catechism against someone." For it is to be feared, in the first place, that in such a case it was but half learned, and even if all of it that is remembered is literally and absolutely accurate, still does not the consequent narrowness of outlook and lack of proportion amount in practice to error? For if, as the whole history of the Church shows and as the doctors, from the first centuries onward, are fond of pointing out, heresy is an occasion of progress for orthodox doctrine, there follows in its train the danger that this progress may be one-sided and the occasion in its turn— history proves this as well—of further error; if salutary inflexibility is not soon followed by an attempt at deeper investigation, the necessary defence of threatened truths, with its *operosae disputationes,* may deflect attention, unless we are careful, from the *orationes quotidianae;* what the Church "has never ceased to proclaim in her prayers" can thus disappear for a time from some theological treatises. Who, then, can estimate the evil done in this way by a heretic or false mystic not only by propagating his opinions but even by provoking his own condemnation, with the inevitable commotion it causes and the prejudices it creates? We have learnt our catechism too much against Luther, against Baius or even against Loisy. For a long time after Luther's desecration of it no one dared even to mention "Christian liberty." In opposing the detractors of the Mass some theologians seemed to think that they must improve upon the traditional idea to which the Council of Trent had just set its seal, and sought on the altar a sacrifice in some sort independent of Calvary, as if at all costs there must be on each occasion a real immolation and, as it were, a destruction of the victim offered.

From decrees like the Bull of St Pius V against Baius strange conclusions have sometimes been drawn; and would not the anti-modernist oath lead to a great distortion were it to be taken, not as the defensive document which it is obviously intended to be, but as a balanced theological synthesis. A reinforced sector of the walls is not the whole city won!

The motherhood of the teaching Church is far from being merely the judicial power which she exercises against error. As products of the extraordinary *Magisterium* the definitions of faith themselves are a result of a "defence-reaction" which controls their choice and the form of their expression. That is what Franzelin recalled at the Vatican Council. "The purpose of the holy Councils," he explained to the twenty-four fathers who were to examine the *schema* prepared by him,

> was never to expound Catholic doctrine as long as it was undisputed . . . but to expose dangerous errors and, declaring the truth directly opposed to them, deny them admittance. Hence decrees almost always contain two parts: a statement of the error with its peculiar features, and its condemnation; and a declaration of the Catholic doctrine under the precise aspect whereby it is opposed to the error. These two parts are so closely related that sometimes they are connected together even in the Canons themselves. It clearly follows from this purpose that in a dogmatic definition not only the choice of doctrinal points, but also the essential character of the exposition necessarily depends on the precise form of the error that is to be exposed and condemned. Thus the Catholic doctrine should be enunciated under that formal aspect in which it contradicts the peculiar character of the error.[10]

So classical theology was never confined to a commentary on and a justification of texts whose authority, however absolute, does not prevent their being incomplete, dependent on circumstances, and often more negative than positive.[11] Unenlightened zeal in these cases would result only in a doctrinal minimism to the prejudice of Christian thought and life. Perfect fidelity to the decisions of the Church in matters of faith is only a starting point. "Bar the way to error," said St Cyril of Jerusalem, "so that we may go forward along the only royal road." [12]

Moreover—and this is less often noticed—"as a very frequent historical phenomenon, through a fresh application, a new verification, of a very ancient law of antinomies," [13] the very conflict between two doctrines nearly always implies certain presuppositions common to both. Whence arises another danger for the theologian who makes too many concessions to the demands of controversy. In his struggle against heresy he always sees the question, more or less, willingly or unwillingly, from the heretic's point of view. He often accepts questions in the form in which the heretic propounds them, so that without sharing the error he may make implicit concessions to his opponent, which are the more serious the more explicit are his refutations. Can it be maintained that Catholic exegesis, in certain instances of narrow-mindedness, was never influenced in that way by the Protestant idea of the Bible? And nowadays, seeing the matter in its proper perspective, don't we realize that the "separated" philosophy of recent centuries has found its correlative in a "separated" theology? The return to the great doctrines of tradition, particularly to Thomism, on this point appears to be an accomplished fact. But for about three centuries, faced by the naturalist trends of modern thought on the one hand and the confusions of a bastard Augustinianism on the other, many could see salvation only in a complete severance between the natural and the supernatural. Such a policy ran doubly counter to the end which they had in view. For on the one hand they failed to observe that the more you separate the less do you really *distinguish*. When the "primitives" separate the soul from the body in so simple a way, do they not make it by that very separation just a "double" of the body? Thus the supernatural, deprived of its organic links with nature, tended to be understood by some as a mere "super-nature," a "double" of nature. Furthermore, after such a complete separation what misgivings could the supernatural cause to naturalism? For the latter no longer found it at any point in its path, and could shut itself up in a corresponding isolation, with the added advantage that it claimed to be complete. No hidden dissatisfaction could disturb the calm of its splendid equilibrium. . . . Such a dualism, just when it imagined that it was most successfully opposing the negations of naturalism, was most strongly influenced by it, and the transcendence in which it hoped to preserve the supernatural with such jealous care was, in fact, a banishment.

The most confirmed secularists found in it, in spite of itself, an ally.

These remarks find their natural application in the subject-matter of this book. We have already noticed that the modern theology of the Church has reflected the Protestant individualism which it sought to correct in too extrinsic fashion. But without emphasizing this last complaint it is easy to see that our treatise *De Ecclesia* in its regular form has been built up in two main stages: one in opposition to the imperial and royal jurists, the other in opposition to Gallican and Protestant doctrines. Consequently there is a certain emphasis upon the rights of ecclesiastical authority in relation to the civil authority, and then to the prerogatives of the hierarchy, and especially of the papacy, within the religious society; or rather, so large a place has been given to these two subjects that the spiritual unity of the members of the Mystical Body has been more than once practically forgotten—and for this very reason the doctrine of authority in the Church could be only partially explored. We know that if the Vatican Council could have finished its programme it would have been easier to restore a juster perspective. St Peter Damian, Cardinal of the Holy Roman Church, a strenuous supporter of the papacy and a collaborator with the future Gregory VII in the great work of ecclesiastical reform, had no hesitation in saying: "The whole Church forms, in some sort, but one single person. As she is the same in all, so in each one is she whole and entire; and just as man is called a microcosm, so each one of the faithful is, so to say, the Church in miniature." [14] *Nos utique sumus Ecclesia,* he also proclaimed in the name of all, priests and layfolk, in one of his sermons. No one could be mistaken about the thought of this great Churchman, the strenuous defender of the sacrament of order and the power of the Roman Church; by it all were awakened to a feeling of their responsibilities together with a holy pride in their Catholicism.

In those days, however, the name "Catholic" was less frequently in use than it is to-day. From the sixteenth century onwards it was increasingly necessary to use it as a symbol of integral Christian fidelity in opposition to not only the denials but also the partialities of heresy. Protestantism, whether primitive or modern, Lutheran or Calvinist, orthodox or liberal generally occurs as a religion of antitheses—and liberal theology is not the least marked by this characteristic. Either rites or morals, authority or liberty, faith or works, nature or grace, prayer or sacrifice, Bible or pope, Christ the Saviour or Christ the judge, sacraments or the religion of the spirit, mysticism or prophecy . . . but Catholicism does not accept these dichotomies and refuses to be merely Protestantism turned inside out. The splendid name of Catholic, that has been so fittingly translated by "comprehensive," a term "as full of welcome as outstretched arms, far-reaching like the works of God, a term of wonderful richness, filled with echoes of the infinite," has not always been perfectly grasped even by the Church's own children. Instead of signifying, in addition to a watchful orthodoxy, the expansion of Christianity and the fullness of the Christian spirit, it came to represent, for some, a sort of preserve, a system of limitations; the profession of Catholicism became linked with a distrustful and factious sectarian spirit. Abbot Rupert's complaint—always to the point because the evil exposed is so very human—became at that time more alarmingly relevant: *Cum Antiquus dierum dixerit: Dabo tibi gentes haereditatem tuam et possessionem tuam terminos terrae—futuri jam erant qui haereditatem ejus nimium vellent angustare.*[15] Certain untheological emphases on the principle of authority in the Church seemed a sort of safeguard to a religion which would be dangerous if left to itself. Except by this weakening of the Catholic spirit in so many minds it is hard to explain their toleration of that sacrilegious antithesis, worked out by non-Catholic writers, between Christianity and Catholicism, some blaming the Church for having betrayed her Founder's spirit, others praising her because, although she did not destroy the Christian spirit, she neutralized it. The fact that among these latter critics this spirit was generally called "the Jewish spirit" or "Protestant spirit" and that its essential nature was always confused with its distortions did not affect the main positions. For it was indeed the real meaning of the Scriptures, it was indeed without any possible equivocation true Christianity that was envisaged. The sacred deposit confided to the Church's care, that she might "give life to the world and quicken all mankind," that deposit, the whole reason for her existence, to safeguard which she has the right to demand any sacrifice of her children, this it was that they rejected in the very act of praising her. She was congratulated on removing all its strength—its "venom"—from that new wine of the Gospel which "ever gives new life to the vessel containing it." Ecclesiastical authority was seen as a merely human institution, in the service of a small party, and as the keeper of a "closed order." But the spirit of unity does not suffer the Bride thus to be parted from the Bridegroom. The Bride was not to be beguiled and the splendour of the *Catholica* to-day shines out in all its brilliance in many Christian hearts.

In Eucharistic theology, also, the narrowing effect of controversy made its influence felt. Many Protestants, in France Pastors Claude and Aubertin especially, were fond of saying that the primitive Church was drawn together and found its unifying force in the celebration of the "Lord's Supper." And even nowadays historians refuse to relate this supper with the institution in the Upper Room. In the beginning, they tell us, it was only a communion of the faithful among themselves in their eager expectation of Christ's coming and of the Kingdom; at the most a meal with Christ already mysteriously present among his own, not a partaking of Christ. Thenceforward, in spite of St Paul's clear teaching and of an unswerving, emphatic tradition, this symbolism of unity, magnified by some to the prejudice of the Eucharistic reality, became suspect to theology which had been for some time past ill-prepared to understand it for the reasons which we have seen. Theologians tended to see in this view of the Eucharist only a "subsidiary symbolism," a secondary significance, even a mere "morality" or "edifying consideration." If, then, this view was preserved with a certain respect as a link with the past, there was often a temptation to relegate it to an appendix so as to concentrate entirely on the proof of the real Presence. The very connexion between this Presence and the reality of the sacrifice was too little regarded for all its lessons to be drawn from it. *Nonne oportuit haec facere, et illa non omittere*? Did not the Fathers of the Council of Trent set that example? [16] Did not St Paschasius Radbertus, a ninth-century witness to Eucharistic realism, Durandus of Troarn, Lanfranc, Guitmond, eleventh-century defenders of the same faith against Berengarius, all make a point of emphasizing strongly the unifying function of the mystery of the altar, while adopting as their own all the symbolisms then current and declaring that they recognized in them the teaching of the Church? And does not this show in the clearest way how inter-dependent are those two truths handed down by tradition, since this unifying function without the reality of the Presence could be only an illusion?

When the causes of an evil have been seen it becomes easier to remedy it. The hoped for cure has already begun. The disappointment caused by the bitter fruits of individualism in all branches of theology, as well as the widely felt need of avoiding minor controversies so as to achieve a synthesis, creates the right atmosphere. A better but still too imperfect knowledge of the patristic period, as well as of the golden age of medieval theology, studied in conjunction with the former, is a considerable guarantee of success. Theologians have set to work. One of them not long since summoned his fellows to this work in no uncertain terms: "Our academic teaching," he said,

> must be saved from the individualism with which for the sake of clarity and the needs of controversy we seem to have allowed it to be associated since the sixteenth century. Our treatises on Grace and the Sacraments, on the Eucharist, even on the Church, are fashioned so as to give the impression that God the Redeemer is never faced with anything but an untold number of individuals, every one of them regulating on his own account the measure of his personal relationships with God, just like the taxpayers, the travellers and the employees who pass successively, with no organic connexion with each other, before the pay-desks and turnstiles of this world. In place of this conception we must bring back to the foreground the dogma of the Mystical Body in which the Church consists, where there are jointed limbs, a single nervous system, a single circulation of the blood and a single head, for the mystery of the Word incarnate is first and foremost the mystery of the New Adam and of the Head of Humanity.[17]

The task may appear heavy. But the preparation has been going forward for some time. An endeavour like that of the Catholic school of theology at Tübingen, begun upwards of a century ago, not to mention other, more isolated or less ambitious efforts, still shows that the sap is strongly rising. In 1819 in the prospectus of its official organ, the *Theologische Quartalschrift*, could be read an attempted definition of the Spirit and Essence of Catholicism: "The central fact is the revelation of the plan realized by God in humanity: this plan is an organic whole with a progressive development in history." Drey, Möhler, and their disciples commented on this definition in magnificent fashion, and the recent work of their successors has remained faithful to the first inspiration of the school. Other publications, coming from all points of the theological horizon, are like so many little streams which promise well for the mighty river that our century needs. But why speak of books and schools? For what gives ground for the greatest confidence is that this is no mere surface agitation, that the theologians themselves, the interpreters of the living tradition, are urged forward by a revival which is reflected primarily in events because it springs from the very depths of the Catholic conscience. Take, for example, the success from a religious point of view of such authors as Péguy or Claudel. Is it not extremely significant? But principally we should realize all the doctrinal implications of those great movements which in our day show so plainly the vitality of the Church: the missionary movement, the liturgical movement—so very different from that archæological sectarian spirit that at one time merely kept it in check—social movements like the J.O.C. in Belgium or in France. But we realize, too, the need in which they stand, if they are to fulfil their promise, of fully enlightened support and guidance. Again we see the urgent necessity of strictly theological doctrinal elaboration.

Just to imitate primitive Christianity or the Middle Ages will not be enough. We can revive the Fathers' all-embracing humanism and recover the spirit of their mystical exegesis only by an assimilation which is at the same time a transformation. For although the Church rests on eternal foundations, it is in a continual state of rebuilding, and since the Fathers' time it has undergone many changes in style; and without in any way considering ourselves better than our Fathers, what we in turn have to build for our own use must be built in our own style, that is, one that is adapted to our own needs and problems. We should gain nothing at all by breaking with an unhealthy individualism if in its place we dreamt of an impossible return to the past, for that is either an illusion which breeds schisms or a childish fancy which dulls the mind. Two conditions must govern our contemplation of the past. We must recognize, in the first place, the great diversity of the theories which have been professed in the course of Christian history on those innumerable subjects where religious truth comes in contact with our human pre-occupations. Secondly, we must realize to how great an extent these theories depend on social, intellectual or cultural conditions in a state of constant development. Only so can we contemplate and admire in all security the imposing unity of the great current of tradition, bearing in its ever-changing waves free from all contamination the same indefectible belief. It is only when we have realized very keenly how different we necessarily are in our human reactions, even towards revelation, and in our human methods of thought, even about dogma—from St Paul or Origen, St Thomas Aquinas or Bossuet, a monk of the Thebaid, a medieval craftsman or a Chinese neophyte—that we shall be conscious of the full intimacy of our profound union with them all in this same dogma by which they lived as we live to-day: *in eadem doctrina eademque sententia.* Then a return to the sources of antiquity will be the very opposite of an escape into a dead past. We shall understand how disastrous it would be if we were to forgo the great heritage which comes to us from the centuries of analysis and scientific research as well as from the definitive results, the clarifications, which emerge from the controversies. We shall not condemn self-examination or spiritual experience as if they derived from a merely individualist psychology or narcissist introspection, any more than, by an analogous method of misinterpretation, we shall confuse transcendental speculation with an abstract discarnate idealism. Even in our criticism of individualism we shall recognize that much of human progress has been bound up with its expansion, and that it is a question not so much of repudiating it as of rising above it. So too shall we reject the notion that the modern age has experienced outside the Church only error and decadence. That is an illusion, a temptation to which we have yielded only too often. The epoch of a "separated" philosophy was providential, like all others, and the fruits of the immense effort of thought which was undertaken in its name, and is still being undertaken, ought not, through our fault, to be left outside Catholicism. Certainly it requires a far more generous perspicacity to give a favourable reception to what has arisen outside our own body than to gather up what had at one time flourished within it and give it new life.

A much keener discernment too is necessary if mistakes are to be avoided. So the work that is called for at the present day is in many respects far more delicate than that required in the patristic age, in St Thomas Aquinas's time or even at the "humanist" epoch. It demands a comprehensive combination of opposing qualities, each of them brought to a high degree of excellence, one buttressed, so to say, on another, and braced with the greatest tension. Who would not feel overwhelmed and disheartened at the very outset in face of such requirements, however unassuming the part which he hopes to play in the great common task? But once again it is faith that wins the victory, and he who realizes his helplessness retires within himself and with the whole Church begs for the grace of the Holy Spirit.

For it is indeed to this grace, in our opinion, that must be ascribed the present fervent propagation and the vigorous life of the traditional doctrine of the Mystical Body. But such a doctrine will produce the results that we have a right to expect from it only if it is established on solid foundations. Great care must be taken lest it should give the impression of being merely a passing craze. Many are already growing impatient with the new scholasticism, the mixture of abstractions and metaphors in which it tends to be entangled. Others are anxious, not perhaps without some semblance at least of reason, at the vague mysticism and the unsystematic speculation that are in some instances the price of its success.[18] But there would be a much more serious danger if the very magnificence of the Pauline definitions and the commentaries on them were to dazzle certain minds, and cause in them the recrudescence of a kind of false gnosis, and if the consequent mental intoxication were to dissipate, as being something too humble, the charm of the Gospel itself. Paul is but a servant, an interpreter. His inspired teaching is not sufficient of itself, and it can never dispense with a continual reference to the only Master, the only Son in whom God has given us all, having expressed himself completely by him. But such a danger, which is entirely hypothetical, may be averted by prudent guidance. In any case, there are many problems to be probed, many applications and careful adjustments to be made if the movement which we are witnessing is not to be compromised. A doctrinal effort is imperative. For although dogma is essentially unchanging, the work of the theologian is never ended.

NOTES TO CHAPTER X

¹ *Marc-Aurèle*, 3rd edn., p. 626.

² The first edition of *Marc-Aurèle* was published in 1881; the *Didache* was discovered in 1883.

³ Cerfaux, *La théologie de l'Eglise suivant saint Paul*, p. 147, note: "Christianity appeared to St Paul not as a sort of initiation into a mysterious rite but as a summons to the whole of humanity. If it is true that Baptism or the Last Supper could be compared to initiations, it is with the reserve that the initiation is that of a new people which must embrace all humanity."

⁴ *Matt.* xxviii. 19. And *Mark* xiii. 10: "And unto all nations the Gospel must first be preached."

⁵ *Acts* ii. 5: there were present at the miracle of Pentecost "Jews, devout men out of every nation under heaven," etc. Cf. also the mention in *Luke* x of the seventy-two disciples; as many as there are nations, according to Jewish tradition.

⁶ *Apoc.* vii. 9; cf. xxi. 24–6; xxii. 17.

⁷ "Dominus universae carnis . . . omnis spiritus creator et visitator, qui multiplicas gentes super terram . . . Oramus te, Domine . . . errantes a populo tuo converte, . . . ut sciant gentes quoniam tu es Deus solus . . ." c. 59 (Latin version ed. by Dom Morin).

⁸ Further particulars on this subject in G. Fessard, *Théologie et Histoire* in *Dieu Vivant*, number 8.

⁹ *Quelques réflexions sur le matérialisme dialectique*, in *Unitas*, Dec. 1935, p. 12.

¹⁰ *Acta et decreta sacr. concil. recent. collectio lacensis*, t. 7, col. 1611–2. A certain exaggeration may be detected in this language. But see *ibid.*, col. 84, 397 and 921, the similar declarations of several Fathers of the Council (Gasser, Bp. of Brixen; Simor, Archbp. of Eztergom; Dechamps, Archbp. of Malines). St Thomas, IIa, IIae, q. 1, a. 9 ad 2; a. 10, c. and ad 1.

¹¹ L. de Grandmaison, *Jésus-Christ*, t. 2, p. 216–7.

¹² *Catech.* 16, c. 5 (P.G. xxxiii, 924).

¹³ Péguy, *L'Argent* (*Œuvres complètes*, p. 395).

¹⁴ *Liber qui appellatur Dominus vobiscum*, c. 5 and 10 (P.L. cxlv, 235 and 239). See Extract 48, p. 273.

¹⁵ *De divinis officiis*, lib. 10, c. 1 (P.L. clxx, 263).

¹⁶ "The Council declared that the Eucharist is also a symbol of the Mystical Body. Nowadays, through fear of misunderstanding, such language is hardly ever used." P. Batiffol, *l'Eucharistie*, p. 243. Mgr Batiffol himself gives a curious explanation of St Augustine's teaching as being a legacy of "an African tradition."

¹⁷ E. Masure, *Semaine sociale de Nice* (1934), pp. 230–1.

¹⁸ L. Cerfaux's analyses in *La théologie de l'Église suivant saint Paul* may help to ward off this danger without diminishing, as some have seemed to fear, the force of Pauline mysticism. I tried to show this in *La Vie Spirituelle* of May 1, 1943, pp. 470–

83: *L'Église dans saint Paul.* In a letter of January 18, 1943, Mgr Groeber, Archbishop of Freiburg-im-Bresgau, showed his anxiety on this subject; cf. Dom Lialine, *Une étape en ecclésiologie, l'encyclique Mystici Corporis* in *Irenikon,* 1946, p. 151 (the Encyclical itself cleared up the difficulty). More recently Fr Louis Bouyer mentioned a similar danger, perhaps with somewhat excessive severity, but with a proper regard for soundness of doctrine: "How are we to regard those speculations, without scriptural or patristic warrant, in which the Mystical Body designated as the σῶμα Χριστοῦ in St Paul, the visible Church herself, extended and explained by the invisible reality which cannot be separated from her, becomes some other undefined reality, first distinct from the visible Church, then separated from her and in a fair way to being in opposition to her." *Catholicisme et Œcuménisme* in *La Vie Intellectuelle,* June 1945, p. 23.

XI

PERSON AND SOCIETY

The first difficulty that occurs is too obvious to pass unnoticed and too serious to be evaded. By bringing out as clearly as we have done the social character of dogma and what might be called the unitary element of Catholicism do we not diminish or dangerously obscure that other no less essential truth that salvation is a personal matter for every individual, that at the Judgement "no one will find help in another" and that individuals are distinct for eternity? The assertions of so many mystics about the "unity" of the soul with God breed a certain obstinate mistrust, and if their utterances are not to be dismissed as pious exaggerations or loose poetical expressions they are condemned as pantheist. And is not the danger of pantheism immeasurably increased if we take too seriously that Augustinian formula *unus Christus amans seipsum* which condenses, as we have seen, the whole doctrine which we have so far set forth? Should it not at least be recognized that in the Christian tradition there are two teachings not easily reconcilable with one another about man's salvation? Not only are the three great scriptural figures—the heavenly Kingdom of the synoptic Gospels, St Paul's social Body, St John's mystical vine—irreducible and impatient of systematization, but the idea that each in its own way conveys seems at the outset incompatible—especially in the cases of St John and St Paul—with that strict personalism which we owe to the Christian revelation alone and which is of supreme practical importance.

Such an antinomy should not surprise us. This is not the only case in which revelation presents us with two assertions which seem at first unconnected or even contradictory: God creates the world for his own glory, *propter se ipsum,* and yet out of pure goodness; man is capable of action and free, and yet he can do nothing without grace, and grace works in him "both to will and to perform"; the vision of God is a free gift, and yet the desire of it is at the very root of every soul; the redemption is a work of pure mercy, and yet the rights of justice are no less respected. And so on. The whole of dogma is thus but a series of paradoxes, disconcerting to natural reason and requiring not an impossible proof but reflexive justification. For if the mind must submit to what is incomprehensible, it cannot admit what is unintelligible, and it is not enough for it to seek refuge in an "absence of contradiction" by an absence of thought. It finds stimulation, then, in its very submission. Despite its natural laziness it is almost obliged to delve beneath these superficial contradictions and to penetrate into those deeper regions where what was hitherto a stumbling-block becomes darkness visible. And when the mind tries to establish that coherent doctrinal statement which is known as theology—provided that it makes no mistake about the nature of its delicate task—the lights which it receives about itself are no small help to it in the work of philosophical consideration to which revelation invites it.

Thus the antinomy which we have mentioned obliges us to consider the relations between distinction and unity the better to understand the agreement between the personal and the universal. The dogmatic "paradox" makes us notice the natural paradox, for the former is a higher intensified statement of the latter. The paradox is this: that the distinction between the different parts of a being stands out the more clearly as the union of these parts is closer. The less they are "fragments" the more they are "members," and the greater is their convergence into unity. That is indeed a paradox for our distinctive—and still imaginative—logic, for a state of intelligence adapted to the consideration of material things. But it is, too, a truth enjoined on us by the twofold converging power of experience and faith—though we can never succeed in grasping it in its ultimate nature.

The experience of our senses puts us on the track. For we find that the higher a living thing rises in the scale of being the more internal unity does it acquire. The undifferentiated, entirely homogeneous being is as little *one* as it is possible to be; it is only a nameless agglomeration. In certain elementary plants, composed of the one same material, unity is so weak that every piece cut from the stalk produces a new plant. On the other hand in those cases where there is a complicated network of cells, the whole organism is concentrated and the greater individuality of the parts works for the unity of the whole.

If we start from the consideration of our higher functions, moral experience leads us towards the same asymptotic term as the observation of life. Does not the psychology of a group of men freely associated in the service of some great cause show entirely different characteristics from those to be observed in crowd psychology, and does not the same term "collective life" mean in the second case purely and simply *fusion* and in the first the exaltation of each personality? Likewise does not the mutual love of two beings complete them both, and call forth in each of them higher and more irreducible qualities? That is, in proportion as this love tends the more to true unity, because it is more spiritualized, so are these qualities more fully, more strictly personal.

Yet observation, whether biological or moral, can only furnish us with analogies; it can discern the truth that we are seeking, but only from afar, and does not allow us to state it in its fullness. The rough approximations of objective analysis, the suggestions of spiritual experience, all these are useless here. It is faith itself, by means of its most hidden mysteries, that brings us right up to the truth, though it cannot let us see it. It sets us in that very centre, to us irremediably dark, whence issues the definitive light. For do we not believe that there are three persons in God? It is impossible to imagine greater distinctions than those of this pure threefold relationship, since it is these very distinctions that constitute them in their entirety. And do they not arise in unity, the unity of one same Nature? [1] The most complete expression of Personality appears to us thus in the Being of whom every being is a reflexion—an image, a shadow, a trace—the consequence as well as the consecration of the highest unity.

Gregory Nazianzen, Gregory of Elvira and others, seeking to vindicate the faith of Nicaea, did not let this pass unnoticed. They considered that in order not to find a contradiction in the doctrine of the Trinity it was sufficient to set oneself free from those habits of thought that contemplation of material things develops. "When we speak of one only

God it is thought that we deny the Persons; but it only seems as if we do so; in reality we do not introduce into the God-head a division such as there is between bodies. Here we are no longer in the material order. . . ." [2] Our reliance on dogma enables us in its turn to strengthen and to amplify the initial suggestions furnished by our consideration of experience. Unity is in no way confusion, any more than dis-tinction is separation. For does not distinction imply a certain connexion, and by one of the most living bonds, that of a mutual attraction? True union does not tend to dissolve into one another the beings that it brings together, but to bring them to completion by means of one another. The Whole, therefore, is "not the antipodes, but the very pole of Personality." [3] "Distinguish in order to unite," it has been said, and the advice is excellent, but on the ontological plane the complementary formula, unite in order to distinguish, is just as inevitable. It is not necessary to fear unitary values in order to preserve personal ones, as if what was granted to the former were so much lost to the latter. "All is one, one is in the other, like the three Persons." [4] Man no more loses himself or disintegrates by becoming an integral part of that spiritual Body of which he must be a member than he does by submitting himself to God and uniting himself with him. On the contrary, he frees himself, he is strengthened in being. And as St Augustine said: *solidabor in Te, Deus meus,* so St Ildefonsus of Toledo could say with equal truth: *in unitate ipsius Ecclesiae solidari.*[5] Union differentiates. Soli-darity binds together.

There seems to be a greater comprehension at the present day—and this certainly is one of the best results of that "Christian philosophy" which is sought for in vain in any definitive system, but gives evidence of its presence by its widespread influence—that a person is not an idealized in-dividual nor a transcendent monad.[6] God "did not create the world apart from himself," nor did he create souls apart from one another. In the first place, does not each one need "the other"—the other whom if necessary he imagines and discovers in all things—so as to be awakened to conscious life? This psychological truth is the symbol of one more pro-found: we must be *looked at* in order to be *enlightened,* and the eyes that are "bringers of light" are not only those of the divinity. Again, does not to be a *person,* if we take the old original meaning of the word in a spiritual sense, always mean to have a part to play? Is it not fundamentally to enter upon a relationship with others so as to converge upon a Whole? The summons to personal life is a *vocation*, that is, a summons to play an eternal rôle. Now perhaps it will be understood how the historical character that we have found in Christianity, as well as the social, emphasizes the reality of this rôle: since the flow of time is irreversible nothing occurs in it more than once, so that every action takes on a special dignity and an awful gravity; and it is because the world is a history, a single history, that each individual's life is a drama.

In the One there is no solitariness, but fruitfulness of life and warmth of presence. *Numquam est sola Trinitas, numquam egens divinitas.* In the all-sufficient Being there is no selfishness but the exchange of a perfect Gift. The created mind, although so faint a copy of him who is, is none the less a reproduction in some sort of his structure—*ad imaginem fecit eum*—and practised eyes can discern the stamp of the creating Trinity. There is no solitary person: each one in his very being receives of all, of his very being must give back to all. *Quid tam tuum quam tu? sed quid tam non tuum quam tu, si alicujus est quod es?* [7] It is like a two-way method of exchange, a twofold mode of presence. Fundamentally, personality can be imagined a network of concentric shafts; in full development, if a paradox may be used as an expression of its interior paradox, it can be called a centrifugal centre. Thus it can also be said, to exalt its inner richness and to make clear its character as an end, which all others must acknowledge, that "a person is a whole world," [8] but it must also be added at once that this "world" presupposes others with which it makes up one world only. If there is not admitted beyond all visible mortal societies a mystical and eternal community, beings are left in their solitary state or are crushed into annihilation; in any case they are destroyed, for suffocation too can cause death.

These indications may enable some to escape from the dilemma in which their desire to safeguard some keenly realized aspect of the whole truth has placed them. Indeed, just as "rebel individualists" and "conformist sociologists" have both been non-suited in their ill-conceived controversy about the nature of the earthly city, so too, and with all the more reason, can we refuse to take sides in any discussion about the heavenly city. In this connexion it is useful to re-call the first principle of Augustinian mysticism: *inter animam et Deum nulla natura interposita.* Each individual needs the *mediation* of all, but no one is kept at a distance by any intermediary. By this principle, which Augustine saw so clearly in the light of his faith, the neo-Platonist idea that pseudo-Dionysius only partially rectified is completely trans-formed: the hierarchic vision of the world is replaced by that of the *Civitas Dei*—a vision by no means individualist, but how much more truly spiritual! Between its different persons, whatever the variety of their gifts, the inequality of their "merits," there obtains no scale of the degrees of being, but in the likeness of the Trinity itself—and, by the media-tion of Christ in whom all are enfolded, within the Trinity itself—a unit of circumincession. It is clear, then, that each person by itself does not constitute a final end, is not a posi-tive, independent little world: God does not love us as so many separate beings—*Sociale quiddam est humana natura.*[9] But we can no more follow the upholders—if there are any —of such a personal atomism than we can those who, in reaction against attributing an excessive value to the human person, would make profession of a kind of transcendent specificism, and would make the end of the person subordi-nate to some other, supposedly higher, end: for it is possible to sacrifice the individual to the species or to require of a man the sacrifice of his earthly life for the community, but to speak of the sacrifice of even one single personal being for the perfection of the universe is to imagine a factitious op-position between two sorts of "good" which can only coin-cide. A universe whose beauty was bought at such a cost would be valueless. The consequences of both attitudes, if they are taken in all the rigour of their abstract meaning, are far-reaching, for whoever rejects the complete subordination of persons to the universe runs the risk, if he does not take care, of falling into an anarchic individualism so long as he has not a clear idea of another universe which is spiritual, while on the other hand whoever perceives that individual good is subordinate to universal good may go so far as to uphold that the perfection of the universe, which is identical with God's glory, requires that some should be damned: and that is a blasphemy which is certainly no better than the idolatry which it seeks to rebut.

The society of persons is not an animal society. Spiritual

unity does not entail a unity of species. If, to define the transcendent city, we were willing to rely without interpretation or reserve on the image of a city built of living stones —*vivis ex lapidibus*—we should be merely deluding ourselves. This figure is indeed traditional, but its meaning is quite different from what we might be tempted to read into it. *Vivis et electis lapidibus*. In the well-known Dedication hymn, as previously in the Apocalypse, the first epistle of Peter and many another similar text,[10] it is in no wise a question of the universe in general, but of the heavenly Jerusalem, of that city of God where none of the elect is sacrificed. For "nothing soiled enters therein," and stones which were not worthy to be used for the building have been already rejected.

"We have learnt from Peter," writes Origen for example,

> that the Church is a house of God built of living stones, a spiritual house for a holy priesthood. Solomon building the temple is in that respect a figure of Christ. Each of the living stones (which are the saints), according to the worth that they have acquired in this earthly life, will have its place in the heavenly temple: one, apostle or prophet, will be laid at the foundation to uphold all that is built upon it. Then another, upheld by the Apostles, will bear along with them the weaker stones. There will be, also, a stone within the building where are the ark and the cherubim. Another will be the stone of the entrance hall and yet another the altar stone of the first fruits.[11]

This temple, this holy city, which the prophet in contemplation saw in all its future glory, and which, unseen, must be built up stone by stone here below—*ad aedificandam Ecclesiam*—is, therefore, quite unlike our human buildings with their foundations beneath the earth, their invisible component parts and their dark crypts: for it is built in heaven, and its foundation is at its pinnacle; it is a city wholly of light—*lucerna ejus est Agnus*—and it needed not the "outer darkness" to enable it to shine forth. Without giving up the analogy of a building, we shall not use in every detail a metaphor which carries with it its own correction. The more we aim at an exact understanding of the spiritual truth, the better shall we realize, thus surmounting that conflict of opinion in which each party tries to preserve some essential aspect of the truth, that

Catholicism and personalism are in harmony and reinforce one another.

Is it not clear, moreover, that these two scales of value, so far from harming each other, have been developed in conjunction? That fact must be acknowledged even though our superficial logic cry scandal. Christian revelation

has extended to the utmost the confines of the human community into which every "I" is born, and has at the same time done the most to consolidate the existence of this "I," the lowest element of that community. It is a revelation of universal brotherhood in Christ and a revelation of the definitive value of each man. . . . The term "person" is suitable in every way to denote the two opposing qualities that follow in this way from our supernatural destiny: on the one hand it serves to show that by reason of this destiny each of us acquires a worth which is not to be compared with that of the whole world of nature below us, so that it becomes for all the object of a sovereign respect; on the other hand, in this absolute value, communicated by Christ, our freedom realizes the only end which is worthy of it; that is, the achievement of perfect community among all men.[12]

The whole history of the Church, if we interpret it aright, testifies to this—all Christianity in action, whether in the experience of its mystics, or in the work of its great Apostles, or in its collective life at the periods of its most vigorous growth, especially those favoured days of its origin to which, in no spirit of archaism, we must always be looking back. The Fathers' meditations about this collective life may indeed be lengthy, and they may never succeed in translating into human language a truth which stands out in all clarity and in concrete form quite explicitly from the beginning. The Holy Spirit that Christ promised to send to his own, his Spirit, is at the same time he who causes the Gospel to penetrate into the soul's depths, and he who spreads this Gospel on all sides. He creates in man new depths which harmonize him with the "depths of God," and he projects man out of himself, right to the very end of the earth; he makes universal and spiritualizes, he personalizes and unifies.

Nowhere else is this twofold movement of the Holy Spirit,

this simultaneous and correlative twofold action, to be seen to better advantage than in the conversion of St Paul in the account that he himself gives of it. Paul uttered one of the most novel and most pregnant of phrases that ever came from the mouth of man on the day when, constrained to present his own *Apologia* in order to lead back his beloved Galatians to the straight path, he dictated these words: "when it pleased him who separated me from my mother's womb, and called me by his grace, *to reveal his Son in me. . . .*" [13] It is not merely to reveal his Son to me, to show him to me in some vision—whatever we may say about the external prodigy recounted in the Acts of the Apostles—or to cause me to comprehend him objectively, but to reveal him *in me*. By revealing the Father and by being revealed by him, Christ completes the revelation of man to himself. By taking possession of man, by seizing hold of him and by penetrating to the very depths of his being Christ makes man go deep down within himself, there to discover in a flash regions hitherto unsuspected. It is through Christ that the person reaches maturity, that man emerges definitively from the universe, and becomes conscious of his own being. Henceforth, even before that triumphant exclamation: *Agnosce, O Christiane, dignitatem tuam,* it will be possible to praise the dignity of man: *dignitatem conditionis humanae.* The wise man's precept "Know thyself" takes on a new meaning. Every man who says "I" gives utterance to something that is absolute and definitive.

Now in the same passage of the Epistle to the Galatians Paul adds: "That I might preach him among the Gentiles." His *conversion* is a *vocation.* He cannot remain in quiet recollection with the Christ whom he has just discovered within himself. By the same token, and with the same urgent need as the service of this Christ, the service of men, his brethren—of all men without respect of persons—calls him. "The whole human race can find room within his heart." That too is a novelty. In this summons to the apostolate of the Gentiles, as in the reproach that Christ, taking to himself the sufferings of his own, had just addressed to the Apostle, there was something implied by which man could complete the exploration of his own true dimensions: for through the Christian revelation not only is the scrutiny that man makes of himself made more searching, but his examination of all about him is at the same time made more comprehensive.

Henceforth the idea of human unity is born. That image of God, the image of the Word, which the incarnate Word restores and gives back to its glory, is "I myself"; it is also the other, every other. It is that aspect of *me* in which I coincide with every other man, it is the hallmark of our common origin and the summons to our common destiny. It is our very unity in God.

If, then, there took place in our past some "decisive" event that the historian must record with "emotion" as having opened out to us the perspective of "the joy of an essentially universal union," we shall know where such an event took place, and shall not seek it in Greece in the discovery by one of Pythagoras's followers of an instrument of calculation—pure arithmetic. Without failing to recognize the immense importance of such an invention we find it impossible to ascribe to it, in itself, any such kind of influence. "The universality of communion in the incorruptible and ineluctable light of the Word" can appear to us in such a context only as a *contradictio in terminis,* for in that Word intelligences coincide but beings are not united. Coincidence is no more union than proximity is presence. There is no real unity without persisting difference. And how can one here speak "unequivocally" of a "solidarity of the personal and the universal" since in fact both these terms are abolished? Would not that be just another way of "making the hard laws of analysis yield to the convenience of synthesis"? Why not confess that this joy is a deceitful dream unless we are to seek it in something better than a purely abstract function—which is itself only conceivable in reference to spatial multiplicity? Anyway, it is a fact that nowhere outside the influence of Christianity has man ever succeeded in defining its conditions; he has always wavered between the imagining of an individual survival in which beings remain separated and a theory that absorbs them in the One. No abstract logic—whether it uses concepts or judgements, the law of identity or the law of participation—will ever completely overcome this dilemma. There must be basically a real apperception which seizes at a single glance, beyond all spatial intuition, the bond between the personal and the universal.

But for the realization of this bond it is not enough for it to be merely apprehended. The idea of unity is not unity itself. The revelation of Christ cannot be dissociated from his action; we cannot gain the advantage of the one while resisting the other. If, as we have seen, an isolated person is meaningless, on the other hand a fully realized, that is, a perfectly universalized, person without Christ is an impossibility. For how can we, left to ourselves, make our way through the corridor which must lead us to the new world, that world "ruled by the mysterious immanence of one in all, and of all in each one"? [14] A twofold obstacle, naturally impassable, rises before us to bar our way into the Promised Land: our egoism and our individuality. There is both a moral and a metaphysical obstacle, the first an intensified expression of the second. For in spite of the desire of our very being we do not wish nor are we naturally able to communicate ourselves whole and entire to all, effecting that miracle of unexclusive choice in which the *Agape* consists. . . . But what is impossible to mere man becomes possible to man made divine, and what natural understanding rejected as fanciful becomes the sacred object of our hope. Christ, by completing humanity in himself, at the same time made us all complete—but in God. Thus we can say, in the end, taking up again St Paul's εἷς and St Augustine's *una persona*, that we are fully persons only within the Person of the Son, by whom and with whom we share in the circumincession of the Trinity. Just as Christ, his victory once accomplished, must hand over the Kingdom to his Father in an eternal act, so— and it is still the same act expressed in other words—he will never cease to make us complete, to make us persons in himself.

Catholic spirituality has not to choose, therefore, between an "interior" and a "social" tendency, but all its authentic forms in their extraordinary variety will share in both. None of us can afford to forget St Paul's poignant phrase: "He loved me and gave himself up for me"; nor Christ's answering words to Pascal in the *Mystère de Jésus:* "I shed this drop of blood for you"; nor the summons of the *Imitation* to silence and retirement. We shall be able to make our own—without being obliged to suspect egocentrism—the phrase that comes like a refrain from Newman's lips, "God and myself"—a phrase that recalls so directly St Ignatius's advice to those who give the *Exercises: Sinat Creatorem cum creatura, et creaturam cum suo Creatore ac Domino immediate operari.*[15] Is not all spiritual life made up of these contrasts, alternating rhythms or, rather, experienced coincidences? Nothing would be more fatal than to believe that a true Catholicity is easily realized. No one attains it save by the narrow way. Its first requisite is to be found in detachment and solitude, and the most charitable of men, the saint, is primarily, according to the ancient etymology, a being apart. A charity fully conscious of its own requirements does not neglect those most hidden tasks, nor hold in low esteem the so-called "duties towards oneself," any more than it forgets justice. If, from the first conversion, all must be enforced by charity, that perfect unity which charity alone effects and which alone merits man's endeavour can only be the end of a race, the victory after many a hard-fought struggle. For

> there exists in us what we ought to love in others—an image of God to be restored. To leave it blemished or defaced in ourselves is a sign that, despite our assertions, what interests us in others is not their true being, but that they provide us merely with an opportunity of satisfying our need of exteriorization. . . . Need one add that an activity of this sort will never produce fruitful results? Deprived of its necessary regulating principle, it merely results in indiscretion, it knows nothing of that respect which a soul deserves. On the religious plane it develops into the clumsiest and most harmful kind of proselytism.[16]

Furthermore, charity can distinguish between those vague dreams that are so harmful to concrete action and that universal intention which, by transforming the humblest task, makes a man give himself up to it wholeheartedly. Charity realizes that great self-denial is necessary for a man that he may have something to give, and that to give is not to scatter oneself abroad—and that many natural bonds must be severed if the divine relationships of grace are to be established. And what is more urgent to-day than to recall man to himself? Just as with culture and thought, so with spirituality: it is useless unless it is disinterested. In all the things of the Spirit we must shun utilitarianism as a cause not only of superficiality but also of corruption, and as an unfailing source of insincerity. "The capacity for presence," on the other hand, "grows with the capacity for recollection." Over and above all agreement on the plane of the perceptible, of words and actions, *spiritual* union takes place only through what is most personal in us, and, it has been said, "through all that is most incommunicable," for there is no real communion in what is externally communicated.

The hidden virtues, those virtues, as Bossuet said, "in which the public has no part," are not without their social justification. Nor are the contemplative orders. Religious who devote themselves to the study of the scriptures and who "meditate night and day on the law of the Lord" do so, according to St Thomas, for the general good of the Church, and that is why they can lawfully live on alms, though they neither preach nor teach: a bold conclusion, obliging one who profits by it to an earnest examination of conscience. But its fundamental principle cannot be contested. As Fr Teilhard de Chardin puts it in a magnificent simile:

> If we were as perceptive of the invisible light as of the thunder clouds, the lightning or the rays of the sun, pure souls would seem to us, in this world, as active by the very fact of their purity as the snowy summits whose impassive peaks continually suggest to us the invigorating currents of the higher atmosphere.

On the other hand personal religion and interior life are by no means synonymous with individualism and religious subjectivism. "True religion is a life hidden in the heart" (Newman), but it has nothing to do with an egotistic introspection. St Cyprian's words about prayer in secret are still true: *Publica est nobis et communis oratio, et quando oramus, non pro uno sed pro populo toto oramus, quia totus populus unum sumus. Deus pacis et concordiae magister qui docuit unitatem, sic orare unum pro omnibus voluit, quomodo in uno omnes ipse portavit.*[17] After having declared *Deum et animam scire cupio*, St Augustine does not fail to add: *Animas nostras et Deum simul concorditer inquiramus.*[18] Ruysbroeck bestows on the highest degree of spiritual life the name of "common life," because in this state man is at the service of all. It was understood in this sense by St John of the Cross, and Eliseus of the Martyrs reports him to us as follows:

> John of the Cross interpreting those words of Christ: "Did you not know that I must be about my Father's business?" said that here the Father's business should be understood to mean nothing else than the redemption of the world . . . and that it is an evident truth that com-

passion for one's neighbour increases in proportion as the soul is united to God by love.[19]

An interest in Catholic mysticism may prove disastrous for a certain spiritual æstheticism and for amateurs of psychological analysis, but it is only such parasites that it injures in this way. It restores to the soul its strength and energy. The same correlation is found between "experience" and "thought," and it would provide a further example of harmful "specificism" to place them in opposition to each other, as if a choice must be made between personal experience without universal value and "depersonalized" universal thought; as if self-awareness and reason had to be sacrificed to one another. For the same awareness could engender the story of the *Confessions* and also think out the *City of God,* and it was St Augustine too who, following St Paul, indissolubly united historical synthesis and reflexive analysis in a whole series of correlations, every attempt at a deeper self-knowledge corresponding to a widening of his outlook upon the universe.[20] The new Man, who is the universal man, is at the same time the interior man: ὁ ἔσω.

The synthesis spoken of by Fr Maréchal in an important passage of his *Studies in the Psychology of the Mystics* thus seems quite traditional. "It was realized at every period, in practice," he writes, "but nowadays it seems on the way to explicit doctrinal formulation." "We understand better," or perhaps we are again beginning to understand better

that the Catholic mystic is not merely a separated being in comparison with the rest of the faithful, an escapist in search of some hazy transcendence; that the mystic ascent is made up of "integrations" rather than "suppressions"; that no specific characterization of the common Christian life should be effaced by it; in short, that the perfect mystic would be as such the perfect Christian, and we mean a Christian whom the highest of divine favours does not withdraw from solidarity in the sufferings and the triumphs of the Church militant.[21]

How indeed could Christian mysticism, the foretaste of the Beatific Vision, the "noviciate" and the "anteroom" of eternity, the secret entry into the City of God and, at the same time, the return to original purity, how could it be anything but the very opposite to Solipsism? The community supports the mystic with it, and in its turn is supported by him. In the end it is an ever more real and more widespread spiritual society that must be rediscovered in the deepest, most abandoned interior silence. Claudel extolled it in his *Cantique de Palmyre*, where we hear the perfect echo of the ancient Fathers:

No one of our brethren, even should he desire it, can separate himself from us, and in the meanest miser, in the heart of the prostitute or the most squalid drunkard there is an immortal soul with holy aspirations which, deprived of daylight, worships in the night. I hear them speaking when we speak and weeping when I fall upon my knees. I accept them all! I take and understand them all; there is not one of them I do not need, not one that I can do without! There are many stars in the heavens and their numbering is beyond all my power of calculation, and yet there is not one that I do not need in my praise of God. There are many living beings, yet we see scarcely any give forth their light, while the rest are whirled around in the dark chaos which contains them; there are many souls, but there is not one of them with whom I am not in communion in that sacred apex where it utters its *Pater Noster*.[22]

NOTES TO CHAPTER XI

[1] Of the Trinity can be said what the council of Fréjus (797) said of baptism: "sociale bonum et individuum sacramentum," for the same council adds: "sacramentum igitur sanctae Trinitatis" (M.G.H., *Concilia*, 2, p. 183).

[2] Gregory Nazianzen, *Orat.* 21, c. 2 (P.G. xxxv, 1084).

[3] Fr Teilhard de Chardin, S.J., see Extract 50, p. 277.

[4] Pascal, *Penses*, Br. fr. 483.

[5] *De cognitione baptismi*, c. 96 (P.L. xcvi, 147).

[6] Gabriel Marcel, *Acte et Personne*, in *Recherches Philosophiques*, t. 4 (1934–5), p. 160.

[7] Augustine in his commentary on the words "Mea doctrina non est mea," *In Joannem*, tract. 29, n. 3 (P.L. xxxv, 1629).

[8] J. Maritain, *Humanisme intégral*, p. 17.

[9] Augustine, *De bono conjugali*, c. 1.

[10] *I Petr.* ii. 5. *Apoc.* xxi.

[11] *In Joan.*, t. 10, c. 39–41 (Pr., pp. 215–9).

[12] G. Fessard, *Pax nostra* (1936), pp. 39–40. See Extract 50, p. 277.

[13] *Gal.* i. 15–6. Cf. *Rom.* vii. 17.

[14] J. Monchanin, *De la solitude à Dieu, op. cit.,* p. 293. Cf. G. Fessard, *Pax nostra,* p. 335.

[15] *Exercitia spiritualis,* annotatio 15 a. Newman, *Apologia,* chap. 4.

[16] Yves de Montcheuil, *Le "ressentiment" dans la vie morale et religieuse d'après M. Scheler,* in *Recherches de Science religieuse,* 1937, p. 149.—It is this caricature of zeal and charity which is the real object of so many of the criticisms of the Catholic apostolate.

[17] *De dominica oratione,* c. 7 (P.L. cxlv, 246C).

[18] *Soliloques,* lib. 1, n. 7 and 20 (P.L. xxxii, 872 and 880).

[19] Quoted by Bruno de J.-M., O.C.D., *Saint Jean de la Croix* (1929), p. 299.—English translation: *St John of the Cross* (London, 1936), p. 290.

[20] See above, Chap. VI.

[21] *Études sur la psychologie des Mystiques,* t. 2 (1937), p. 15, and pp. 253–4.

[22] *Conversations dans le Loir-et-Cher* (1935), p. 119.

XII

TRANSCENDENCE

The progress effected in the last century or two by the social sciences has accustomed us to a better realization of the dependence of the individual upon those various communities that are far more than a mere framework or external support to him, especially upon the great human community, of which the others are, each in its rank, only the necessary distributions. At the same time, progress in the physical and natural sciences combined with the increasing use of the genetic method in all branches of science has enabled us to discover not only the immensity but also the fecundity of the historical process. In that way too we have become more fully aware of the extent and the depth of the social bond. We see every individual rooted in humanity as humanity itself is rooted in nature, and the scientific enrichment of this perception provides a natural basis of great value for a better understanding of our Catholicism. On every side, moreover, in our divided world there are appearing desires for unity which are themselves the outcome of the fruitful conjunction between an ever-active though frequently repudiated Catholicism and the immense progress of our knowledge of man both in time and in space: desires which are powerless, when they are not also mischievous, in the secularist and entirely materialist shape which they are wont to assume. But that is no reason for refusing to perceive and for not trying to elucidate the germs of genuine truth which these desires cannot completely destroy without dying themselves. Whence arise both those "harmonies" which it would be most wrong to leave in the shade and, at the same time, the risks of misunderstanding which it is no less important to avert. For the twofold historical and social character that we have recognized in Catholicism should no more hide from our eyes the continual presence of the Eternal and his unchanging transcendence than it should allow us to belittle the value of each person in whom shines the image of the Eternal.

In face of these contrasting but complementary difficulties we can see taking shape not, indeed, a new apologetic but a renewal of the most traditional form of apologetics—and should not apologetics, just like any other discipline, enjoy constant renewals if it is to remain alive?

We have often been told—and in tones of finality—that all the paltry ideas of our Christian forebears about human history have been swept away by modern discoveries, which have shown to us the vastness and the complexity of this history. Even to-day theologians are to be found who perpetuate the objection by their timorous attitude to these discoveries. Do not we see some of them—incredible as it may seem—afraid to acknowledge in all simplicity that man's existence on our planet is of much longer standing than the authors of the biblical chronologies ever suspected? Man, "whose archives are the earth. . . ." But defence of our faith requires of us to be neither timorous nor blind. We realize that the men of each generation could possess no more than the science of the time, that revelation makes no difference here: its light is of another order. Neither the biblical writers nor the Fathers nor the medieval theologians could have known, obviously, about Neanderthal man or *Sinanthropus,* nor could they have had precise knowledge about the Chinese. But the material narrowness of their view was no hindrance to its formal breadth. And it is this latter which is proper to Catholicism; however remote the horizons which modern science discovers Catholicism spontaneously incorporates them. Discoveries in astronomy, at first so disturbing, have resulted in the freeing of Christian thought from the confines of an ancient cosmology, ill-suited to its genius; and what was at first taken to be a dogmatic crisis was only a wholesome surprise. Thus we can be assured that the fresh conclusions forced upon us about our history and our empirical origins will help us, after their own fashion, to probe more deeply into the meaning of our Catholicism, in its concern for the whole history of man and its solicitude for each member of the human family.

The unity of this human family as a whole is the subject,

we have said, of some of the deepest yearnings of our age. It longs to organize it, to bring it to complete awareness of itself, in fine to humanize it by making it fully one. The Catholic cannot adopt this programme as it stands, nor can he simply reject it as a disastrous illusion. But just as he can use man's aspirations to go beyond himself and "play the God" to persuade him to accept that death to self which is the indispensable condition of entering on Life, so can he use the no less profound, no less natural desire for human unity—often stifled, often perverted as it is—to lead men of good will to the threshold of Catholicism, which alone can effect this unity in its highest sense.

The first step would be to show to those who have realized that no end short of humanity itself deserves absolutely to be loved and sought—and there are many such men in many different camps, even in those which are most opposed to one another—that they are obliged to look higher than the earth in the pursuit of their quest. For a transcendent destiny which presupposes the existence of a transcendent God is essential to the realization of a destiny that is truly collective, that is, to the constitution of this humanity in the concrete. Otherwise it is not really for humanity that the sacrifice is made; it is still, despite assertion to the contrary, for other individuals, who in their transitory outward form contain nothing that is absolute and do not stand for any essentially higher value than those who are sacrificed to them; in the last resort it is all for one generation of humanity—the last—which is yet no greater than the others, and which will pass away like the others. There are two reasons for discouragement which explain easily enough why a humanitarian optimism can offer no resistance to the solvent of reflective thought. "I have no wish to sacrifice myself to that terrible God called future society," exclaims a character in a contemporary Russian novel.[1] That is a very natural protest, possibly inspired by egoism, but one which cannot be reproved by reason. For no unselfishness can be sustained in face of an absurdity, and to require a worthy object for one's sacrifice is not to transform the sacrifice into self-interest. On such reasoning perspicacity and generosity would be mutually exclusive. It is absolutely necessary, then, that humanity should have a meeting-place in which, in every generation, it can be gathered together, a centre to which it can converge, an Eternal to make it complete, an Absolute which, in the strongest and most real sense of the word, will make it *exist*. It needs a magnet to attract it. It needs—but this last point would involve us in fresh considerations—Another to whom it can give itself.

"Becoming," by itself, has no meaning; it is another word for absurdity. And yet, without transcendence, that is, without an Absolute actually present, found at the heart of the reality which comes to be, working upon it, really making it move, there can only be an indefinite "becoming"—unless of course complete disaster makes an end of all things and absurdity discovers at last the truth of its being, if one may so speak, by becoming nothingness. If there is "becoming" there must be fulfilment, and if there must be fulfilment there must have been always something else besides "becoming." The Christian more than all others looks forward to the new Man. But he does not desire this new Man on the earthly horizon, for on that level he would be only a myth, since he cannot be what he must be if he is to remain new: completed, perfected Man. If we want to renew our hope of the coincidence of these two terms, new and perfect, which together and indissolubly sum up our human ideal, we must go back to St Paul: we too must believe in Christ.

In the bringing together of these very simple ideas there is contained, it seems, in principle a refutation of that social humanism which is the present phase of man's hopeless endeavour to save himself by his own efforts. Not indeed the only refutation, but a variety of the only valid one; of that which sets free the truth within the error by which it was enslaved and makes it appear greater and more beautiful in the eyes of those who had been already unwittingly attracted by it, that which refutes by bringing salvation.

But complete refutation can be achieved only by the revelation of the complete truth, and to this end we might follow the suggestions that Canon Masure puts forward in a page which contains a whole programme. In this author's view (and it is the legitimacy and importance of just such a view which we have been trying to show):

Christ is not only the bearer of an eternal message which he repeats to the astonished ears of successive individuals, but also he in whom humanity finds an unexpected answer to the problem of its organic unity. The Church is not only Christ's foundation; she is also his Body and he is her Head and her Life. Christianity is not only the perfect religion rising upon the ruins of all the defeated religions, in particular upon the debris of abrogated Judaism; it is primarily the conversion of all the ancient moral and mystic efforts of humanity into a higher religion, which, in fulfilling their aspirations, transcends them. And man, instead of seeing Catholicism appear at the conclusion of a series of inexorable syllogisms as an obligation superimposed upon his natural duties, welcomes it as soon as it tries to satisfy in him those limitless higher appetites which God has placed in his soul, and in the first place this need of social unity, of a holy union with all the members of an organism of which we are but the personal cells. The sacramental system, instead of seeming the final humiliation imposed upon fallen reason, is proffered, on the contrary, as the unique and divine means for the transmission, in a human manner, of God's grace to our souls as they live in our flesh, to our bodies as they live in society.

And so with all our great dogmas: the divinity of Christ, the foundation of the Church, the unity of faith, the sacramental system—instead of seeming so many isolable sections of a composite and possibly arbitrary system—combine with one another to provide what is certainly the most unlooked for and the least necessary solution, but at the same time the most logical, and the most in conformity with the fundamental laws of our being. We are members of a single race and together we seek union with God in our bodies and in our souls. "So the Wisdom of the invisible God is the head of the body of the Church. . . . The fullness of the divinity dwells in the flesh, so that God may be all in all, and that all may be summed up in Christ." [2]

Having thus identified ourselves with the genuinely human characteristics of the preponderant movement of our time, which seeks to set it right by making plain both its end and the conditions of its development, we must now have the courage to bring more direct criticism to bear upon the by-paths into which this movement has been ensnared. In examining this entirely secularized concept of society, which at the present time dominates men's minds everywhere and only degrades what it has inherited of the historical and social character of our faith, we must have the courage to show ourselves resolutely reactionary.

At the present day we are submerged in time. The enormous success of the philosophies of "becoming" as well as the distressing results which have lately imperilled their authority have had in this respect the same effect. Empty dreams and fears, exacerbated by the violence of their contrast, hope in the future and anxiety for the morrow, have laid hold of our consciousness. Visions of concord among men and of indefinite progress, or tragic realization of the chaos in which we flounder, weighed down by the intolerable burden of the day, our terror of approaching catastrophes or our straining towards an unknown future from which every advantage is expected, all hide the present reality from our eyes, and in an age when man, as a reward for his immense effort, has at last achieved a degree of repose, he is no longer able to achieve that fundamental repose that would save him from himself and at the same time enable him to find himself. Even in these times of intoxication mingled with anxiety, amidst the most pressing necessities, it is the rôle of the Christian, a man among his brother men, buoyed up by the same aspirations and cast down by the same anxieties, to raise his voice and remind those who forget it of their own nobility; man is only himself, he only exists for himself *here and now* if he can discover within himself, in silence, some untouched region, some mysterious background which, whether gloomy or cheerful, commonplace or tragic, is not encroached upon by the cares of the present. To seek to give him back an understanding of this is not to plunge him in the waters of Lethe, to stupefy him with opium, or to give him Dutch courage. And to call back to the duties of the day one who lives entirely in a future which he sees rising out of his own creative energy is by no means to try to snatch from him his faith in man. On the contrary, it is to make him have a respect for man wherever he is found. It is to forbid his ever making use of the man of to-day as a mere instrument for the purposes of the man of to-morrow.[3] Above all, it is to prevent him, both now or in the future, whether rich or poor, successful or unsuccessful, from being entirely absent, completely estranged from himself.

Here we come face to face with the quasi-religious ideologies which are struggling to-day for the conquest of the world, and particularly with Marxism, the most powerful of them all. In the short statement of his "Fifth Thesis on Feuerbach" Marx, relating his thought to his predecessor's, unconsciously summed up the most fatal of the objections which lie against himself. "Feuerbach," he wrote in that spring of 1845 when Marxism was born, "dissolves the religious being into the human being. But the human being is not an abstraction that inheres in isolated individuals. It is found in reality only in the whole body of social relationships." [4] We may interpret: Feuerbach dissolved the religious being into the human being; Marx, completing the process, dissolved the human being into the social being. What was to exalt man ended in his ruin.

There is in man an eternal element, a "germ of eternity," which already "breathes the upper air," which always, *hic et nunc,* evades the temporal society.[5] The truth of his being evades his being itself. For he is made in the image of God, and in the mirror of his being the Trinity is ever reflected. But it is only a mirror, an image. If man, by an act of sacrilege, inverts the relationship, usurps God's attributes, and declares that God was made to man's image, all is over with him. The transcendence that he repudiates was the sole warrant of his own immanence. Only by acknowledging himself to be a reflexion could he obtain completeness, and only in his act of adoration could he find his own inviolable depths. Henceforth, then, he is estranged from himself, *dispersed,* separated from himself, and far more grievously and fundamentally than in Marx's description! We will suppose this man completely "emancipated." We will suppose him, *per impossibile,* freed from all economic constraint, from all exploitation by his fellows, from every tyranny of the state. He is not therefore set free. Society no longer weighs upon him, in the sense that he is no more dominated, exploited by other men. Yet it weighs upon him more heavily than ever, since he is entirely absorbed by it. Previously, something within him could evade constraint and exploitation; now he is no more than a social function, a "network of social relationships."

That is not, we are well aware, the ideal cherished by those who dream of a stateless and classless society. They seek, on the contrary, a future age when "man shall be for man the supreme being," when human intercourse shall be "exchanges of confidence and of love," when the "free development of each individual shall be the condition of the free development of all." Yet of a certainty what was described in the last paragraph is the logical development of that initial negation that they no longer dare call in question. In a non-transcendent society, the reduction of man to his "social relationships" will work inevitably to the prejudice of his personal interiority, and will beget a tyranny of some kind, however novel. Moreover, have we not already the right to think, short as is our experience of this sort of thing, that it provides our analysis with its first confirmation? When Marx's followers eventually become aware of this, they will have no longer any inclination to extol that "total revolution" that they suppose themselves to have achieved in human intelligence before implanting it in society. They will have no longer any inclination to sing of their deliverance from "metaphysical agony" and from the "obsession of God." They will have to return to "those accursed eternal questions," as Dostoievski called them, and they will understand why a revolutionary as radical as themselves, as much an opponent of transcendence to all appearances, and as unmystical as themselves, could have exclaimed: "Ever since I existed I have thought of God." In this exclamation of Proudhon's [6]—Marx jeered at him for dallying with the outworn ideas of metaphysics—it is the whole of humanity which testifies to itself and which, even in its denials, demands the air without which it suffocates.

The happiest and most perfect form of social existence would be the most inhuman of conditions if it were not ordered to the spiritual life, just as the latter would be, on a final analysis, only a mystification if it retired into itself in a sort of refined egoism. In accordance with the negation taken over from Feuerbach and already prepared for by Hegel, Marx's system reaches its consummation in a socialism that is an absolute temporalism. It is true that it comes to this point by running directly counter to the inner demands of a thought that was too vigorous not to break down its self-made prison; this was established some ten years ago, by a penetrating piece of exposition, which, it is to be hoped, will be the beginning of a salutary process of evolution for the Marxist doctrine. But if we consider the system as explicitly constituted it must be said that its temporalism not only indulges chimerical hopes and is untenable in itself; it is also something which cannot possibly be desired by mankind. It is the vision of an entirely monotonous world. It would be a most incomprehensible retrogression if men were satisfied with it, and the most frightful torment if they were not. Marx's social, historical man has only two dimensions,[7] but the sense of the Eternal, the consciousness of the Eternal Presence which he must regain, will repair his loss.

How grateful must we be to the Church for reminding us always, *opportune, importune,* of the essential condition of our existence, for that continual *sursum,* that continual *redi ad cor,* which she presses upon us. Nothing is more superficial than the charge made against her of losing sight of immediate realities, of neglecting man's urgent needs, by speaking to him always of the hereafter. For in truth the hereafter is far nearer than the future, far nearer than what we call the present. It is the Eternal found at the heart of all temporal development which gives it life and direction. It is the authentic Present without which the present itself is like the dust which slips through our hands. If modern men are so *absent* from each other, it is primarily because they are absent from themselves, since they have abandoned this Eternal which alone establishes them in being and enables them to communicate with one another.

That, then, is first and foremost the social rôle of the Church; she brings us back to that communion which all her dogma teaches us and all her activity makes ready for us. Nevertheless, if it is true that the communion of persons is, in the deepest sense, *society,* it is no less true that it is a society whose structure is quite different from that of the temporal societies which are necessary for the life of humanity. Now it is evident that the Church, which is not "of this world," has but a very general jurisdiction over the smooth running of those societies, a jurisdiction which does not extend to technical details. So that if in the first case the expression "social Catholicism" seems to smack of pleonasm, in the second its use requires not, doubtless, limitation, but perhaps some reserve. It defines an attitude, a trend, rather than a doctrine settled in all its particulars. For the Church's proper mission is not to assume the general direction of social movements any more than of intellectual ones, though she may exert on both, in many different ways, an influence

without compare. Thus, for example, it was not entirely false
to say that she was sometimes taken by surprise by the
new problems that were raised in the nineteenth century by unprecedented economic development; and, doubtless, it is not entirely right, in face of the increasing in-
credulity of the masses combined with the success achieved
among them by so many disastrous utopian schemes, to say
by way of total explanation: "If only people had listened to
the Popes!" Obedience, necessary as it is, is not always
enough, and the Papacy has not always spoken at once. That
does not mean that it was lacking in its duty. But among
Catholics there were not always to be found enough men living their faith so intensely and so intimately in touch with
the life of their times as to feel at once particular difficulties
as they arose, and to find, within their own province and on
their own responsibility, the required solutions. Lack of initiative preceded lack of submission, and this latter was sometimes only too real and far too easily discernible. Of course
it is desirable that the Church herself, by virtue of that
maternal instinct by which she anticipates her children's ills,
should herself encourage and hasten on the necessary work.
But no one would be scandalized that it does not always
happen like this, nor can he make it an excuse for his own
abstention. Can we reasonably ask of the authority of the
Church anything more than the assertion of the moral law,
the careful control of private initiative, the support of all
those efforts in which she recognizes her own Spirit, and,
finally, such interventions as are necessary to settle eventual
disagreements and to sanction what proves to be definitive
in the solutions adopted? [8]

The Church has made pronouncements, in this way, on
many points of social teaching. Nevertheless, she does not
take the place of statesmen and formulate "programmes,"
in the precise, complete sense of the word, or suggest
"plans." Nor can all her children be authorities on social
matters or social reformers. Moreover, it is quite usual to
find among them a great diversity both in opinions and in
functions. But even on the plane of earthly societies the
Church contributes, in fact, much more than a programme,
and her authentic children contribute to the best of programmes much more than an outward agreement or a mere
technical competency. For, according to a saying of St Gregory the Great, which sums up all the traditional teaching con-

tained in this book, *in sancta Ecclesia unusquisque et portat alterum et portatur ab altero.*[9] Now this sense of a common salvation and of a fellowship of all in relation to all is the best possible preparation for social tasks—it is the best introduction for everyone to "social Catholicism." There can be no question, we must repeat, of merely transposing into the natural order what faith teaches us about the supernatural world: that would be to transform the divine reality, which must be believed and lived in mystery—*mysterium unitatis*—into a dangerous kind of secularization which might well lead us to speak again of Christian truths gone mad; though when Christians become too much impressed by the reasoning of the wise men of this world God sometimes makes use of this madness, itself by no means in accordance with his wisdom. But an anxiety to make a clear distinction between the two orders, natural and supernatural, must not prevent faith from bearing its fruit. Faith is not a repository of dead truths which we may respectfully set aside so as to plan our whole lives without them. If in the upward direction a discontinuity between the natural and the supernatural is fundamental, there must be an influence in the downward direction. Charity has not to become inhuman in order to remain supernatural; like the supernatural itself it can only be understood as incarnate. He who yields to its rule, far from giving up his natural qualities, contributes to those societies of which he is naturally a member an activity that is all the more effective because its motive is more free. No human problem, no human anxiety can find in him a stranger: all awake within him an echo that is all the deeper for his realization of their eternal consequences. The service of his brethren is for him the only form of apprenticeship to the charity which will in very truth unite him with them. However free he may be from all illusion, suspicious of all dreams of materialistic progress, proof against all visions of utopia, or all kinds of social eudemonism, yet he cannot remain satisfied—no more satisfied with the world than with himself. The spiritual union for which he longs is not within but beyond that social harmony for which he must strive. Whatever freedom he may justly claim for the details of his task, it is impossible for him not to aim at establishing among men relationships more in conformity with Christian reality. In the measure of his strength and according to his own vocation—for the gifts of the one Spirit differ, and in the unity of one same body each member has a different function—he will labour heart and soul to achieve it. If he fails, he will feel it as a wound in his own flesh, and even if he despairs of success, he will never give up.

NOTES TO CHAPTER XII

[1] Novel by Rikatchoff. Quoted in *L'Ordre nouveau*, March 1, 1937.

[2] *Bulletin des anciens élèves de Saint-Sulpice*, Nov. 15, 1931, p. 581.

[3] See N. Berdiaeff, *Personne humaine et Marxisme*, in *Le Communisme et les chrétiens*, 1937, p. 197.

[4] *Thèses sur Feuerbach*, thèse 6 (French translation in Marx and Engels, *Études philosophiques*, 1935, p. 73).

[5] J. Maritain, *Humanisme intégral*, 1935, p. 10.

[6] *De la justice dans la Révolution et dans l'Église*, new edn., vol. i, 1930, p. 283.

[7] Marx is mentioned here only as an example, though he is the most important for the vigour of thought and the extent of influence. Cf. B. Mussolini, *Le Fascisme, doctrine, institutions,* first part, n. 6: "Outside history man is nothing" (French trans., 1933, p. 17). There is an excellent study on the historical character of man according to Marx in *La Vie Intellectuelle* of Sept. 10, 1937, by P.-L. Landsberg, *Marx et le problème de l'homme.*

[8] See Extract 53, p. 280.

[9] *In Ezechielem*, lib. 2, hom. 1, n. 5 (P.L. lxxvi, 939).

MYSTERIUM CRUCIS

Wherever a Christian's meditations may have led him, he is always brought back, as by a natural bias, to the contemplation of the Cross.

The whole mystery of Christ is a mystery of resurrection, but it is also a mystery of death. One is bound up with the other and the same word, Pasch, conveys both ideas. Pasch means passing over.[1] It is a transmutation of the whole being, a complete separation from oneself which no one can hope to evade. It is a denial of all natural values in their natural existence and a renunciation even of all that had previously raised the individual above himself.

However genuine and unsullied the vision of unity that inspires and directs mankind's activity, to become effective it must first be dimmed. It must be enveloped in the great shadow of the Cross. It is only by abandoning all idea of considering itself as its own end that mankind can be gathered together. For does not man, in reality, will and love humanity with the same natural impulse that he wills and loves himself? Now God is essentially a jealous God, who must be loved pre-eminently, under pain of not loving him at all.[2] And if it is true that in the last analysis humanity will be loved for its own sake, and not with a love that is self-centred, only by being loved in God the only Beloved, this truth does not appear automatically with such obvious clarity that it does away with the reality of the sacrifice. Humanism is not itself Christian. Christian humanism must be a *converted humanism*. There is no smooth transition from a natural to a supernatural love. To find himself man must lose himself, in a spiritual dialectic as imperative in all its severity for humanity as for the individual, that is,

imperative for my love of man and of mankind as well as
for my love of myself. *Exodus* and *ecstasy* are governed by
the same law. If no one may escape from humanity, humanity whole and entire must die to itself in each of its
members so as to live transfigured in God. There is definitive
brotherhood only in a common adoration. *Gloria Dei, vivens
homo;* but man will attain to life only by means of the *soli
Deo gloria.* That is the universal *Pasch,* the preparation for
the City of God.

Through Christ dying on the Cross, the humanity which
he bore whole and entire in his own Person renounces itself and dies. But the mystery is deeper still. He who bore
all men in himself was deserted by all. The universal Man
died alone. This is the consummation of the *Kenosis* and
the perfection of sacrifice. This desertion—even an abandonment by the Father—was necessary to bring about reunion.
This is the mystery of solitude and the mystery of severance,
the only efficacious sign of gathering together and of unity:
the sacred blade piercing indeed so deep as to separate soul
from spirit, but only that universal life might enter.

"O You who are solitary among the solitary, and all in
all!" [3]

"By the wood of the Cross," concludes St Irenaeus, "the
work of the Word of God was made manifest to all: his
hands are stretched out to gather all men together. Two
hands outstretched, for there are two peoples scattered over
the whole earth. One sole head in the midst, for there is
but one God over all, among all and in all." [4]

NOTES TO "MYSTERIUM CRUCIS"

[1] See Extract 54, p. 281.
[2] See St John of the Cross, *Ascent of Mount Carmel,* book
3, chap. 12.
[3] Pseudo-Chrysostom (Hippolytus?): Extract 55, p. 282.
[4] *Adversus Haereses,* 5, 17, 4 (P.G. vii, 1171–2). Cf. Rhabanus
Maurus, Poem 80:

> Expansis manibus sic totum amplectitur orbem
>   In cruce confixus Christus in arce Deus.
>   (M.G.H., *Poetae latini aevi carolini,* vol. 2, p. 234.)

APPENDIX

EXTRACTS, MAINLY FROM PATRISTIC SOURCES

1

GREGORY OF NYSSA
The Double Nature of Man

"In Christ Jesus," says the Apostle, "there is neither male nor female." Yet Scripture says that mankind was divided in that way. It follows that our nature is constructed on a twofold plan: united in the common possession of human nature, by which man is like to God; yet divided into the two sexes. There is a hint of this truth contained in the order of the expressions which Scripture uses. The first account says, "God created man, to the image of God he created him"; but when the account is repeated, something is added: "male and female he made them"; and the latter division is not one of the characteristics of God.

In this passage Holy Scripture contains, it seems to me, a deep and profound lesson, namely, that man's nature lies midway between two extremes—between the divine, incorporeal nature, and the irrational nature of the brute creation. Examine the compound which is man, and you will find that he has a share in each of these opposite elements. From the divine nature we receive reason and understanding, which are not divided according to sex; from the irrational nature of the brutes, we receive our bodily structure, divided into male and female. Each of these two elements is to be found complete in every human being. From the order of the account of man's first creation we learn that in man the power of understanding takes first place, while his sharing in the nature of the brute creation, his similarity to the brutes, is something superadded. First we are told that "God made man to his own image and likeness," to indicate that, as the Apostle says, in God there is neither male nor female; then a special characteristic is added to human nature— "male and female he made them." What lesson are we to

211

learn from this? I would ask the reader's indulgence if I go back some way to explain the point we are discussing.

God is, by his very nature, all the good it is possible to conceive; or rather he surpasses in goodness all that it is possible for our minds to understand or grasp. And his reason for creating human life is simply this—because he is good. Such being the nature of God, and such the one reason why he undertook the work of making man, there were to be no half measures when he set about to show forth the power of his goodness. He would not give a mere part of what was his own, and grudge to share the rest. The very utmost limit of goodness is displayed in this work of bringing man into being out of nothing, this heaping on man of all that is good. In fact, so many are the benefits bestowed on every man that it would be no easy task to list them all. And so Holy Scripture sums all up in one phrase by saying that man was created to the image of God; which is the equivalent of saying that God made human nature a sharer in all that is good. . . .

Now, one of these good things is freedom. Man is not subject to any overmastering yoke of necessity. We are our own masters, to choose what seems good to us. Virtue is something we choose for ourselves, not something forced upon us from outside. . . . But if an image bears in every point the impress of the beauty of the Prototype, it can no longer be called an image at all, but is the very Prototype itself, since there is no means of telling the two apart. Wherein, then, lies the distinction between God and the image of God? In this: that God is uncreated, the image of God created. This difference gives rise in turn to other differences. All are agreed that the uncreated Nature is also unchangeable, while for a created nature to exist is to change. The very passage from not-being to being is a kind of movement, a kind of change. By the will of God that which was not begins to be. . . . That which came into being through change has a natural affinity to change. And so the Creator, who, as the prophet says, knows all things before they come to be, when he created man saw, or rather foresaw, what human nature would incline to, following its self-determining, self-mastering power. And as he looked upon the creature that was to be, he added to his image and likeness the division into male and female. To this division nothing corresponds in the divine archetype. It is borrowed, as I have said, from the nature of irrational creatures. The true reason for this additional structure is something that could only be given by those who had received a view of the truth, and handed it down to us in inspired Scripture. All we can do is to give the best picture we can, based on conjecture and likelihood. We shall give it not as the last word on the subject, but as a sort of exercise, submitted to the reader's kind consideration.

Our suggestion is this: when Scripture says that God created man, this indefinite expression *man* means *universal human nature*. Adam is not yet named as the new creature, as he is later on in the account. The creature is called man —not any particular man, but man in general. This general term, used for the nature created, indicates that God by his foreknowledge included the whole human race in this first fashioning. We may not suppose that anything made by God is left indefinite. Every actual creature must have some definite measure of perfection assigned to it by the wisdom of its Maker. And just as an individual man is made with a body of a definite size, enclosing his human nature within the limits of a definite quantity, namely, the dimensions of his body, so it seems to me the whole range of humanity was enclosed, as it were, in one body by the foreknowledge of the God of all things. This is what Scripture intends to convey by saying that God made man and made him to the image of God. The gracious gift of likeness to God was not given to a mere section of humanity, to one individual man; no, it is a perfection that finds its way in equal measure to every member of the human race. This is shown by the fact that all men possess a mind. Everybody has the power to think and plan, as well as all the other powers that appear distinctively in creatures that mirror the divine nature. On this score there is no difference between the first man that ever was and the last that ever will be: all bear the stamp of divinity. Thus the whole of humanity was named as one man, since for the Divine Power there is neither past nor future. What is still to come, no less than what is now, is governed by his universal sway.

The whole of human nature, then, from the first man to the last, is but one image of him who is. The division into male and female was something superadded to the work, made, it seems to me, for the reasons I have given.

On the Formation of Man, ch. 16 (P. G. xliv, 181–5)

2

GREGORY OF NYSSA
Universal Human Nature

Whether what I am about to say on this question comes near to the truth or not, he knows best who is Truth itself. The following at any rate is what suggests itself to me. First I repeat what I said earlier on. God said, "Let us make man to our image and likeness." This image of God finds its fulfilment in human nature as a whole. Adam had not yet come into being. The word Adam means "formed from the earth" according to Hebrew scholars. The Apostle Paul, well versed in his native Hebrew, turned the name Adam into Greek by the word γοϊκόν, i.e. *of the earth*.

By man, then, is meant the universal nature of man, this God-like thing, made in the likeness of God. It was not a mere part of the whole that came into being through the all-powerful wisdom of God, but the whole extension of the created nature at once. He saw it all who holds all things within his hand, even to the uttermost limits of creation (as the Scripture says, "in his hands are all the ends of the earth"). He saw it who knows all things even before they come to be; saw before his mind in one all-seeing glance the whole extent and number of the human race. And since he also saw the inclination which our nature would have towards evil, and how we should, of our own free choice, fall away from a dignity equal to that of the angels to consort with lower creatures, he mingled with that image of himself an irrational element. In the blessed nature of God this distinction of male and female had no part. But God transferred to man a characteristic of the brute creation, imparting to our race a means of increase quite out of keeping with our lofty nature as first created. When God made man to his image and likeness, he did not add the power of increasing and multiplying; it was only when he divided man into male and female that he said, "Increase and multiply and fill the whole earth."

On the Formation of Man, ch. 22 (P.G. xliv, 204–5)

3

SEVERUS OF ANTIOCH
The Common Grave

(This ceremony) is the Commemoration of the poor men and strangers who in the course of the ages, up to the present day, have brought their lives to a close, and fallen into that last ineluctable sleep; who have put up, as at an inn, in the one common grave, and entrusted to earth that flesh which was formed out of clay and joined with a rational soul created in the image of God.

Let us not see only the outward form of this commemoration, but let us search out the spirit that lies within. Now, those who originally laid down a law for its celebration did so with the clear knowledge . . . that Christ did not die and rise again for the sake of one class of men or another, but for all mankind. . . . Keeping in thought close to their own Master, and showing in practical action the common avail of divine succour, they recommended and decreed a Commemoration Service for all, in a body, who were cut off from all kindred and worldly friendship; having in view the same union as Paul, when he said: [1] "where there is no question of Gentile or Jew, circumcised or uncircumcised, barbarian, Scythian, slave, freeman; but all, and in all, is Christ."

It was fitting, therefore, in the first place because of our common nature, to come together and render to the holy burial of those who were first to depart the same service which others will later do for us. In the second place, we should be filled with awe . . . at the succour brought by Christ in dying and rising again for the sake of all; and should give due consideration also to the fact that it is Christ who is honoured through the poor and the stranger, the same Christ who said: [2] "As often as you have done it to one of these my least brethren, you have done it to me." And we should mount in thought, and rise to this sublime reflexion, that these dead, who were reckoned of no account, we find to be dignified by the likeness and dignity of God: for Christ . . . came to us, in his Incarnation, in the guise of a stranger and a poor man, and . . . being rich, became

[1] *Col.* iii. 11.
[2] *Matt.* xxv. 40.

poor for our sake, that we might be enriched by his poverty: became so poor that he cried : [8] ". . . the Son of Man has nowhere to lay his head. . . ." He was not laid in a tomb of his own, but Joseph of Arimathea received him into his own tomb like a stranger.

Homily 76 (*Patrologia Orientalis*, XII, 136–8)

4

ST AUGUSTINE
Adam Broken Up and Gathered Together

"For with righteousness shall he judge the world," not a part of it only, for it was not merely a part that he redeemed; the whole of the world is his to judge, since for the whole did he pay the price. You have heard what the Gospel has to say, that when he comes "He shall gather together the elect from the four winds" (*Mark* xiii. 27). He gathers all the elect from the four winds, that is to say, from the whole world. Now Adam's name, as I have said more than once, means in Greek, the whole world. For there are four letters, A, D, A, and M, and with the Greeks the four quarters of the world have these initial letters. They call the East, "Anatole"; the West, "Dusis"; the North, "Arctus"; and the South, "Mesembria," and these letters spell Adam. Adam is thus scattered throughout the globe. Set in one place, he fell and, as it were, broken small, he has filled the whole world. But the Divine Mercy gathered up the fragments from every side, forged them in the fire of love and welded into one what had been broken. That was a work which this Artist knew how to do; let no one therefore give way to despair. An immense task it was indeed; but think who the Artist was. He who remade was himself the Maker; he who refashioned was himself the Fashioner. "He shall judge the world in righteousness and the nations in his truth."

On Psalm 195, n. 15 (P.L. xxxvii, 1236)

5

DURANDUS OF MENDE
The Threefold Wall Thrown Down

The *Gloria in excelsis* is the hymn not only of the Angels,

[8] *Matt.* viii. 20; *Luke* ix. 58.

but also of men, rejoicing with one another because the woman has now lit her lamp to look for the groat which was lost, and the shepherd has now left his ninety-nine sheep in the desert and come to look for the single lost one.

For before Christ's birth there were three walls of enmity: one between God and man, one between the Angels and man, and the third between man and man. The reason for this was that man had offended his creator by disobedience, by his fall had hindered the restoration of the Angels, and by the diversity of his cults had separated himself from his fellow men (since the Jews used ceremonial worship, while the Gentiles practised idolatry).

But our Peace by his coming destroyed these walls, and thus united what had been separated. This he did by taking away sin, and thus reconciling man with God; by repairing the effects of the Fall, and thus reconciling man with the Angels; and by destroying diversity of worship, and thus reconciling men with each other.

Therefore, in the words of the Apostle, "He restored the things that are in heaven and those that are on the earth," and it is for this reason that the multitude of the heavenly army sang: "Glory to God in the highest," that is, among the Angels who have never sinned or been at enmity with God; and "on earth" Christ makes "peace with men," that is, Jews and Gentiles, "of good will," because before his birth their sins put them at enmity with God and with the Angels. This also explains why the Angel speaks to the shepherds and rejoices with them, for peace is made again between man and the Angels; God is born as man, and so peace is re-established between man and God; he is born in the manger of an ox and an ass, and so peace is restored between men themselves, for the ox stands for the Jewish people and the ass for the Gentiles.

Explanation of the Divine Offices, Book iv, ch. 13. Cf. ch. 33, on the Preface

6

CARDINAL DU PERRON
Salvation through Unity

God of his inestimable bounty and incomprehensible wisdom has vouchsafed to watch over us and to prepare and direct us even in this life towards that eternal happiness that it has pleased him to promise us and reserve for us in the other; and to this end he has chosen the method which best corresponds with the excellency and dignity of his nature. And since he is one, the principal of all unity, and even unity itself, instead of saving us by so many distinct and separate ways, he has obliged us to embrace the means of our salvation and its conditions in unity. "He is one," said St Augustine (*In Psalm*. 101), "the Church is unity, nothing corresponds to the one save unity." That is, he was not content to win us and possess us separately as so many scattered and dispersed individuals, but willed that by the terms of that same covenant between him and ourselves we should be bound up together in a common society, to constitute, under the authority of his name, a sort of spiritual body, and a form of Estate and Republic. Jesus died, said St John, "not only for the nation, but to gather together in one the children of God, that were dispersed" (*John* xi. 52).

Replique à la Response du Serenissime Roy de la Grande Bretagne

(Paris, 1620), Preface

7

ST FULGENTIUS OF RUSPE
The Miracle of Tongues

Now let us see why it was that at that time the sign of the presence of the Holy Spirit was this, that they who received it should speak in every tongue. For the Holy Spirit has not ceased to be given. Yet the recipients nowadays do not speak in every tongue. The Holy Spirit does not renew in them the striking miracle by which, formerly, he proved his Presence.

We must realize, my dear brethren, that this Holy Spirit it is who pours forth charity into our hearts. By this charity the Church of God was to be assembled from every corner of the globe. Now united by the Holy Spirit, the Church by her very unity speaks in every tongue, as then each recipient of the Holy Spirit spoke. If then anyone were to say to one of us: "You have received the Holy Spirit, why do you not speak in every tongue?" he ought to answer "I do. For I am part of the Body of Christ, the Church, I mean, and she speaks in every tongue. What else did God mean the presence of the Holy Spirit to convey if not this, that his Church should one day speak in every tongue? . . ."

Celebrate, then, this day as members of the unity of the Body of Christ. For you will not celebrate it in vain, if you are what you celebrate by adhering together to that Church which God fills with the Holy Spirit; that Church which by its growth throughout the world he recognizes as his own and by which he in turn is recognized. . . . To you of every nation who constitute the Church of Christ, the members of Christ, the Body of Christ, the Spouse of Christ, to you it is that the Apostle says: "Supporting one another in charity, careful to keep the unity of the Spirit in the bond of Peace" (*Eph.* iv. 2–3). Notice how he links mutual tolerance with love, and the hope of unity with the bond of peace. This is the house of God, built with living stones, the house in which he loves to dwell as Father of his Household. The ruins of division must never be allowed to sadden the eyes of such a Father.

Sermon 8, on Penetcost, n. 2 and 3 (P.L. lxv, 743–4)

8

HERMAS
The Stone Quarried from the Twelve Mountains

Why, Lord, are these mountains all of different shapes and colours?

Listen, the Shepherd replied. These twelve mountains are twelve tribes which inhabit the whole world. The Son of God was preached to them by the Apostles.

But, Lord, tell me why they are of different colours and shapes.

Listen, said he. These twelve tribes which inhabit the whole world are twelve nations. Now these nations differ in outlook and spirit. The variety of form which you saw among the mountains represents the diversity of spirit and outlook among these nations. I shall now describe to you the manner of life of each of them.

First tell me this, Lord, I asked: Seeing that the mountains are so varied, how is it that when their rocks were built up into the tower they became all of one colour, glistening like pebbles thrown up from the depths of the sea?

The reason, he replied, is that all the nations that dwell beneath the sky, when once they heard the gospel and believed, were called in the name of the Son of God. In receiving the seal they took on one mind and one spirit, in the unity of one faith and spirit of love. . . . In this way the tower came to be built of one colour and to shine like the sun.

The Shepherd, Similitude 9, c. 17, n. 1–4

9

ST IGNATIUS OF ANTIOCH
Christian Prayer

Let everyone have reverence one for another, making God the rule of your conduct: not with merely human eyes should you regard your neighbour, but have love always one for another in Jesus Christ. Do not allow any cause of division to spring up in your midst, but let your union with the bishop and those who preside over you be an example and an object-lesson of incorruptibility.

Just as our Lord, being one with the Father, did nothing on his own or by means of the Apostles without the Father, so neither should you do anything without the bishop and the presbyters. Do not try to persuade yourselves that you can do anything good on your own; on the contrary, do all in common: one prayer, one petition, one mind, one hope in the unity of love and in innocent joy—this is Jesus Christ than whom there is nothing higher. Make haste, all of you, and gather in the same temple of God at the one altar, the one Jesus Christ who came forth from the one Father and, remaining one with the Father, went back to the unity of the Father.

Letter to the Magnesians, c. 6–7

10

ORIGEN
The Science of Harmony

"We, thy servants, have reckoned up the number of the fighting men, whom we had under our hand, and not so much as one was wanting" (*Num*. xxxi. 49).

. . . Not of the mere rank and file do you hear it said that not one of them was wanting, but only of those who are acclaimed as "picked champions of the fight." Amongst these true champions not one is wanting, amongst them is no breath of discord. Of such it was said: "The multitude of believers were of one heart and soul, and not one of them said that he possessed anything of his own, but they held all things in common." Champions, therefore, because each was of one mind with the rest. In the battle they have won great booty in gold, and all this gold, whether crowns for the head, bracelets for the arm, rings for the finger, they offer to God as symbol of all that their intellects have to offer, all that their hearts and hands have found to do. But unless they were of one mind and heart, they could not offer any gift to God. They represent, I believe, those who diligently observe the precept of our Lord and Saviour, "If in offering your gift at the altar you remember that your brother has anything against you, leave your gift there at the altar and go first to be reconciled to your brother. Then come and offer your gift"—that thus they may "lift their hands to God in prayer free from anger and discord." Such men can say, "We have numbered the pick of our fighting men, not one has failed the others. We have offered our gift to God."

It is for us then earnestly to lay to heart this lesson of mutual harmony. For, as in music, if each chord chimes harmoniously with the rest, the whole harmony is pleasing and true, but if there be but one note out of harmony, then discordant noise is the result and the whole joy of the song is lost, so with those who fight for God. If they allow dissension and discord to exist among them, then nothing they have is pleasing or acceptable to God—no matter how many battles they may win or spoils they bring home, nor however numerous the gifts they make to God.

Homily 26 *on the Book of Numbers,* n. 2 (ed. Baehrens, pp. 244–5)

11

ST MAXIMUS THE CONFESSOR
The Three Laws

There are three common laws, the law of nature, written law and the law of grace, each imposing a particular outlook and a consequent discipline on those submitting to them.

Natural law, where the sensitive appetites do not dominate reason, leads a man without the help of any other master to have a fellow-feeling for all beings of a nature similar to his own, and teaches him to succour those in need. It induces a common will in man to render to all the treatment he would wish to receive from them. Our Lord, too, teaches this in the words: "Do unto all men as you wish them to do unto you." For in all men whom reason governs there arises a common outlook; this in turn gives rise to a common moral code and way of life; and where these are found there appears a consciousness of men's mutual bond in the rationality of human nature. Then there can be no place for the prevailing dissension, which is grounded on a narrow egoism.

Written law restrains disordered impulse, in those whose moral sense is undeveloped, by fear of penalties; and, by accustoming them first to have a regard for justice, in the narrow sense, goes on to implant a wider sense of righteousness, which in time takes root and becomes natural, whereas the initial fear yields little by little to recognition of the good. This in turn, when it becomes a habitual outlook, gives rise to love of other men. This is the end and fulfilment of this law, viz. to bind together all who share the same human nature in mutual love, and through this love to enthrone natural reason in man. Thus the goal of this law is to cherish the natural law with the warmth of affection. Hence our Lord says: "Love thy neighbour as thyself"—and not merely "treat him as thyself": for the second formulation only suggests that men are socially dependent for their mutual subsistence; whereas the former emphasizes the real concern which each should have in the welfare of all.

But the law of grace teaches its devotees to imitate God himself directly, without intermediary steps—for he has loved us, dare one say, even more than himself. . . . "For there is no greater love than this, that a man lay down his life for his friends."

To sum up. Natural law is natural reasoning, keeping control over sense appetite and eliminating that irrational behaviour which is the disruption of what is naturally coherent. And written law, too, is natural reasoning which, after eliminating the same irrationality of sense, rises to a spiritual love which is the bond of union with our fellow men. But the law of grace is a reasoning which rises above nature, and un-

swervingly fashions nature into the likeness of God. . . .
Questions to Thalassios, No. 64 (P.G. xc, 724–8)

12

BALDWIN OF CANTERBURY
Prayer for Fraternal Union

Guard me, O Lord, from grave sin which I fear much. Guard me from the hatred of thy love, lest I should sin against the Holy Spirit who is the bond of love, who is unity, peace and concord: let me not separate myself from the unity of thy Spirit, from the unity of thy peace, by committing the sin which is forgiven neither here nor hereafter. Keep me, Lord, among my brethren and neighbours to tell of the peace which is from thee. Keep me among those who keep the unity of the spirit in the bond of peace.

Dearly beloved, let us anxiously attend to all that concerns the profession of our common life, keeping the unity of the spirit in the bond of peace, by the grace of our Lord Jesus Christ and the love of God and the imparting of the Holy Spirit. From the love of God comes the unity of the spirit; from the grace of our Lord Jesus Christ comes the bond of peace; from the imparting of the Holy Spirit comes that communion which is necessary to those who live in common, if they are to live in common.

. . . This unity which the love of God works in us is preserved in the bond of peace by the grace of our Lord Jesus Christ. He is our peace who made of two peoples one; at whose birth the angels sang: Glory to God in the Highest and on earth peace to men of good will; who when about to ascend into heaven said: My peace I leave with you, my peace I give you.

What is this peace given us by Christ in the bond of which the unity of the spirit is preserved? It is mutual charity by which we love one another, which remains unbroken if we are all of one mind and there are no divisions among us. St Peter exhorts us on this point: Above all things, preserve constant charity among yourselves. What is this charity, if not what is mine and thine, so that I speak of it to him whom I love? . . .

This, then, is the law of the common life, the unity of the spirit in the love of God, the bond of peace in the mutual and constant love of all our brothers, the sharing of all our goods, with every opportunity of possessing things as our own far removed from us by the rule of holy religion. That this may be our abiding intention, that we may have but one heart and one soul and all things in common, "the grace of our Lord Jesus Christ, and the love of God, and the imparting of the Holy Spirit be with us all. Amen."

I believe, O Lord, in the Holy Ghost, the holy Catholic Church, the Communion of Saints. This is my hope, this is my trust, this is my confidence, this is the whole of my security in the professing of my faith: in the goodness of the Holy Ghost, in the unity of the Catholic Church, in the Communion of Saints.

If I am allowed moreover to love thee and to love my neighbour, though my merits are small and few, yet will my hopes reach beyond them. I am confident that the merits of the saints will help me by the communion of charity, so that the Communion of Saints will make up for my insufficiency and imperfection. The prophet comforts me saying: To all things I see a limit, but thy commandment is exceeding large. O large and widespread charity, how great is thy dwelling, how immense the place of thy possession. Let us not be straitened in our bowels, let us not confine ourselves within the bounds and limits of any justice whatever. Let charity expand our hope as far as the Communion of Saints in the sharing of merits and rewards; but the sharing of the latter belongs to the future, for it is the sharing in the glory which shall be revealed in us.

Since, then, there are three communions—the first of nature, which includes the sharing of guilt and anger, the second of grace and the third of glory—by the communion of grace that of nature begins to be remade and the sharing of guilt to be excluded: but by the communion of glory that of nature will be perfectly restored and the communion of anger will be entirely excluded, when God will wipe away every tear from the eyes of the saints. Then among all the saints there will be one heart and one soul and all things will be in common, when God will be all in all. That we may all arrive at this communion and that we all may be one, "the grace of our Lord Jesus Christ and the love of God, and the imparting of the Holy Spirit be with us all for ever. Amen."

Treatise on the Conventual Life (P.L. cciv, 554–6, 562)

13

CLAUDIANUS MAMERTUS
Mutual Presence in God

Now that this proof enables you to appreciate how utterly different and inferior is physical sight [to that of the soul], you should no longer be disturbed by the doubt that, when you are thinking of your absent friend (to use your own example), you have to believe him to be absent from you just because he is not bodily there before you. For if he is dear to you in that aspect of himself which makes you both human, and makes you love one another with a reciprocal love, then you are both equally present to one another: for your friend is precisely one with you in nature.

Now, the soul's faculty of vision is the intellect; if you see yourself [in this spiritual way] you see your friend too, for he is in no way different from yourself. Were he physically before you, you would be able to recognize him by clear and visible physical characteristics. But supposing these characteristics were signs which led you to recognize him for an enemy, surely your soul would be repelled with antipathy, and would in a manner recoil from his. In spite of your both being physically in the closest possible proximity, you would really be separated by no small distance, through your wills being in opposition to one another.

Therefore, one cannot maintain that it is distance that separates hearts, when we see there can be separation even with the bodies close to each other. Besides, the obstacle created by the body to the mutual union of hearts is a small one, unless you would either use the body to look for the image of God in yourself, or desire the body for its own sake. For it would be sadly opposed to the truth to be using the body to look for the image of God, that is, the truly human part of man, instead of using this truly human part itself in your search. But you do use the truly human part and your search will be successful, if you use the image of God. Now, every rational soul is this image of God, so that he who seeks the image of God in himself, is seeking both himself and his friend at the same time: and if in seeking this image he finds it in himself, he will recognize it in all other men too. As for you, you have good reason for maintaining that your friend seems to be absent: for you fix your thoughts

on the body and can only love the body, when you think that
he is nothing more than a body.

Love your God, and in your God love your friend, who is
the image of your God, and may he, likewise loving God,
love you in God. If you both seek and aim at the one single
object, you will always be united to each other, for you are
rooted in this object. And I do not see how it could be
that, if bodies brought together to one place can be present
to each other, hearts fastened on one single object can fail to
be united.

On the State of the Soul, Book I, Chap. 27

14

ST PETER DAMIAN
The Unity of the Body of Christ

During the actual celebration of the Mass, shortly after he
has pronounced the words *Memento, Domine, famulorum
famularumque tuarum,* the priest adds, *Pro quibus tibi
offerimus vel qui tibi offerunt hoc sacrificium laudis.* These
words make it quite clear that this sacrifice of praise is
offered by all the faithful, men and women, even though it
may seem to be offered, in an especial way, by the priest
alone. What he offers to God with his hands, the multitude
of the faithful offer in spirit by their earnest devotion. That
this is really so is evident also from the words: *Hanc igitur
oblationem servitutis nostrae, sed et cunctae familiae tuae
quaesumus, Domine, ut placatus accipias.* From these words
it is as clear as day that the sacrifice which the priest places
on the altar is offered by all God's family in general.

The Apostle sets forth clearly the Church's unity when he
says, "We, being many, are one bread, one body." So great,
in fact, is this unity of the Church in Christ, that throughout
the whole world there is but one bread of Christ's body and
one Chalice of his Blood. The Divinity of the Word of God,
though it fills the whole world, is yet everywhere the same.
So too, though Christ's Body is consecrated in many different places and on many different days, there are not many
bodies but one only. Just as the bread and wine are truly
changed into the Body of Christ, so also do all the members
of the Church who receive that Body worthily, become, beyond all doubt, one Body in Christ. He himself bears witness

to this when he says, "He that eateth my flesh and drinketh my blood abideth in me and I in him."

If then we are all one body in Christ, if we remain in him, we cannot be separated from one another, even though, as far as bodily appearance goes, we seem to live apart. I do not see, therefore, why each individual should not follow the common usage of the Church since, thanks to the Sacrament of Unity, we are never separated from her. When I utter in solitude the common prayers of the Church, I truly show that I am one with her, that I am always with her in spirit. For if I am a member, there can be nothing incongruous in my exercising the functions of the whole body to which I belong.

The Dominus Vobiscum, c. 8 (P.L. cxlv, 237–8)

15

WILLIAM OF SAINT-THIERRY
The Threefold Body of Our Lord

. . . Whenever the intelligent reader finds in a book anything about the flesh or body of the divine Jesus, he may apply this threefold definition of his flesh or body. I have not presumed to invent or fashion it according to my own notions, but have extracted it from the writings of the Fathers. . . .

For he must think *in one way* of that flesh or body which hung on the cross and is sacrificed on the altar, *in another way* of his flesh or body which is abiding life to the person who receives it in Communion, and *in yet another way* of that flesh or body which is the Church. . . .

Not that we would depict Christ as having three bodies, like Geryon in the fable, since the Apostle testifies that the body of Christ is one. But the mind or heart makes the distinction with a certain relation to faith, though the reality maintains the undefiled truth in its simplicity. For this threefold nature of the body of the Lord is to be understood exactly as the body of the Lord himself is understood, according to its essence, its unity and its effect. For the body of Christ, exactly as it is in itself, is offered to all as the food of eternal life, and unites in its life those who receive it faithfully, both by the love of the spirit and by a sharing in its own nature, the living head of the body of the Church.

On the Sacrament of the Altar, c. 12 (P.L. clxxx, 361–2)

16

THEODORE OF MOPSUESTIA
The Priest Invokes the Spirit of Unity

Next the priest asks that the grace of the Holy Spirit descend upon the whole congregation, so that all those who were brought together in one body by the symbol of regeneration may now be also bound up as in a single body by partaking of the body of our Lord; that they may come together in concord and peace and zeal to serve one another, lest, while each of us turns the whole gaze of his spirit upon God, it should yet be for our punishment that we receive the communication of the Holy Spirit, being divided in thought, contentious and quarrelsome, prone to jealousy and envy, and heedless of propriety. (He asks) on the other hand, that we may be deemed worthy to receive him, because we turn the eyes of our soul on God in concord and peace and zeal for the good, in a perfect spirit; and that we may so be made one by taking part in the holy mysteries, and thus together be joined to our Head, Christ our Lord, whose body we believe we are, and through whom we believe that we enter into a share of the divine nature.

6th Liturgical Homily

17

ST FULGENTIUS OF RUSPE
Unity through the Trinity

At no time may the spiritual building of the Body of Christ, which charity effects, be implored more opportunely than when Christ's Body, the Church, in the sacrament of the bread and of the chalice, offers the very Body and Blood of Christ. For "the chalice of benediction which we bless is it not the communion of the blood of Christ? And the bread which we break is it not the partaking of the body of the Lord? For we, being many, are one bread, one body: all that partake of one bread." This is why we pray that by that same grace, which has made the Church the Body of Christ, all its members may persevere, held fast by the cement of charity in the unity of his Body.

Rightly do we ask that this should be brought about in

us by the gift of that Spirit, who is the one Spirit of the Father and of the Son: because that Holy Unity of Nature, that Equality and Love, that is the Trinity, the one true God, sanctifies in unanimity those whom it adopts. In this one substance of the Trinity there is unity in the origin, equality in the Son, but in the Spirit of Love a fusion of equality and unity: the unity knows no division, the equality no difference, the love no shadow of dislike. There is no discord there: for the equality, which is love and unity, the unity, which is equality and love, and the love, which is unity and equality, continue for ever in one unchanging nature.

It is by this fusion (of unity and equality) in the Holy Spirit, if one may use such language, that the love of the Father and the Son is seen to be one, and because of this the Apostle writes: "Because the Charity of God is poured forth in our hearts by the Holy Spirit who is given to us." That Holy Spirit indeed, the one spirit of the Father, and the Son, works in those to whom he grants the grace of divine adoption what he worked in those of whom the Acts tell us: "The multitude of the believers had but one heart and one soul." This one heart and one soul were the work of him who is the one Spirit of the Father and the Son as he is likewise, with the Father and the Son, one God. That is why the Apostle asserts that this spiritual unity is to be preserved by the bond of peace. "I therefore, a prisoner in the Lord, beseech you that you walk worthy of the vocation in which you are called: with all humility and mildness, with patience supporting one another in charity; careful to keep the unity of the spirit in the bond of peace." This spirit they lose by their desertion, who, led astray by vice or puffed up by pride, sever themselves from the unity of the body of the Church. That these men have lost the Holy Spirit the Apostle Jude states clearly where he says, "These are they who separate themselves, sensual men, having not the Spirit." For the same reason, St Paul remarks, "The sensual man perceiveth not these things which are of the Spirit of God." Such men are prone to division, for they lack that Spirit in whom alone the members of Christ preserve their loving unity. It is in the sacrifices of the Church alone, the sacrifices offered by her spiritual unity, that God takes pleasure. Just as true faith admits no discord in the Trinity, so does peace hold us brothers in the harmony of charity.

To Monimus, Book II, Chap. XI (P.L. lxv, 190–1)

18

ST FULGENTIUS OF RUSPE
The Sacrifice and the Summoning of the Spirit

Realize what is taking place when the sacrifice is being offered. Then you will understand why we invoke the Holy Spirit.

The sacrifice is offered to proclaim the death of the Lord, that the memory of him who gave his life for us may live again. When, in this sacrifice, we commemorate his death, we pray that by the coming of the Holy Spirit love may be bestowed on us, for whom Christ died of love. Humbly and earnestly we pray, that by that same love which made it seem to Christ worth dying on the cross for us, we too, having received grace of the Holy Spirit, may be crucified to the world and having imitated our Lord in his death may walk in the newness of life. . . . Thus does it come about that all the faithful, who love God and their neighbour, even though they do not drink the chalice of bodily suffering, drink none the less the chalice of the love of the Lord. . . . For the chalice of the Lord is drunk when holy love is cherished, and without it giving one's body to be burnt is of no avail. But with the gift of love is given us the grace to be in truth what in this sacrifice we celebrate in mystery. This the Apostle affirms when, after saying "for we being many are one bread, one body," he adds "all that partake of one bread."

As warrant for our asking this at the moment of sacrifice, we have the salutary example of our Saviour. He has willed that in the commemoration of his death there should be made that same petition which, on the eve of that death, he himself, the true High Priest, made on our behalf, saying, "Holy Father, keep them in thy Name whom thou hast given me: that they may be one as we also are." And adding shortly after, "and not for them only do I pray, but for them also who through their word shall believe in me. That they all may be one as thou, Father, in me and I in thee; . . . that they may be made perfect in one." When we offer the Body and Blood of Christ, we ask what he asked on our behalf when he deigned to offer himself for us. Read the Gospels carefully and you will see that as soon as our Redeemer had finished this prayer, he entered the garden and was there taken captive at the hands of the Jews. . . . Thus does he show us that we ought to ask, especially at the time of this sacrifice, what he, the supreme High Priest, deemed it fitting to ask when he established the law of sacrifice. Now, that which we ask, that we may be one in the Father and the Son, we receive through the grace of spiritual unity which the blessed Apostle commands us to preserve with care when he says, "Supporting one another in charity, careful to keep the unity of the spirit in the bond of peace." We pray then that the Holy Spirit may come, not in person, in the Immensity of the Godhead, but by his gift of personal charity. . . .

So the Holy Spirit is said to come at the request of the faithful whenever he deigns to increase, or to give anew, the gift of charity and unanimity. This is the function which is, so to speak, proper to the Holy Spirit. By this especially is he recognized. When, therefore, the holy Church, in the sacrifice of the Body and Blood of Christ, prays that the Holy Spirit may be sent her, she is simply asking for that gift of charity by which she is enabled to preserve spiritual unity in the bond of peace. Since also it is written, "Love is stronger than death," in order to promote the love of mortification in those of her members who are still on earth, she asks for that charity which, as she recalls, led her Redeemer to go freely to his death for her sake. Thus does the Holy Spirit sanctify the Sacrifice of the Catholic Church; because of this, the Christian people continue in faith and charity. Each one of the faithful, thanks to the gift of the Holy Spirit, eats and drinks worthily the Body and Blood of Christ. For each holds the right beliefs concerning God, and by his good life is far from deserting the unity of Christ's Body, the Church.

Against Fabianus, Fragm. 28 (P.L. lxv, 789–91)

19

ST AUGUSTINE
The One City of God

An orderly exposition of the faith demanded that the Church should be joined to the Trinity as a house to its owner, as a temple to its god, as a city to its founder. The Church is here to be considered not in any partial aspect but as a whole; not only as the Church on earth as it jour-

neys on towards its goal, praising the name of the Lord
from the rising of the sun even to its setting, singing a new
song after its liberation from the old captivity; but also as the
Church in heaven which ever since its foundation has cleaved
to God and has never suffered in itself the evil of a fall.
Set among the angels in blessedness it ever endures, and
brings help, as is but right, to that part of itself which is still
in its pilgrimage. For both will be one by sharing eternity
together, are one already in the bond of love, seeing that
the whole Church was founded for the worship of the One
God.

Enchiridion, c. 57 (P.L. xl, 258–9)

20

ST HILARY
The "Natural" Unity of Christians

There were those whose heart and soul were one, and it
was faith which made them so. This faith is itself one, witness the Apostle who proclaims one faith even as one Lord,
and one baptism and one hope and one God. If then it is
through faith, that is through the nature of one faith, that
all are one, why not admit a natural unity in them, seeing
that they are one through the nature of a unique faith?
For all were born again unto innocence, unto immortality,
unto the knowledge of God, unto faith, unto hope. Now these
things cannot differ within themselves, for there is one hope
and one God, as also there is one Lord and one baptism of
regeneration. If, however, these things are one by common
consent rather than by their very nature, then to such as receive a new birth unto them, ascribe a simple unity of will.
But if they have been born again unto the nature of one
eternal life, then there is in them no longer a mere unity
of will, but they are one by being reborn with one and the
same nature.

These are not our own conjectures which we are offering,
nor do we seek to delude our hearers with falsehoods based
on distorted interpretations; but holding fast to essentially
sound doctrine we know and preach the things which are
true. For the Apostle teaches that this unity of the faithful
arises from the nature of the sacraments when he writes to

the Galatians: "As many of you as have been baptised in Christ have put on Christ. There is neither Jew nor Greek, there is neither bond nor free, there is neither male nor female. For you are all one in Christ Jesus." Surely this unity among such diversity of race and circumstance and sex is not the result of free consent, but of the unity of the sacrament, in that they share one baptism and have all put on the one Christ. What part can mutual agreement play when they are one by putting on the one Christ in the one baptism?

Our Lord prays to his Father that those who believe in him may all be one, and that as he is in the Father and the Father in him, so all may be one in them. Why speak of harmony of soul, why bring in here a unity of mind and heart based on agreement of will? Our Lord had an unlimited vocabulary and knew the precise meaning of words. If their unity was to be an affair of will he would have prayed thus: "Father, even as we will one and the same thing, so let them will one and the same, so that we all may be one through the oneness of our wills." Perhaps the Word did not know the meaning of words or he who is truth could not say what was true? He announced the true and unsullied mysteries of the Gospel faith; and he not only made his meaning clear but spoke to be believed when he said: "That they all may be one, as thou, Father, in me, and I in thee; that they all may be one in us." First of all it is for them that he prays, that they all may be one; and then he points out the nature of that unity: as thou, Father, in me and I in thee; so that, even as the Father is in the Son and the Son in the Father, so, as a result of and based on the pattern of this unity, all may be one in the Father and the Son.

Our Lord did not leave the minds of the faithful in doubt: "That they may be one as we also are one; I in them and thou in me; that they may be made perfect in one." I ask those who assert a unity of will between the Father and the Son, whether Christ is in us to-day truly by nature or by the concord of wills? For if the Word was indeed made flesh and if in Holy Communion we really receive the Word-Flesh, surely he is to be considered as "naturally" abiding in us? For, born as man, he has taken unto himself inseparably the nature of our flesh and has conjoined the nature of his own flesh to the nature of the eternal Godhead in the Sacrament by which his flesh is given to us. Thus we are all one, because the Father is in Christ and Christ is in us. We therefore who are united inseparably in his very flesh must proclaim the mystery of a true and natural unity. . . .

We do not, of course, deny unanimity between the Father and the Son; it is the heretics, with their lying tongues, who assert that because we do not accept concord by itself as the bond of unity we therefore declare them to be at variance. If they attend they will see that unanimity is not denied by us. The Father and the Son are one in nature, in glory and in power, and one and the same nature cannot will things that are contrary. . . .

On The Trinity, Book 8 (P.L. x, 241–50)

21

GREGORY OF NYSSA
In the Perfect Dove

But if perfect love casts out fear, as Scripture says, fear being transformed into love, then whatever attains to salvation will be found to constitute a unity. All its elements will be gathered up into one by being grafted on to the one Good, in the perfect unity which is typified by the dove. This we learn from the words that follow: "My dove is one, my perfect one." And the same is declared even more clearly in the Gospel in the words of our Lord, when he proclaims to his disciples that they should all become one by being grafted on to the one and only Good; so that through the unity of the Holy Spirit, as the Apostle says, bound together by the bond of peace, they should all become one Body and one Spirit.

Better still, in the very words of Christ in the Gospel, "that they all may be one, as thou, Father, in me, and I in thee." Now, the bond of this unity is spoken of as "glory"; and that by glory is meant the Holy Spirit no man of discernment will deny, in view of the words of our Lord, "The glory which thou hast given me, I have given to them." This, it is certain, is the glory which he gave to his disciples when he said to them, "Receive ye the Holy Ghost. . . ."

And he is the perfect dove upon whom the bridegroom looks, saying, "My dove is one, my perfect one."

15th Homily on the Canticle (P.G. xliv, 1116–7)

22

EUSEBIUS OF CAESAREA
The Sacerdotal Prayer

The prayer which our Saviour makes to the Father on our behalf teaches us the nature of his great mission—that wherever he may be, there we may be with him and may gaze upon his glory; that he may love us even as his own Father loves him, and may give to us all that he receives from the Father, even his glory, making of us all a unity in which we will be no longer many individuals but one, bound together in his divinity and in the glory of the Kingdom—not, indeed, by our merging into one substance, but by the consummation of perfected virtue. . . . For in this way, made perfect by him in wisdom and justice, in holiness and all virtue, we shall be united with each other and with the unfailing radiance of the Father's godhead, ourselves taking light from this union and becoming sons of God, fashioned by our participation in the union of God with his only Son, and in the splendour of the godhead.

"The Father and I are one," he tells us. So too he prays that all of us may share in this union by following and imitating him. . . . "The glory you have given me," he goes on, "have I given to them, that they may be one as we also are one. . . ." Thus the Father and the Son are one through the glory they share, and by giving to his followers a part in their glory, God has found them worthy even of this union itself.

On the Theology of the Church, Book 3, Chaps. 18, 19
(P.G. xxiv, 1042–3)

23

ORIGEN
In Expectation of the New Wine

Once we have understood what is meant by this "inebriation of the saints" and how it is held out to them as a joy in store, we can now consider how it is that our Saviour can be said to drink wine no more until he drinks this new wine in the Kingdom of God.

Understand, then, that at this very moment my Saviour is grieving over my sins. There can be no joy for him while I remain in my evil doing. Why not? Because he is the advocate for our sins with the Father, as John his closest friend declares, saying, "If anyone sin, we have an advocate with the Father, Jesus Christ the just. And he is the propitiation for our sins." How then could he, as the advocate for my sins, drink the wine of joy while I grieve him by my sinning? How could he possibly rejoice as he approaches the altar to make propitiation for me a sinner, while all the while there mounts to his heart the misery of my sins? "I shall drink this wine with you," he says, "in the Kingdom of my Father." So long then as our steps are not set towards that Kingdom, he cannot in solitude drink that wine which he has promised to drink with us. While we remain in sin, he must remain in grief. If his Apostle grieves over "many that were in sin before and have not repented," how much more he who is called "the Son of Love," who humbled himself for the love that he had for us, and though he was equal to God sought not his own but our advantage, and to that end emptied himself. Do you think that having gone so far in seeking our good, he now ceases to seek it, that now he gives us no further thought and is not filled with sorrow when we leave his side? Will he who wept over Jerusalem and said of her: "How often would I have gathered together thy children, as a hen gathereth together her chickens under her wings, and ye would not" have now no tears to shed for our loss? Once as the healer of our bodies and souls he took upon himself our stripes and grieved over us. Is he now unconcerned at the foulness of our sores? "There is no soundness in my flesh, no health in my bones because of my folly," wrote the Psalmist. For all those sins of ours he now takes his stand before the face of God, interceding for us. He stands at the altar making propitiation for us to the Father. It was for this very reason that on the eve of his sacrifice he uttered the words, "I shall not drink of this fruit of the vine until the day when I drink it new with you." He is in suspense then until we are converted, till we have begun to follow the steps of his example, that then at last he may rejoice in our company and drink that wine with us in the Kingdom of his Father. And since the Lord is "compassionate and gracious" "he weeps with those that weep and rejoices with those that rejoice" with a depth of feeling beyond the range of his own Apostle. But over "the many that were in sin before and have not repented" his grief is greater still. It is inconceivable that Paul should grieve over sinners and weep over those who fall away, while my own Lord Jesus should be dry-eyed as he approaches his Father, when he stands by the altar and offers propitiation for us. "He who approaches the altar does not drink the wine of gladness," that is to say he still tastes the bitterness of our sins. He has no heart to drink that wine alone in the Kingdom of God—he is waiting for us; for did he not say, "until I drink with you"? It is we then who by the negligence of our lives delay his happiness.

It is for us he waits that he may drink "of the fruit of this vine." What vine does he mean? He means the vine of which he is the figure. "I am the vine, you are the branches." Wherefore he also said: "My blood is drink indeed and my flesh is food indeed." And in very truth "He has washed his garment in the blood of the grape." What then is he waiting for? For happiness. How long will he wait? "Until," he says, "I shall have finished the work God gave me." When does he finish that work? Only then when he has finished and perfected his work in me, the worst of all sinners. For as long as I am imperfect, his work too is imperfect. Nor, finally, is he said to be "subject to the Father" until I too am "subject" to the Father. Not that there is in him any lack of submission to the Father, but in so much as I, his work, am not yet finished, he himself is said not to be "subject." We read in the Scriptures that "we are the body of Christ and his members in part." Consider what is meant by "in part." Suppose, for example, that I am subject to God according to the spirit, that is, in my will and intentions, then while in me "the flesh lusteth against the spirit and the spirit against the flesh," and I am unable to bring the flesh into subjection to the spirit, then I am "subject" to God, it is true, yet not wholly but only "in part." But if I succeed in bringing the flesh likewise with all my members into harmony with the spirit, then I shall become perfectly "subject." If you have understood what perfect subjection and subjection only "in part" mean, consider now what I have said about our Lord's subjection and observe that as long as some of us are not yet in perfect subjection, he, whose body and members we are, is not said to be perfectly subject. But when he has finished his work and brought all his creation to the height of its perfection, then he too will be said to have attained his full subjection in us whom he has made subject to the Father and in whom he has consummated the work which the Father gave him, that God might be all in all.

And what is the point of all this? It is to bring you to an understanding of the reason of what we have treated above: namely, why he drinks wine and why he does not drink wine—drinking it, that is, before he enters into the tabernacle and before he approaches the altar, but not drinking it now because he stands before the altar in grief for my sins; yet he will drink it again in the future when all things shall have been made subject to him, when all have been saved and when with the abolition of the death of sin it will no longer be necessary for him to offer sacrifice for sin. Then will come the time for gladness and rejoicing, then "the bones which have been crushed will rejoice" and Scripture will be fulfilled, "Sorrow and sadness and mourning are no more."

But we must not lose sight of a further point. Not of Aaron alone was it said that he would not drink wine. His sons are included when they in their turn enter into the sanctuary. For not even the Apostles have entered as yet into their joy, but they must wait till I become a sharer in their joy. Nor do the saints when they leave this world receive the full reward of their merits, but they stand in wait for us, tardy and sluggish though we be. There can be no perfect joy for them while they still weep over our truancy and grieve for our sins. Perhaps you hesitate to take my word for this, for who am I to presume to establish such lofty doctrine on my own authority! So I call upon the most unimpeachable testimony—the teacher of the Gentiles in faith and in truth, the Apostle Paul. When writing to the Hebrews, after enumerating all those holy patriarchs who had been justified by faith, he adds: "All these, though through their faith they had gained approbation, yet they did not receive the fulfilment of the promise, for God intended that for our greater good they should not come to their perfection without us." You see, then, that Abraham is still waiting to receive his perfection. Isaac is waiting, Jacob and all the prophets are waiting for us, that with us they may receive their perfect happiness. Here is the reason why this mystery is kept till the Last Day, and why the Judgement is deferred till then. For it is one single body that awaits its justification, one body that is promised a future resurrection. "There are many members, yet one body. And the eye cannot say to the hand I have no need of thee." For even if the eye is a healthy one and without any defect of vision, what joy can it have if its fellow members are missing? What sort of perfection will it seem to have if it has no hands, if its feet are gone or the rest of its members missing? The eye, indeed, has a certain pre-eminence of glory, yet this lies chiefly in its being the guide of the body and is completely dependent on the eye not being deprived of the support of the other members. This I think is the lesson for us of that vision of the prophet Ezechiel where he says "that bone must be united with bone, joint to joint, and that nerves, veins and skin are all to be restored each to its proper place." Notice that last phrase of his—"these bones," he says; not, mark you, "all men," but "these bones" are the House of Israel. You will enter into joy then if you leave this life in holiness. But your full joy will only come when not one of your members is lacking. Wherefore you must wait for others, just as others have waited for you.

Surely, too, if you who are a member have not perfect joy as long as a member is missing, how much more will he, our Lord and Saviour, consider his joy incomplete while any member of his body is missing. This was the reason for his earnest prayer to the Father, "Holy Father, glorify me with that glory, which I had before the world was, with thee." He is loath to receive his perfect happiness without you, that is, without his people who constitute his body and his members. His wish, then, is to take up his dwelling as the soul of that body his Church and of those members his people, so that he may rule all their actions and works into accordance with his will, whereby that saying of the Prophet may be realized in us, "I shall dwell in them and walk amongst them." But while we are not yet perfect and are "still in our sins," he is only in us "in part" and so "we know in part and we prophesy in part" until each of us merits to arrive at that measure of which the Apostle speaks, "It is no longer I that live but Christ that liveth in me." "In part," then, as the Apostle says, "we are Christ's members," and "in part" we are his bones. But when bone shall have been joined to bone and joint to joint, as we have read above, then he will bring that prophecy to its realization in us, so that "all my bones will say, 'Lord, who is like unto thee?' " For all these bones give voice in song and thanks to God, mindful of the favour he has done to them. Then all my bones shall say, "Lord, who is like unto thee, who delivereth the needy from those too strong for him?" Of these bones, when they were still scattered apart before the coming of him who was to collect and gather them into one, this further prophecy was made, "Our bones have been scattered at the mouth of the nether-world." And it was by reason of this scattering that it was said by another prophet, "They shall be joined together, bone to bone, joint to joint, and veins and nerves and skin shall once more cover them." When this has been brought about, then "all these bones shall say, Lord, who is like unto thee, who delivereth the needy from those too strong for him." For each of those bones lay powerless, crushed beneath the hand of a too powerful adversary. For the joint of Charity, the veins of the living soul, the sinews of patience, the vigour of faith, all these were lacking. But when he comes who is to gather together that which was dispersed, joining bone to bone and joint to joint, then will he begin to build up that holy body which is the Church.

All this may seem a digression, but I found it necessary to introduce it in order to bring out more clearly how it is that our High Priest drinks no wine as he enters upon the sanctuary, nor will drink of it again till his priestly task is accomplished. Afterwards he will drink, but it will be new wine, and a new wine in a new heaven and a new earth, as a "new man" with "new men" and with those who will sing him a new song. Now you see how impossible it is for him who has not yet put off the "old man with his deeds" to drink the new draught from the new vine. "None," he has said, "puts new wine into old skins." If you too wish to drink of this new wine, then make yourself a new man, and say, "Even if our outward man suffers corruption, yet the inner man is ever renewed afresh."

Homily 7 on Leviticus, n. 2 (ed. Baehrens, pp. 374–80)

24

GREGORY OF NYSSA
When the Son also himself shall be subject . . .

When, therefore, like our first-fruit, we have put off from ourselves all evil, then the whole of our nature will be absorbed in him who is our first-fruit, and we shall become one continuous undivided body with him, admitting no other governor but the one and only Good. In this way the whole of our bodily nature will become mingled with the incorruptible divine nature, and the subjection attributed to the Son will also come about in us. When, I say, the subjection accomplished in his body is attributed to him as working the grace of subjection in us . . . then he absorbs into himself all who are made one with him by sharing the same body. He makes them all members of his own Body, so that there are many members, but one Body. When he has made us one with himself, and himself one with us, he becomes identified with us in all his operations, and makes all that is ours his own. Now the chief good that we possess is our subjection to God, when the whole of creation sings together in unison. . . . Then Christ makes his own the obedience which his whole Body gives to the Father. Let no one take this explanation amiss: we too instinctively attribute to the soul things that come about through the Body. . . . By making all men one with himself, through himself he makes them one with the Father, "As thou, Father, in me, and I in thee; that they also may be one in us. . . ." The words in the Gospel context are in complete harmony with what has been said: "The glory which thou hast given me, I have given to them."

By "glory" in this passage I hold that he means the Holy Spirit which he gave to his disciples when he breathed upon them. There is no other possible means of uniting district souls than by bringing them together into the unity of the Spirit: "Now if any man have not the spirit of Christ, he is none of his." And the Spirit is called glory, as Christ says to the Father in another place, "Glorify me with the glory which I had from the beginning before the world was, with thee. . . ." Nothing existed before all ages except the Father, the Son and the Holy Spirit; and so Christ says in the pas-

sage previously quoted, "The glory which thou hast given me,
I have given to them," that through it they may be made
one with me, and through me with thee.

*Treatise on the Text: "Then the Son himself shall be
subject"* (P.G. xliv, 1316–21)

25

JULIAN OF NORWICH
The Ghostly Thirst of Jesus

. . . Thus shall the ghostly thirst of Christ have an end.
For this is the ghostly thirst of Christ: the love-longing
that lasteth and ever shall, till we see that sight [the oneing
of all mankind that shall be saved unto the Blessed Trinity]
at Doomsday. For we that shall be saved and shall be Christ's
joy and his bliss, some be yet here and some be to come,
and so shall some be, unto that day. Therefore this is his
thirst and love-longing, to have us all together whole in
him, to his bliss—as to my sight. . . .

For we know in our Faith . . . that Christ Jesus is both
God and man. And anent the Godhead, he is himself highest
bliss, and was from without beginning, and shall be without
end: which endless bliss may never be heightened nor low-
ered in itself. . . . And anent Christ's manhood, it is known
in our Faith . . . that he with the virtue of Godhead, for
love, to bring us to his bliss, suffered pains and passions and
died. . . . Anent that Christ is our Head, he is glorified
and impassible; and anent his Body in which all his members
be knit, he is not yet fully glorified, nor all impassible.
Therefore the same desire and thirst that he had upon the
Cross (which desire, longing and thirst, as to my sight, was
in him from without beginning) the same hath he yet, and
shall, unto the time that the last soul that shall be saved is
come up to his bliss. . . . The ghostly thirst is lasting in
him as long as we be in need, drawing us up to his bliss.

Revelations of Divine Love, ch. 31

26

ADELMAN OF BRESCIA
Growth of the Body of Christ

Let us believe from our hearts and proclaim it by our
words that the power of Christ, which is invisible, works

through the visible ministry of his priest, and creates out of material bread the true body of Christ. Let us also believe that all who are born again of water and of the Holy Ghost are, by partaking of this food, incorporated into Christ himself. For in the words of the Apostle: "As the body is one and has many members, and all the members of the body, whereas they are many, yet are one body, so also is Christ." Such is clearly the man of whom Paul speaks in another place, "Until we all meet unto the perfect man": he does not say "perfect *men*," but "perfect *man*." The Head of this man is none other than he who was born of the Virgin Mary, died and rose again; the members are the elect, from the beginning of the world to the end.

Now just as in our own bodies the head is the seat of all the senses and of the intellect itself (whereas the rest of the body possesses only the sense of touch, each of the members having its own particular function to carry out), so is it, according to the Apostle, with him who is our Head: "In him are hid all the treasures of wisdom and knowledge"; and again: "He is the head of the body, the Church." About the members, on the other hand, this is what Paul says: "To every one of us is given grace according to the measure of the giving of Christ." And about himself, assuredly a true member of this Head, he says: "to fill up those things that are wanting of the sufferings of Christ in my flesh," calling the sufferings he himself is enduring the "sufferings of Christ." Therefore Christ suffered in Paul and was crucified in Peter, both Peter and Paul being in Christ citizens of heaven; "our fatherland is in heaven," says St Paul. And elsewhere he shows his hope even more clearly: "He hath quickened us together in Christ . . . and hath made us to sit together in the heavenly places." We may well be surprised: he was still being buffeted on earth by an angel of Satan, and yet he gloried in that he was, in Christ, risen and sitting in heaven. Now he could say this because of the union which obtains between all the members dependent on one another, as he explains more clearly in another passage: "If one member suffer anything, all the members suffer with it; or if one member glory, all the members rejoice with it."

This same teaching is frequently given by our Lord himself in the Gospels. When he says: "I am the vine, you the branches"; or: "unless the grain of wheat falling into the ground die, itself remaineth alone. But if it die, it bringeth forth much fruit." He can only imply by these examples this same interdependence of all who are united to him, which he in his goodness and love procured for them, giving them to share in his own glory. . . .

Again, the vision of King Nabuchodonosor seems to contain this same idea: he saw a small stone (this stands for Christ) which, cut out from the mountain without being touched by human hand (as Christ was conceived without human seed), increased in size till it became itself a great mountain and filled the whole earth (*Dan.* ii. 34–5). The meaning of this is that our Lord's Body, which had its origin in a minute fragment of matter taken from the single mass of the human race, has had added to it a great number of the faithful, so that, multiplying itself many times, it goes on growing until the end of the world, when it will have filled the whole earth.

This Body, then, is even now fully and perfectly glorified in its Head, and also in those of its members of whom it is written: "and many bodies of the saints that had slept, arose"; these are now at rest in perfect happiness in heaven. But other members are still suffering—those, that is, who are yet in this mortal life and imprisoned in the body, "mourning, and desiring to be dissolved and to be with Christ." Further, there are amongst the members of this immense Body (it may well be called "gigantic," according to the Psalmist: "He rejoices as a giant") some who, although they have been cleansed from all stain of sin and now enjoy the glory of the blessed, yet abide in the firm hope of their happiness being increased, for they look to the end of time when their bodies will at last rise again, to be harmoniously united with each other in a deathless life.

It is likely that the Psalmist is referring to the striking diversity of the members of this Body, when, under the inspiration of the Holy Ghost, he says: "The queen stood on thy right hand in gilded clothing, surrounded with variety." Surely this queen is the consort of the King who is referred to a little after: "And the king shall greatly desire thy beauty, for he is the Lord, thy God."

This King is her God, her Spouse, her Head; while she is his Church. By nature his servant, by grace she has been made his Spouse and his Body, and we can say that now is fulfilled that mysterious thing which was promised in the beginning of the world: "they shall be two in one flesh." What surrounds her is the great variety of her different members, some reigning in bliss, others suffering—"sowing in tears"—as they await the redemption of their bodies. Yet their present state is not to last for ever: otherwise they would be in the most wretched condition imaginable. But how long will it go on? And when will it end? It will last as long as the King remains resting on his couch, tarrying it may be, but bound inevitably to come in the end; and when he does show himself, at the same time the queen will appear with him in glory. Then this great variety of her members will finally disappear, for, with "death swallowed up in victory," the whole Body will be clothed with the glorious state of immortality, and all the members will be conformed to their Head, all of one accord rejoicing in an honour at once special to each and reflecting back from each to the whole. On that day, our Lord Jesus Christ, having delivered the kingdom to God and the Father, and reduced to nothing all principalities and powers, will introduce his Church without spot or wrinkle into his presence, and God will be all in all.

Adelmanni ex scholastico Leodiensi episcopi Brixiensis, de Eucharistiae sacramento ad Berengarium epistola. (*See* R. Heurtevent, *Durand de Troarn et les origines de l'hérésie bérengarienne,* 1912, pp. 298–302.)

27

COURNOT
The Historical Character of the Bible

The other religions of antiquity have not, properly speaking, a historical side to them, and although of necessity they have their own history, just as every sect or institution has, they are not founded on history; in their sacred writings, when they have any, it is only cosmogonies and myths that are recorded. By contrast there is nothing more imposing, nothing simpler and briefer than the purely cosmogonic portion of the Jewish people's sacred books. And the genealogies which follow, if they are not exactly historical in every way, are very much more so than all other accounts of the same kind. Lastly, the books of a national history which reciprocally verify and are verified by the historical records of other peoples—and in this they are unique—play a considerable and fundamental part in the scheme of the canonical books. Later on, as the Jews became involved with the great empires of antiquity, they linked up their prophecies and their hopes for the end of time with the break-up of these empires; so that even in the dreams of an oppressed people there appears and is developed the idea of a plan of historical events.

Traité de l'enchaînement des idées fondamentales dans les sciences et dans l'histoire, ed. Hachette, 1911, pp. 655–6

28

RUPERT OF TUY
Jacob's Ladder

On this Christmas night there is read before Mass the genealogy of Jesus Christ from St Matthew's Gospel—a custom handed down by holy Church with a beauty and mystery of its own. For behold how in truth the authors of the divine office by this reading put before us at dead of night that ladder which Jacob saw at night in his sleep. Supported on the topmost rung of the ladder where it reached heaven the Lord appeared to Jacob and promised him that his posterity would inherit the earth. This vision took place when he was on his way, at his father's command, to assure that posterity by taking a wife from the family and kin of his father and mother. . . . Now, as we know, "all these things happened to them in figure." The ladder by which the Lord appeared to be supported prefigured the family-tree of Jesus Christ which the holy Gospel-writer so drew up as to come through Joseph. It is by Joseph that our Lord as a small child is supported. . . .

Through the gate of heaven—a gate to which the topmost rung of the ladder, meaning St Joseph, is joined by his dignity of spouse—through this gate, that is, through the Blessed Virgin, our Lord, a tiny child for our sake, comes crying. He comes supported by the ladder, as I have said above, and in proof of his blessing promises our salvation, that is the salvation of the Gentiles: rather he fulfils that promise. For the words which Jacob in his sleep heard the Lord say, "And in thy posterity shall all the nations of the earth be blessed," are fulfilled by the birth of Christ.

The divine writer, bearing in mind this very point, put the names of Rahab the prostitute and Ruth the Moabite into his genealogy. For he saw that Christ was made flesh not for the Jews alone, but also for the Gentiles, inasmuch as he deigned to accept mothers from among the Gentiles. The prophets had previously borne witness to this. David, for example, says: "I shall remember Rahab and Babylon": that is, the wide extent and confusion of the Gentiles, for Rahab means "wide extent" and Babylon "confusion." And Isaias in his vision over Moab: "Send forth, O Lord, thy lamb, the ruler of the earth, from Petra in the desert to the mount of the daughter of Sion," as if he were to say plainly: "Thou shalt send forth, O Lord, thy lamb Christ from the midst of the Gentiles, to prevent carnal Israel from boasting that Christ is exclusively her own—Israel to whose notions it is clearly repugnant that thou shouldst send the same Christ from the Gentiles to the mount of the daughter of Sion." For Petra in the desert represents Ruth the Moabite who, standing fast on the rock (*petra*) of a firm faith, forsook her own people and her native gods and going with Noemi married Booz of Bethlehem, by whom she was the mother of Obed, the grandfather of David; and so also the ancestor of the Saviour.

Sprung therefore from two races, Jew and Gentile, as from two sides of the ladder, the ancestors from their different rungs support Christ our Lord emerging from heaven. The holy angels come up and go down and all the elect are first humbled to receive faith in his Incarnation that they may be afterwards lifted up to see the glory of his divinity. Hence our Lord himself says elsewhere, "Amen I say to you, you will see heaven opening and the angels of God going up and coming down upon the Son of Man." That is to say, you will see all the saints going up to God supported and raised up by the Son of Man, since the barriers of heaven have been opened by his redemption. But to be able to go up, they first go down in a spirit of humility to adore his cross and passion.

This double movement of ascent and descent seems to be hinted at by Matthew and Luke when the former composed the genealogy in a descending order, the latter in an ascending order. For God-made-man, crying in his crib, invites us to humble ourselves by the example of his humility: but once baptized and beginning to be famous by his heavenly miracles, he raises up the humble to the understanding of his divine glory.

De divinis officiis, lib. 3, c. 18 (P.L. clxx, 75-7)

29

ORIGEN
The Water of Mara

"They came to Mara but they could not drink its waters because they were bitter, whereupon he gave the place an appropriate name, calling it Mara, that is, bitterness. And the people grumbled against Moses, saying, 'What shall we drink?' But Moses cried to the Lord who showed him a tree. And when this had been cast into the waters they were turned into sweetness." (*Exodus* xv. 23-5.) The Old Law, then, is an exceeding bitter draught to drink. . . . But if God should reveal a tree which when cast into this bitterness should turn it into a law of sweet waters, then one might drink of it. Moreover, we know the tree that the Lord has revealed, for Solomon teaches us when speaking of wisdom that it is a tree of life to those that embrace it. If then the tree of the wisdom of Christ be cast into the waters of the Old Law and show us what we are to think of circumcision, what are the obligations of the law of the Sabbath, the law of leprosy, the distinction between things clean and unclean, then the water of Mara is made sweet and the bitterness of the letter of the law is turned into the sweetness of a spiritual understanding so that we of God's people can drink of it. For unless we understand such things in a spiritual sense then a people which has abandoned idols and turned to God, on hearing of a law enjoining sacrifices, will have none of that law, and will refuse to drink of it, finding it bitter and harsh.

To make this water of Mara drinkable, then, God has revealed a tree that may be cast into it so that he who drinks of the water may neither die nor find any bitterness in it.

Clearly, then, if anyone wishes to drink of the letter of the law without this tree of life, that is, without the mystery of the Cross, without faith in Christ, without spiritual understanding, then he will die of its exceeding bitterness. This is what St Paul had in mind when he said that it is the letter that killeth, plainly declaring that the water of Mara is deadly if drunk unsweetened and unchanged.

In Exodum, homily 7, n. 1 (Baehrens, pp. 205–6)

30

GREGORY OF NYSSA
The New Myth of the Cave

The Church receives the light of truth through the porch of prophecy and the lattice of the Law. The Law was a wall of partition through which the original revelation came. The very truth could not pass through, but only a type or foreshadowing. But behind this wall of partition stands the truth which the type foreshadowed. The Church received the first rays of the Word of Truth through the Prophets. But the time came when the very Truth was revealed in the Gospel, and in its light the shadowy outlines of the type of prophecy fade, and the wall of partition is broken down. The house is thrown wide open, and the light of heaven pours in, mingling unhindered with the inner air. No longer need we contrive to catch a few dim rays through a tiny casement; for now the Gospel glory of the true Sun sheds its brightness on all within the house.

On the Canticle of Canticles, homily 5 (P.G. xliv, 865D)

31

PAUL CLAUDEL
The Everlastingness of the Old Testament

The Old Testament, which is made up of history, lyrical and devotional poetry, moral and ritual regulations, cannot be understood without that invisible, future presence which co-ordinates it and settles its direction, even in its slightest shades of meanings and its most colourless passages, surrounding it in its entirety with an atmosphere of prophecy. The Old Testament cannot be understood without the New, which comes to fulfil, to justify and to explain. "I am not come," said our Lord, "to destroy but to fulfil . . . one jot or one tittle shall not pass from the law, till all be fulfilled." And, as in truth the letter has passed away, it must indeed be admitted that, if something remains, that something is its spiritual meaning, dominating, and inherent in, the text of the Old Testament, right down to its smallest details. If

every jot and tittle are to be endowed with perpetuity, it is
because their claim to it comes from God, whom, we are told,
they show forth, rather than from their intrinsic worth; it is
because the dead letter must give way to the spirit which
quickens. . . .

So, nowadays as in all other times, Holy Scripture still
remains the seed of the Church and has lost nothing of its
power to take root and grow. It is not a historical document addressed exclusively to its contemporaries. Himself
above all time, our Lord never ceases to testify that his
whole mission is to fulfil and bring to completion. Deprived
of its opportunities, the original circumstances of its composi-
tion and its proper season, the substance of the written word,
even to every jot and tittle (St Augustine), is still addressed
to us as it was to our fathers. "Unless the grain of wheat
. . . die . . ." says the Gospel, unless it loses its husk to dis-
close before our eyes starch and gluten. . . .

Scripture is concerned throughout with Jesus Christ; sometimes it is Jesus Christ who manifests himself and makes himself known; at others it is we who perceive him, answering
his summons to press forward on the path that he shows us.

> *Introduction au livre de Ruth, Le sens figuré de*
> *l'Écriture, pp. 87–8, 110–1 and 114*

32

PSEUDO-EPIPHANIUS
The Light of the Cross

What is this? To-day there is a great silence in the world;
a great silence, and a stillness over all, because the King
slumbers. The earth is fearful, and has grown still, because
God, falling asleep in his flesh, has awakened those who have
slept from the world's beginning. . . .

Christ our God, our Sun, has sunk to his setting, and has
brought for the Jews an endless night. This day has brought
salvation for those upon the earth, and those who have
been below the earth for generations; it has brought salvation for the whole universe, visible and invisible. . . . Christ
is among the dead; let us go down with him, and gaze upon
the mysteries hidden there. . . .

Listen now to the deeper meaning of Christ's suffering;
listen, and sing your hymn of praise; listen, and extol the
wonderful works of God. See how Law gives way, and

Grace begins to flower; see how the ancient Types recede, how the shadows scatter, and our Sun now fills the whole world; see how the Old Law passes, and the New is ratified, how the past fades before the bright coming of the present.

At the house of Christ's Passion, there were two peoples met together in Sion, the Jews and the Gentiles; there were two kings, Pilate and Herod; there were two chief-priests, Annas and Caiphas, so that two Paschs might be kept together, the one on the point of ceasing, the other—the Pasch of Christ—to be celebrated for the first time. Two sacrifices were offered on that same evening; so was there wrought a double salvation, salvation of the living and of the dead. The Jews were binding a lamb for sacrifice and slaughter; the Gentiles were binding God made Man. The Jews were still gazing into darkness; the Gentiles were hastening towards the Light, towards God himself. The Jews were recalling their deliverance from Egypt; the Gentiles were proclaiming their deliverance from all untruth. . . .

And where did this take place? In Sion, the city of the great King. There, at the world's centre, was accomplished the world's salvation; there, between the two Living Beings, Father and Spirit, Jesus was seen to be the Son of God. Angels and men were round the manger at his birth; and he, set as a corner-stone for both peoples, heralded alike by Law and Prophets, seen upon the mountain with Moses and Elias, recognized as God as he hung between the two thieves —he, this day, in the midst of the living and the dead, to both alike has brought life and salvation.

He has united in peace his two peoples, linking the things of heaven with the things of earth. . . . With symbols merely, and in darkness, as the Paschal night came down, Israel kept her Pasch; in clearer truth and light, do we keep ours, while Time's long day moves to its close.

Homily II for Holy Saturday (P.G. xliii, 440-1 and 468-9)

33

ST AMBROSE
The Church, the Mystic Eve

Moses tells us that after the creation of man God also made woman. "Then the Lord cast a deep sleep upon Adam; and when he was fast asleep, he took one of his ribs and filled up flesh for it. And the Lord God built the rib which he took from Adam into a woman" (*Gen.* ii. 21, 22). This way of acting on the part of God forces me to see something more which I cannot quite grasp. Such passages as "Bone of my bones and flesh of my flesh," "She shall be called woman because she was taken out of man," left me in doubt as to their meaning. St Paul came to my help and inspired by the Holy Spirit gave me the clue with the words: "This is a great mystery." The mystery of which he is speaking is contained in the words: "They shall be two in one flesh" and "For this cause shall a man leave his father and mother and shall cleave to his wife" and "Because we are members of his body, of his flesh and of his bones" (*Eph.* v. 30–2). What man and what woman is he speaking of? The woman who leaves her parents is the Church, composed as she is of Gentiles, the Church to whom it was said in prophecy, "forget thy people and thy father's house" (*Ps.* xliv. 11). And for what man if not for him of whom John spake, "After me there cometh a man who was before me"? (*John* i. 27–30).

From his side as he slept God took a rib; it was he indeed who slept, took his rest and rose again, for the Lord raised him up. And this rib of his is nothing but his power, his virtue. When the soldier opened his side there came forth at once blood and water, which was poured forth for the life of the world. This life of the world is the rib of Christ, the rib of the second Adam; for the first Adam was made a living soul, but the second Adam a life-giving spirit. The second Adam is Christ and the rib of Christ is the life of the Church. We therefore are members of his body, of his flesh, and of his bones; and it may have been of this rib that he said one day: "I know that virtue is gone out from me" (*Luke* viii. 46). This is the rib which came from Christ without mutilating his body, for it was not a bodily but a spiritual rib, and the Spirit is not divided but gives to others according as he wills. This rib is no other than Eve, mother of all the living, and the mother of the living is the Church. God built her upon the supreme corner-stone, Jesus Christ, on whom every well-built structure rises up to form the temple of God.

Come then, dear God, and fashion this woman, this helper for Adam . . . for Christ. Not that Christ is in any need of help, but because we seek and long to find, through the

Church, the grace of Christ. At this very moment the Church is a building and taking shape; the woman is being fashioned and made. And so the Scripture makes use of a new term: we are "built up upon" the foundation of the apostles and the prophets (*Eph.* ii. 20). At this very moment a spiritual building is rising into a holy priesthood. Come, Lord God, fashion this woman, build this city; and let thy Son come, for I believe thy word: "It is he who shall build my city" (*Isaias* xliv. 13).

Lo! the woman, mother of all; lo! the spiritual dwelling, lo! the city that shall abide for ever, for it knows not death. It is the city of Jerusalem, the city which appears now upon earth, but will be lifted higher than Elias, higher than Enoch. He indeed was carried aloft, lest his heart be changed through malice; but that other, the Church, is loved by Christ as his spouse, glorious, holy, immaculate and without spot. And if one man was carried on high, shall not the whole body be even more so? Such is the hope of the Church. It shall indeed be carried on high, it shall be lifted up, translated to heaven. In a burning chariot was Elias taken up; so shall it be with the Church. You do not believe me? Then believe Paul in whom Christ has spoken: "We shall be taken up in the clouds to meet Christ" (*I Thess.* iv. 16).

For the building of this city how many are sent by God! The Patriarchs and prophets, the Archangel Gabriel and countless angels—and the whole heavenly host gives praise to God because the perfection of the city draws nigh. Many are sent, it is true, but it is Christ alone who is the builder, though indeed he is not alone, for the Father is with him. And if he is the only builder, yet he does not usurp to himself the glory of so great a labour.

It is written of Solomon's temple, which is a type of the Church, that when it was building there were seventy thousand men to carry the materials on their shoulders, eighty thousand stone-cutters and three thousand six hundred overseers (*II Paralip.* ii. 2). Let his angels come then, heavenly stone-cutters; let them cut off all that is superfluous in us and remove all our roughnesses. Let them come and lift us on their shoulders, for it is written: "On their shoulders shall they be carried" (*Isaias* xlix. 22).

Exposition of the Gospel according to St Luke, Book 2, n. 85–9, (P.L. xv, 1666–8)

34

PAULINUS OF NOLA
Christ Suffering in His Members

From the beginning of time Christ has been suffering in his followers. He is, in fact, the beginning and the end, veiled in the old law, revealed in the Gospel, the Lord ever wonderful, suffering and triumphing in his saints: in Abel, slain by his brother; in Noe, mocked by his son; exiled from his land, in Abraham; in Isaac, offered as a victim; made a slave, in Jacob; in Joseph, sold; in Moses, exposed as an infant and later a fugitive; in the prophets, stoned and slain; in the apostles, afflicted by land and sea and slain time and again in the manifold tortures of the Martyrs. It is always he, as in the past so in the present, who bears our afflictions and carries our griefs; always is he, the Man covered with wounds for us, bearing that infirmity which we, without him, could never bear, even if we knew how to. He, I say, at this very moment, for us and in us, endures the malice of the world, that endurance may have the victory and power be made perfect in infirmity. He, in you, suffers contumely, and it is he in you who is hated by the world.

Letter 38, n. 3 (P.L. lxi, 359)

35

SEVERUS OF ANTIOCH
The Good Samaritan

"A certain man was going down from Jerusalem to Jericho." The use of the specific noun is to the point: not "somebody was going down," but "a certain man"; for the whole of humanity is in question, inasmuch as it has fallen, through the disobedience of Adam, from the height of the abode of Paradise—lofty and calm, passionless and godlike, here aptly called "Jerusalem," which means "peace of God"—to the depth of Jericho, low-lying and stifled in heat—meaning the ardent life of this world, which separates from God and drags down, which causes suffocation in the heat of shameful desire, and chokes to death.

Once humanity had gone astray towards this life, and had

lost her balance and been drawn down, borne little by little to the lowest point of the downward path, as I have said, there settled on her a swarm of savage demons, like a band of brigands; and they stripped her of the cloak of virtue, leaving her not a vestige of fortitude or temperance or justice or prudence, or of anything that represented the image of God; and so they hacked her to death with the repeated wounds of various sins, leaving her cut to pieces; in a word, half-dead. . . .

So while humanity was lying prostrate and all but fainting to death, she was visited by the Mosaic Law; for this is of course the meaning of the priest and the Levite, since it was the Law that taught the Levitic priesthood. It did indeed visit her, but it fell short in competence, and was not equal to a full treatment; it did not even raise the prostrate form, but went perforce, in its incompetence, on an ineffectual round. For sacrifices and gifts were offered through it, as Paul said, which were unable to perfect the worshipper in conscience; because, again, it was impossible that the blood of bulls and goats should entirely take away sin. . . .

At last "a certain Samaritan who was going on a journey came to where he was. . . ." Now it was to the point that Christ here called himself a Samaritan; for since he was dealing with a lawyer, who prided himself greatly on the Law, he took care to show by his words that it was not the priest or the Levite, or indeed, to speak in general terms, those who thought to model their conduct on the Mosaic statutes, but himself who was come to fulfil the will of the Law, and to show by actual practice who was really one's neighbour, and what it was to love him as oneself—he to whom the Jews said as an insult: "Thou art a Samaritan, and thou hast a devil." . . .

This Samaritan, then, who was going on a journey—that is, Christ—visited the prostrate man. For he had in fact really *come* on the journey; he was not just passing by, as he was making the journey for that very purpose—to visit us, the people for whom he came down to earth and with whom he dwelt. For he did not merely show himself, but also lived among mankind, becoming man in truth, without figure or fancy; for it is distinctive of true and charitable physicians to live among the sick, and not leave them before they are cured. . . . When pouring wine on the wounds—the Word, instructive but pungent, . . . "the wine of repentance"— . . .

since . . . the severity . . . of the wounds could not bear a strong astringent, he tempered it with oil. That was why he sat at table with publicans and sinners, and told the contentious Pharisees, when they brought his human kindness against him as a reproach: "Go and learn what this means: It is mercy I want, not sacrifices." Next, he says, he mounted him on a beast; meaning that because "man," as the Scripture says, "when he was well off, did not use his intelligence, but imitated the senseless beast, and became like it," and fell sick of every beastly and unclean desire: so Christ, who knew not sin, having become the first-fruits of our race, showed first in himself that having trampled down these beastly passions we have mounted and risen above them; for he has taken the weight of our infirmities and borne the load of our ills. That is why he said that he mounted him, when he had received treatment, on his own ass; for he was bearing us in himself, because we are members of his own body.

But what is more, "he brought him to an inn." Now, πανδοχεῖον —that is, "inn," literally "all-receiving"—is his name for the Church, which has become receptive and holds all mankind: for no longer do we hear, in the restrictive manner of the foreshadowing in the Law and the worship by symbols, "the Ammonite and the Moabite shall not enter the Assembly of the Lord," but: "Go and teach all nations . . ." and "in every nation, he that fears him and does what is right is acceptable to him." And having brought him to the inn, he showed still more solicitude for him. For, indeed, when the Church had been assembled from nations dying of polytheism, Christ himself was in it, dwelling and moving, as the Scripture says, and giving every spiritual grace.

So "to the man in charge of the inn"—let us take him as standing both for the Apostles and for the shepherds and teachers their successors—as he was ascending to heaven, "he gave two coins," bidding him take especial care of the sick man, and adding, "if you incur any further expense, I will repay you on my return." By "two coins" he meant the two Testaments, the Old and the New: that is, the one given in the Mosaic Law and the Prophets, and the one given in the Gospels and the Apostolic Constitutions; both of which are of the same God, and bear, like coins, the same image of the same king on high, and with their sacred words imprint in our hearts the stamp of the same royal likeness. Away,

then, with Manes and his predecessor Marcion, the godless
ones who assigned each of them to a different God. These
two coins were of the same king, given by Christ to the
man in charge of the inn together and without distinction of
value.

Now, since the pastors of the holy Churches have received
these, and developed their teachings with labour and sweat,
and have gone on paying out from their own store, rather
increasing it by the expenditure (for the money of the mind
has this property, that instead of growing less and less with
expenditure, it grows more and more), each of them will say,
when Christ has come again at the last day: "Lord, thou
gavest me two coins; see," by continuing to pay out of my
own account, "I have gained two more," whereby I have
increased and multiplied the flock; and he will say in reply:
"Well done, good and faithful servant; thou hast been faithful in charge of a few things, I will give thee charge over
many: enter upon the joy of thy Lord."

Homily 89 (Patrologia Orientalis xxiii, 105–14)

36

MAXIMUS OF TURIN
The Woman at the Mill

The woman hid the leaven in the dough, as it is written.
Who is this woman? Is she not the Church who day after
day seeks to hide the teaching of Christ in the depths of our
hearts?

The Church is indeed she and she is also that other woman
sitting there at the mill, she to whom our Lord referred
when he said, "Two women shall be grinding at the mill:
one shall be taken, and one shall be left."

Holy Church is sitting at the mill and her millstones are
the Law, the Apostles and the Prophets. When she teaches
her catechumens she is picking out and crushing the hard
grain of paganism.

Then she grinds men into a smooth flour, so that this flour
may be ready to receive the unifying leaven of the divine
Blood.

The leaven, I mean, is all our Lord's Passion. The leaven
of salvation is the Creed which is delivered to the newly
baptized.

Without the leaven of the Blood and the leaven of faith there is no one who can become by grace the substantial bread of eternal life.

But if the message of glad tidings speaks of two women busy at the mill, and if one of the women is the Church who turns the stones of the mill of salvation, is not the other woman the synagogue? She too turns the mill of Moses and the Prophets, but she turns it in vain, as the Apostle says of the Jews: "They are zealous for God, but with a zeal without understanding."

The synagogue works the mill in vain, for she does not mix with her dough the leaven of Christ's teaching.

Holy Church is led onwards to eternal rest; for she has made ready for the Lord the peace of holiness.

The hard-hearted synagogue is left by her mill, sentenced to turn for ever the stones of her unbelief.

Homily cxi (P.L. lvii, 514 B–D)

37

ISAAC DE STELLA
Mary, the Church and the Soul

. . . Head and body: one single whole, Christ: of one God in heaven and one mother on earth. Sons both many and one: for as the head and members are one son, as well as more than one, so Mary and the Church are one mother and more than one, one virgin and more than one.

Each of the two is mother, each of the two is virgin. Each conceives by the same spirit without carnal attraction, each without sin brings forth an offspring to God the Father. Mary without sin provides the head for the body: the Church by the remission of all sins provides the body for the head. Each is the mother of Christ, but neither gives birth to the whole without the other.

Therefore, in the divinely inspired Scripture, what is said universally of the Church, virgin and mother, is also said individually of Mary; and what is said in a special way of Mary, virgin and mother, is understood by right, but in a general way, of the Church, virgin and mother: so that, when the Scripture is understood to be speaking of either, it can be applied to one or the other almost indifferently and in a mixed manner.

Also each faithful soul is the spouse of the Word of God, the mother, daughter and sister of Christ. Each faithful soul is understood in its own sense to be virgin and fruitful.

The same thing is therefore said universally for the Church, in a special way for Mary, individually for the faithful soul: and it is the Wisdom of God who speaks, the Word of the Father.

. .. It is also said: "And I shall dwell in the heritage of the Lord." For the heritage of the Lord, in a universal sense, is the Church, in a special sense, Mary, in an individual sense, each faithful soul.

Christ dwelt for nine months in the tabernacle of Mary's womb. He dwells till the end of the world in the tabernacle of the Church's faith. He will dwell for ever and ever in the knowledge and love of the faithful soul.

Sermon 61, on the Assumption (P.L. cxciv, 1863 and 1865)

38

WILLIAM OF AUVERGNE
The Slow Coming of the Worship of God

But why did God leave the divine cult imperfect and wanting for so many thousands of years? Why did he not take thought sooner for his glory and for our salvation?

One answer to such questions is this: if but a small fraction of the peoples of the world, the Jewish race alone, was capable of understanding, in the most simple and elementary way, wherein lay the perfection of the divine cult, and if to do even this they needed the persuasion of miracles, and something of the compelling power of many great afflictions, not to mention the help gained from knowledge handed on by their ancestors; surely the whole world and society of mankind was far more incapable of attaining to the required perfection in so great a matter. And so God permitted his cult to be imperfect until the fullness of time was come (*Gal.* iv), just as he permits children to be immature and the seed of plants and of animals to be small, till by gradual growth they reach their full and perfect stature.

To go further, the fundamental meaning of the question we are answering is this: why are we born as infants, instead of as fully developed and mature men? Why do certain animals lay eggs instead of bringing to birth fully developed

offspring? When God's cult, the true religion, was first established in the world, it existed rather in the manner of a seed
or an infant, because the community of mankind itself was
immature and unfitted for anything more advanced.

On the Sacrament of the Eucharist, Chap. 2 (*Opera*, Paris,
1674, t. 1, p. 437, col. 2)

39

CARDINAL FAULHABER
Why the Saviour was Born so Late in Time

"Why was our Saviour born so late in time?" "My Father
worketh until now . . ." (*John* v. 17). In carrying into effect
the divine economy of salvation there is no interruption, but
neither is there precipitation. There is no loitering, but neither
is there impetuous haste.

The Man-God was born only when the light of the messianic prophecies had shone through a long Advent and the
world was ready to receive its Saviour and its King. Ask no
longer, then, why our Saviour was born so late! He was to
be not only the dew from heaven and the gift from on
high, but the "fruit of the earth" (*Isaias* iv. 2) and was to
"bud forth" from the earth (*Isaias* xlv. 8). He was not to
speed to earth like a shaft, but to "bud forth" slowly from
the earth like a plant. . . . At the same time pagan Humanity
had first to endure the wretchedness of being separated from
God and brood over all the bitterness of that state. . . .
The educative activity of Divine Providence needed time for
its accomplishment. That is why our Saviour was born so
late in time.

From French trans.: *Juifs et chrétiens devant le racisme*,
1935, pp. 81–2

40

ST GREGORY NAZIANZEN
From Idols to the Trinity

In the history of religion there have been two revolutions,
called the two Testaments or, by St. Paul, "tremors of the
earth." In the first man passed from idolatry to the Law,
and in the second from the Law to the Gospel. And now

we proclaim a third cataclysm, the transference from the present order to that beyond, where there can be no further change or disturbance.

One element the two Testaments have in common. They were established without any abrupt or instantaneous transformation.

It is well to realize the reason for this. God did not wish us to be coerced, but persuaded. For that which is not voluntary is not enduring, as we may see by comparison with the forceful repression of a stream or a plant. On the other hand, a transformation undertaken voluntarily is more lasting, more surely grounded. Coercion is the work of an external and tyrannical power, but choice is our own and is consonant with the goodness of God.

God, then, did not desire us to conform to the good under compulsion, but to choose the good. Hence, in the manner of one instructing children or tending the sick, he withdrew some of our traditional practices while condoning others, yielding to us on some small point to keep us happy. . . . For it is not easy to abandon customs which long usage has invested with dignity and veneration.

Thus, the first Testament abolished idols, but allowed the traditional sacrifices; the second suppressed these, but did not forbid circumcision. In this way men accepted the suppression and then came to give up of their own accord what had been condoned—sacrifices under the old law, circumcision in the new. From pagans they became Jews, from Jews Christians, led furtively, one might say, towards the Gospel by these gradual changes. . . .

With this process I may compare the development of the notion of the Godhead, except that here the process is reversed. In the former instance transformation came by way of suppression; but here perfection was approached by gradual increment. . . . This is what I mean.

The Old Testament unambiguously proclaimed the Father, the Son more obscurely; the New Testament gave full revelation of the Son, but put forward more tentatively the divinity of the Holy Ghost. But to-day the Holy Spirit is resident and active in our midst, giving us a clearer manifestation of his nature.

For it would have been misleading to proclaim decisively the divinity of the Son at a time when that of the Father was not openly admitted, or to add that of the Holy Ghost before the Son had been fully recognized, as an additional burden to our intellects, if I may use so bold an expression. We might, as children given food beyond their power of assimilation or as men of weak sight turning their gaze upon the sun, have imperilled what here and now lay within our grasp. It was more fitting that by piecemeal additions and, in the words of David, by gradual advance from splendour to splendour, the full radiance of the Trinity should come to shine on us. . . .

In this way one can understand the progressive illumination of our understanding, and trace the line of development in the expanding notion of the Godhead. It would be well for us, too, to keep to this line of advance in instructing others, neither displaying the full doctrine from the beginning, nor keeping it from them to the very end. The former course of action would be imprudent and would bewilder unbelievers, the latter impious and it would estrange the faithful.

I will add one consideration which, though it has probably occurred to others, comes to me as the fruit of my own reflexion. There were some truths which our Saviour, perhaps for the reasons I have outlined, told his disciples that they were as yet unable to bear, abounding as they were already in the riches of his teaching. And elsewhere he says that the Spirit of God, dwelling in us, will teach us all truth. Now one of these truths was, I think, the divinity of the Holy Spirit himself, which was made plain later; for the comprehension of this fact could only become firm when our Lord's triumph no longer left room for doubt as to the marvel of his own divinity.

Discourse 31 (*5th Theological Discourse*), Chaps. 25, 26, 27 (P.G. xxxvi, 160–4)

41

CHARLES MIEL, S.J. († 1934)
Man is Adult

. . . We must make no mistake about it. For, if I may put it thus, the Catholic system looks well. It stands up, it is attractive. Still, I don't think there is any advantage in hiding from others, any more than from ourselves, the fundamental strangeness of the redemptive economy. It may even be beneficial to realize this strangeness to the full. We must acknowledge to ourselves that as really believing Catholics we appear to those outside, to-day no less than in the past, as people who accept monstrous beliefs. We must not be astonished, still less worried, if people look on us with amazement, and if sometimes we are asked: "Honestly now, *do* you believe all that?" It is to be expected. A book which caused something of a sensation thirty years ago, and some amusement to those with a sense of humour, for it is rather ridiculous to claim, by the title of one's book, to be the representative of the modern mind—this book did nothing else, in effect, than adduce new reasons for the rejection of Christianity as inadmissible folly. No cause for surprise there, no reason for fear. Paul realized that from the beginning. There was a modern mind in his day. He realized that, and pointed out that this mind, confronted by the Cross, would cry "folly."

Yet he, "an ugly little Jew," as Renan called him, set out to preach that folly. He set out with full realization and great enthusiasm, saying to himself of his future hearers: "Humanly speaking they ought not to listen to me. All the same they shall listen to me." And listen to him they did. Because what was folly to man was at the same time the wisdom of God. And this wisdom of God, to win acceptance, had to find a point of insertion into man's mind. What was it? This is what it was, and it is one of Paul's finest conceptions.

The world is corrupted certainly. But the wickedness of the world matters little. For precisely from the depths of this abyss a desire appears, an appeal arises, a cry goes up: "Who shall deliver us from ourselves?" In Paul's eyes, and it is a wonderful idea, the world will listen to the Good News. Why? Because the world is no longer in its infancy. It is grown up. Yes, grown up. Not by any means because it is strong, because it knows or thinks or can organize. All that can be done by a child. It is grown up, because, being feeble of heart and poor of soul, it knows its wretchedness and that it cannot cure itself. A wonderful truth that is ever true! At what moment in the destiny of the individual does the child become a man? Do you think that your manhood dates from the day when by some act of violence or rebellion, some success or other, you asserted yourself before your fellows or yourself? Nonsense! How often are such things

but childish pranks. In reality, the precise moment at which
we become adult is rather that in which after some personal
failure, struck by the feeling of our own helplessness, we at
last exclaim: "Lord, deliver me from myself, I am only a
poor, wretched man." It is only at that moment of honest
humility that childhood comes to an end. Then man has
grown up. It is then that the divine folly of Christianity
can be manifested; in its presence we can no longer play at
being clever, we are mature and can understand its higher
wisdom.

   *Fourth Sermon from Lenten Course at St Joseph's, Mar-
   seille,* 1927

42

ST LEO THE GREAT
The Universal Sacrament of Salvation

   It would be a good thing if those who murmur about the
dispensations of God gave over their complaints and ceased
their silly chatter about the lateness of our Lord's Nativity.
They talk as if that which has come to pass in the last age
of the world had no bearing on the times that are past.
But the Incarnation of the Word produced its effects not
only after but also before its realization in time, and the
mystery of man's salvation was never, in any age of antiquity,
at a standstill. What the Apostles preached had been foretold by the prophets, nor did fulfilment come too late for
that which had always been believed. Indeed, the wisdom and
loving kindness of God made us more able to receive his
call, by delaying the work which brought salvation. For thus
what was foretold by many signs, by many voices, by many
mysteries, throughout so many ages, would not be doubtful
in these days of the Gospel; and the birth of our Saviour,
which surpasses not only all other miracles but also the very
grasp of human thought, would work in us a firmer faith
precisely because it had been preached so frequently and so
long ago.

   It was therefore by no new design, by no tardy mercy
that God took thought for man, but from the foundation of
the world he ordained one and the same cause of Salvation
for all. For the grace of God, whereby the whole body of
the saints is ever justified, was augmented by the birth of

the Baptist, himself the voice of one crying in the wilderness and pointing to the Saviour; finally this great Voice was made flesh. Then it gave utterance with ever greater clearness and force to many expressions—doctrines and miracles—and in the end, to show that for the sake of truth even the most terrible fate of all—the death of the body—must be chosen, with a loud cry it gave up the ghost.

> *Exhortations*, Book 3: extract from a sermon preached at Trèves in 1443 on the text: "But Jesus, crying with a loud voice, yielded up the ghost" (*Opera*, Basle, 1565, pp. 411–2)

45

PSEUDO EUCHARIUS
The Sixth Age of the World

God completed his work in six days and on the seventh he rested. Similarly the human race proceeds in this world through six ages; from Adam to Noah, from Noah to Abraham, from Abraham to David, from David to the Babylonian captivity, from that to the lowly advent of our Lord Jesus Christ, and the present one from that advent till the end of the world, when the Most High will come as Judge. By the seventh age is understood the repose of the glorious which has no evening.

. . . Now the sixth age comes into being with the advent of our Lord Jesus Christ. For as on the sixth day Adam, the first man, was fashioned from the slime of the earth in the image of God, so in the sixth age of the world the second Adam, that is Christ, was born in the flesh of the Virgin Mary: the former into a living soul, the latter into a life-giving spirit. And as on that day there came into being a living soul, so also in this age there come into being those who desire eternal life. And as on that sixth day the earth produced the different species of serpents and animals, so in this sixth age of the world the Church has begotten the different nations eager for eternal life. And as on the sixth day man was created, male and female, so in this age Christ is made manifest with the Church. And as man on that day was placed over the animals, the serpents and the birds, so also is Christ in this age lord of the nations, peoples and races, that they may be governed by him, whether they be in subjection to the concupiscence of the flesh like animals, or blinded by earthly curiosity like serpents, or carried away by pride like birds. And as on that day man and the animals with him fed on plants, fruit and green herbs, so in the sixth age of the world the spiritual man, who is the good servant of Jesus Christ, feeds on the spiritual food of the sacred scriptures and the law of God. . . .

May the evening of this age no longer find us here! For it is of that evening that our Lord says: But ah, when the Son of Man comes, will he find faith left on the earth?

Commentaries on Genesis, Book 1 (P.L. 1, 903–4)

46

MACARIUS THE EGYPTIAN
Prayer at Evening

O God, who didst come in the fullness of time to save us, who didst cast Adam forth from Paradise at the decline of day, and didst likewise at the decline of day restore him to his inheritance: by thy Crucifixion have pity on me, now that the end of my life is drawing near, and evening comes upon me.

(*Prayer inserted in the Office of the Jacobite Church, at None, and attributed to Macarius the Great, "the Egyptian," d. 390*)

47

NEWMAN
Catholic Fullness

Now, the phenomenon, admitted on all hands, is this: that great portion of what is generally received as Christian truth is in its rudiments or in its separate parts to be found in heathen philosophies and religions. For instance, the doctrine of a Trinity is found both in the East and in the West; so is the ceremony of washing; so is the rite of sacrifice. The doctrine of the Divine Word is Platonic; the doctrine of the Incarnation is Indian; of a divine kingdom is Judaic; of Angels and demons is Magian; the connexion of sin with the body is Gnostic; celibacy is known to Bonze and Tala-poin; a sacerdotal order is Egyptian; the idea of a new birth is Chinese and Eleusinian; belief in sacramental virtue is Pythagorean; and honours to the dead are a polytheism. Such is the general nature of the fact before us; Mr Milman argues from it—"These things are in heathenism, therefore they are not Christian": we, on the contrary, prefer to say, "These things are in Christianity, therefore they are not heathen." That is, we prefer to say, and we think that Scripture bears us out in saying, that from the beginning the Moral Governor of the world has scattered the seeds of truth far and wide over its extent; that these have variously taken root, and grown up as in the wilderness, wild plants indeed but living; and hence that, as the inferior animals have tokens of an immaterial principle in them, yet have not souls, so the philosophies and religions of men have their life in certain true ideas, though they are not directly divine. What man is amid the brute creation, such is the Church among the schools of the world; and as Adam gave names to the animals about him, so has the Church from the first looked round upon the earth, noting and visiting the doctrines she found there. She began in Chaldea, and then sojourned among the Canaanites, and went down into Egypt, and thence passed into Arabia, till she rested in her own land. Next she encountered the merchants of Tyre, and the wisdom of the East country, and the luxury of Sheba. Then she was carried away to Babylon, and wandered to the schools of Greece. And wherever she went, in trouble or in triumph, still she was a living spirit, the mind and voice of the Most High; "sitting in the midst of the doctors, both hearing them and asking them questions"; claiming to herself what they said rightly, correcting their errors, supplying their defects, completing their beginnings, expanding their surmises, and thus gradually by means of them enlarging the range and re-fining the sense of her own teaching. So far then from her creed being of doubtful credit because it resembles foreign theologies, we even hold that one special way in which Provi-dence has imparted divine knowledge to us has been by en-abling her to draw and collect it together out of the world, and, in this sense, as in others, to "suck the milk of the Gentiles and to suck the breast of kings."

How far in fact this process has gone is a question of his-tory; and we believe it has before now been grossly exaggerated and misrepresented by those who, like Mr Milman, have thought that its existence told against Catholic doctrine; but so little antecedent difficulty have we in the matter, that we could readily grant, unless it were a question of fact not of theory, that Balaam was an Eastern sage, or a Sybil was inspired, or Solomon learnt of the sons of Mahol, or Moses was a scholar of the Egyptian hierophants. We are not distressed to be told that the doctrine of the angelic host came from Babylon, while we know that they did sing at the Nativity; nor that the vision of a Mediator is in Philo, if in very deed He died for us on Calvary. Nor are we afraid to allow, that, even after His coming, the Church has been a treasure-house, giving forth things old and new, casting the gold of fresh tributaries into her refiner's fire, or stamping upon her own, as time required it, a deeper impress of her Master's image.

The distinction between these two theories is broad and obvious. The advocates of the one imply that Revelation was a single, entire, solitary act, or nearly so, introducing a certain message; whereas we, who maintain the other, consider that Divine teaching has been in fact, what the analogy of nature would lead us to expect, "at sundry times and in divers manners," various, complex, progressive, and supplemental of itself. We consider the Christian doctrine, when analysed, to appear, like the human frame, "fearfully and wonderfully made"; but they think it some one tenet or certain principles given out at one time in their fullness, without gradual accretion before Christ's coming or elucidation afterwards. They cast off all that they also find in Pharisee or heathen; we conceive that the Church, like Aaron's rod, devours the serpents of the magicians. They are ever hunting for a fabulous primitive simplicity; we repose in Catholic fullness.

Essays Critical and Historical, XI: *Milman's View of Christianity* (1871, Vol. II, pp. 231–3).

48

ST PETER DAMIAN
The Church and Ourselves

The cohesive force of mutual charity by which the Church is united is so great that she is not merely one in her many members but also, in some mysterious way, present in her entirety in each individual. So true is this that we rightly consider the Church as the unique Spouse of Christ and yet rightly believe that through this Sacramental mystery the Church is fully present in each individual. For it was the Church wholly present (in each individual) that Isaac prophetically scented when he said of the person of his son, "Behold the smell of my son is as the smell of a plentiful field." The debtor woman, too, was certainly a figure of the Church when, at the bidding of Eliseus, she sowed her scanty stock of oil, as if it were seed, and reaped the rich harvest of overflowing vessels. Explore the fields of scripture carefully: you will often find there some individual man or woman who symbolizes the Church. For although the Church seems to have many parts by reason of the many nations (she enfolds) she is nevertheless not made up of parts. She is made one by the mystery of one faith and one (sacrament of) divine regeneration. Though seven women have received a single husband, we speak of them as a single virgin betrothed to the Heavenly Spouse. Thus the Apostle says, "For I have espoused you to one husband that I may present you as a chaste virgin to Christ."

The conclusion is evident. Since the Church is symbolized by a single individual, and since, in consequence, she is called a virgin, this Holy Church must be one in all and entire in each. Indeed, by reason of her unity of faith, she has not, in her many members, many parts, and yet through the close-knit bond of charity and the varied charismatic gifts she shows many facets in her individual members.

Though the Holy Church is thus diversified in many individuals, she is none the less welded into one by the fire of the Holy Spirit. Even if one part of the Church seems to be separated from another in space, the full vigour of the Sacrament of unity can never be impaired. It is this Holy Spirit, dwelling in the Church, who makes her one in her universal extension yet entire in each part. For beyond all doubt the Holy Spirit himself is one, yet manifold: one in the majesty of his being, manifold in the diversity of his charismatic gifts. The Word of Truth himself revealed the secrets of this undivided unity when, speaking to his Father, he said of his disciples, "Not for them only do I pray, but for them also who through their word shall believe in me. That they all may be one, as thou, Father, in me, and I in thee; that they also may be one in us: that the world may believe that thou hast sent me. And the glory which thou hast given me, I have given to them: that they may be one as we also are one."

If then those who believe in Christ are one, wherever there appears, to the natural eye, even one member of the Church, there, by the mystery of the Sacrament, the whole body is present. Whatever belongs to the Church as a whole belongs, in some measure, to each member. At any rate, there is no absurdity in an individual saying in private what is said usually by the assembled Church; and whatever may be asserted with truth by an individual may be uttered without any impropriety by many together. Thus, when we are gathered together for prayer, we say quite correctly, "Incline thy ear, O Lord, and hear me: for I am needy and poor. Preserve my soul for I am holy." Yet when we are by ourselves, each one of us may sing without any incongruity, "Rejoice to God our helper: sing aloud to the God of Jacob." Nor is it inappropriate for many together to say, "I will bless the Lord at all times: his praise shall always be in my mouth." Likewise in solitude we often express ourselves in the plural, saying, "O magnify the Lord with me; and let us extol his Name together," and many other things of that sort. In fact, he who prays alone may say "we," and the multitude may say "I." For, by the power of the Holy Spirit who dwells in each and fills us all, the individual is a multitude and the multitude an individual.

What do we find strange in the fact that a single priest, who is undoubtedly but a part of the Church, should fill the rôle of the whole Church in her work of salvation, as he does when he says "The Lord be with you" and answers immediately "and with thy spirit"? What is there strange in the fact that he alone asks and gives the blessing? Is it not true that the Church, by reason of the Sacrament of unity, is wholly present wherever there exists a single individual who shares her faith and devotion? Indeed, the unity of faith does not suffer solitude in the individual any more than schism in the multitude. What is to prevent many voices speaking through one mouth if, at the same time, many tongues profess, in turn, a single faith? For the whole Church is without doubt a single body, as I have already said. It is the Apostle who assures us of this. . . .

If then the entire Church is the one body of Christ, and we are members, what is to hinder any one of us from using the manner of speaking of our body the Church, seeing that we are truly one with it? For if we, though many, are one body in Christ, then, in Christ, the whole body is the property of each. Consequently, though, as far as bodily presence counts, we may appear to be isolated and far removed from the Church, we are nevertheless, through the inviolable Sacrament of unity, ever very close to her. Hence it is that what all together possess is possessed by each: and what is the peculiar possession of a few, the indissoluble unity of charity and faith renders common to all. Rightly then do the people cry, "Have mercy on me, O God, have mercy on me," and "O God, come to my assistance, O Lord, make haste to help me," and justly may a single individual say, "My God, have mercy on us and bless us." Our holy Fathers wished us to be so sure of the necessity of this communion of the Faithful in Christ, that they included it in the Creed of Catholic Belief and ordered us to think of it often as one of the very rudiments of our faith. For as soon as we have said, "I believe in the Holy Ghost, the Holy Catholic Church," we add immediately "the Communion of Saints," so that in the same act in which we give God testimony of our faith, we may include the testimony of our faith in the communion of the members of the Church who is one with him. Now the Communion of the Saints in the unity of faith means simply this: all believe in one God, all are reborn again by the same Baptism, strengthened by the same Holy Spirit, and introduced by the grace of adoption into the same Eternal Life.

Just as man is said to be a microcosm—a term derived from a Greek word meaning "little world"—because he is made up of the same four elements as is the Universe, so too each of the faithful is the Church in miniature, when in the mystery of the hidden unity he receives all the sacraments which have been conferred by God on the universal Church. If then it is beyond dispute that each individual receives the Sacraments, common to the whole Church, what is to prevent his using, as an individual, words used by the whole Church in common, since Sacraments are so much more important than words?

> *The Dominus Vobiscum,* Chaps. 5, 6 and 10 (P.L. cxlv, 235–6, and 239–40)

49

ST BERNARD
Order in Love

"He ordered love in me." This saying was made effective
when in the Church "he gave some apostles, and other some
prophets, and other some evangelists, and other some pastors
and doctors for the perfecting of the saints." It is fitting that
love should bind them all together and arrange them harmoniously in the unity of the Body of Christ; and that can
come to pass in no case if love itself is not ordered. For if
each individual allows himself to be led by his personal
whim, and betakes himself to what pleases him taking no account of the judgement of reason, and still more if no one is
content with his allotted function, but if all wish to be concerned with everything which attracts them by an indiscreet
exercise of activity, then surely there will be no unity but
rather confusion and disorder.

May the Lord Jesus order in me that small degree of
love that he has granted me; so that I may set my heart on
the whole, which belongs to him, in such a way that I may
attend before all things to that part which he has allotted
me in the scheme of duties; but that the precedence given
to this shall not prevent my dwelling with great interior interest on the many other duties which are no concern of
mine in the performance of my own function. For what we
must principally apply ourselves to is not always what we
must love the most. It often happens that what is primarily
our own concern is of itself the least important and that,
consequently, we should not bring our greatest interest to
bear on it.

Forty-ninth Sermon on the Canticle, n. 5 and 6 (P.L.
clxxxiii, 1018–9)

50

PIERRE TEILHARD DE CHARDIN
Christianity and Personalism

The most serious danger to humanity on its present course
is that it should finally forget the essential thing, that is, its

spiritual concentration, faced as it is by the cosmic discoveries made for it by science, and by the collective power revealed to it by social organization. For does not the secularist neo-religion strive, in its confused fashion, to represent the Deity as a sort of diffusive energy, or even as a heartless and shapeless super-society? At this dangerous stage, which threatens the existence of souls, it is, I suppose, Christianity which will, and can, intervene, to bring back human hopes and desires to the only path which conforms to the fundamental laws of being and of life. Until quite recently it could be held that nothing was so unfashionable, so anthropomorphic, as the Christian's personal God. Yet now, in what was apparently the most outworn, yet the most fundamental, of its tenets, the Christian Gospel discovers that it has become the most relevant of religions. Christianity, faced by a humanity that runs the risk of allowing that consciousness which has been already awakened in it by the developments of modern life to be absorbed in the "second matter" of philosophic determinisms and social techniques, upholds the primacy of reflective, that is, personalized, thought. And it does so in the most effective way of all: not only by a speculative defence, through its teaching, of the possibility of a consciousness which is at the same time central and universal, but still more by conveying and developing through its mysticism the meaning and, in some sort, the direct intuition of this centre of total convergence. The very least that an unbeliever must admit to-day, if he understands the biological condition of the world, is that the figure of Christ (not only as it is described in a book, but as it is concretely realized in the Christian consciousness) is the most perfect approximation yet achieved of a final object towards which the universal effort of mankind may tend without fear of weariness or deformation.

Thus, contrary to current notions, it is by its dogma as well as by its moral system that Christianity is human and can be called upon once more to save the world in the immediate future. . . .

La Crise présente, Réflexions d'un naturaliste, in *Études*, Oct. 20, 1937, p. 164

51

FRIEDRICH VON HÜGEL
For a Person Came

As to Christianity, it is really impossible to compare it directly with Hellenism without at once understating its originality. For its originality consists not so much in its single doctrines, or even in its teaching as a whole, and in the particular place each doctrine occupies in this teaching, as in its revelation, through the person and example of its Founder, of the altogether unsuspected depth and inexhaustibleness of human Personality, and of this Personality's source and analogue in God, of the simplicity and yet difficulty and never-endingness of the access of man to God, and of the ever-preceding condescension of God to man. Hence if Christianity is thus throughout the Revelation of Personality; and if Personality is ever a One in Many (and more deeply One and more richly Many, in proportion to the greatness of that spiritual reality): then we need not wonder at the difficulty we find in pointing out any one particular doctrine as constitutive of the unique originality of Christianity.

For a Person came, and lived and loved, and did and taught, and died and rose again, and lives on by his Power and his Spirit for ever within us and amongst us, so unspeakably rich and yet so simple, so sublime and yet so homely, so divinely above us precisely in being so divinely near—that his character and teaching require, for an ever fuller yet never complete understanding, the varying study, and different experiments and applications, embodiments and unrollings of all the races and civilizations, of all the individual and corporate, the simultaneous and successive experiences of the human race to the end of time.

The Mystical Element of Religion, 1st edn., Vol. I, pp. 25–6

52

SIMEON THE NEW THEOLOGIAN
I Knew a Man . . .

Brethren, let us strive to worship God by our love for each other. All effort is vain which does not lead to this . . . for the disciples of Christ are recognized by their mutual love. This is their characteristic mark: "By this shall all men know that you are my disciples. . . ." It was because of love that the Word was made Flesh and dwelt amongst us; for the Son of God became Man, freely and gladly enduring those sufferings which brought us life, in order to remake his creature, that human nature which the devil had shattered and torn apart. . . . This is the true and irreproachable Wisdom of God, which has for its ends the good and the true: the good, a kindness towards our fellow men; the true, a worship of God in accordance with faith. These are the marks of that charity which unites men among themselves, and binds them to God.

Brethren, I knew a man who, in his love, made it his chief work to rescue his intimate companions from their evil thoughts and actions. This he would attempt to do by various means, as occasion offered; he would seek to influence one by his words, another by his acts of kindness. . . . I have known such a man weep over one, mourn for another—clearly, because he had taken upon himself their personality, and now charged himself with the faults which they had committed. . . .

I have known a man rejoice so heartily over the struggles and conquests of others, show such pleasure in their progress in virtue that it seemed as though not they but he himself was going to receive the reward of their merits and labours.

I have known a man possess such a burning desire for his neighbours' salvation that he often begged the Divine Goodness with his whole heart, with warm tears and a lofty zeal worthy of Moses, either to grant them salvation or to condemn him too, along with them. For he was bound to them, in the Holy Spirit, with such a saintly love that he was unwilling even to enter the kingdom of heaven, if this should mean he must be separated from them.

Sermon XXII (P.G. cxx, 423–5)

53

ST AUGUSTINE
The Demands of Charity

Whatever we love in the way of food, we love it to this end that it be consumed and we ourselves refreshed. But men, surely, are not to be loved in this way? There is, indeed, a certain love of well-wishing which urges us at some time or other to do good to those whom we love. But what if there be no good that we can do? To the lover, the benevolence, the mere wishing well, is more than enough. We should not desire that men be in affliction in order that we may practise works of mercy. You give meat to the hungry; but it were far better that there were no hungry and that you had no one to feed. You clothe the naked; oh, if only all were clothed and you had no need to clothe them! You bury the dead; if only that life were come wherein there is no death! You reconcile those who are at variance; ah, that eternal peace were at last here, the peace of the heavenly Jerusalem, wherein none shall disagree! For all these services answer to some necessity. Take away the wretched, and works of mercy are at an end. They indeed are at an end, but the fire of love, shall that ever be quenched?

With a truer love do you love a happy man to whom there is no good work that you can do; purer will be that love, and more sincere. For if you do good to anyone in distress, it may well be that you wish to raise yourself in his eyes and that you are glad that he, who is the occasion of your benefactions, should be inferior to you. He was in need and you came to his help; you, who brought assistance, appear greater than he who had to receive it. Long rather to be equal, that you may both be under the one Lord on whom nothing can be bestowed.

On the First Epistle of St John, Treatise 8, n. 5
(P.L. xxxv, 2038–9)

54

ST BERNARD
The Passover of the Lord

On this, the chief solemnity, we should seriously consider what is set before us: that is, a resurrection, a passing-over, a change of dwelling. For to-day, my brethren, Christ did not remain lying dead, but he rose up: he did not come back, but passed over; he did not establish himself afresh, but he raised his dwelling-place aloft; and, in fine, this Pasch that we are celebrating does not mean Return but Passing-over: and that Galilee in which he who rose up promised to let us see him does not mean that he stayed behind, but that he had changed his dwelling.

And it is to that place, so it seems to me, that the minds of many among you have gone before me, surmising rightly where my words would lead you.

If Christ the Lord, after the consummation on the Cross, had lived again to return once more to our mortal nature and the sufferings of our present life, I should say most certainly, my brethren, that he had not passed over, but that he had come back; that he was not established in a higher state but that he had taken up his pilgrimage again in his former state. On the contrary: he is now raised up to a new life, and that is why he calls us too to the Passing-over, he calls us into Galilee.

Easter Sermon, n. 14 (P.L. clxxxiii, 281)

55

PSEUDO-CHRYSOSTOM
The Cosmic Tree

This Tree is my eternal salvation. It is my nourishment and my banquet. Amidst its roots I cast my own roots deep: beneath its boughs I grow and expand, revelling in its sigh as in the wind itself. Flying from the burning heat, I have pitched my tent in its shadow, and have found a resting-place of dewy freshness. I flower with its flowers; its fruits bring perfect joy—fruits which have been preserved for me since time's beginning, and which now I freely eat. This Tree is a food, sweet food, for my hunger, and a fountain for my thirst; it is a clothing for my nakedness; its leaves are the breath of life. Away with the fig-tree, from this time on! If I fear God, this is my protection; if I stumble, this is my support; it is the prize for which I fight and the reward of my victory. This is my straitened path, my narrow way; this is the stairway of Jacob, where angels pass up and down, and where the Lord in very truth stands at the head.

This Tree, vast as heaven itself, rises from earth to the skies, a plant immortal, set firm in the midst of heaven and earth, base of all that is, foundation of the universe, support of this world of men, binding-force of all creation, holding within itself all the mysterious essence of man. Secured with the unseen clamps of the spirit, so that, adjusted to the Divine, it may never bend or warp, with foot resting firm on earth it towers to the topmost skies, and spans with its all-embracing arms the boundless gulf of space between.

He was All, and in all, filling it with himself; stripped naked for battle against the powers of the air. . . .

With him two thieves were extended, bearing within themselves the marks of those two peoples, the marks of those two types of mind. . . .

When this cosmic combat came to an end . . . the heavens shook; almost, the stars fell from the skies; the light of the sun was extinguished for a time; rocks were split asunder; the entire world was all but shattered. . . . But great Jesus breathed forth his divine Soul, saying: "Father, into Thy hands I commend my spirit." And lo, even while all things shuddered and heaved in earthquake, reeling for fear, his divine Soul ascended, giving life and strength to all; and again creation was still, as if this divine Crucifixion and Extension had everywhere unfolded and spread, penetrating all things, through all, and in all. O thou who art alone among the alone, and all in all! Let the heavens hold thy godhead; and paradise, thy soul; and earth, thy blood. For the Indivisible has become divided, so that all might be saved, and the world below might not remain ignorant of the coming of God. . . .

We beseech thee now, Lord God, Christ, eternal King of souls: stretch forth thy mighty hands over thy sacred Church, and over a holy people for ever thine.

Sermon VI for Holy Week (P.G. lix, 743–6)